Science Fiction

THE GREENHAVEN PRESS COMPANION TO
Literary Movements and Genres

Science Fiction

Jesse G. Cunningham, *Book Editor*

Daniel Leone, *President*

Bonnie Szumski, *Publisher*

Scott Barbour, *Managing Editor*

David M. Haugen, *Series Editor*

Greenhaven Press, Inc., San Diego, CA

Every effort has been made to trace the owners of copy-
righted material. The articles in this volume may have
been edited for content, length, and/or reading level. The
titles have been changed to enhance the editorial purpose.
Those interested in locating the original source will find
the complete citation on the first page of each article.

The editor of this volume wishes to express his gratitude to Dr. Stephen W. Potts, whose
knowledge, guidance, and assistance helped to make this book possible.

Library of Congress Cataloging-in-Publication Data

Science fiction / Jesse G. Cunningham, book editor.
    p. cm. — (The Greenhaven Press companion to
literary movements and genres)
    Includes bibliographical references and index.
    ISBN 0-7377-0571-X (pbk. : alk. paper) —
ISBN 0-7377-0572-8 (lib. bdg. : alk. paper)
    1. Science fiction—History and criticism. I. Cunning-
ham, Jesse G. II. Series.

PN3433.5 .S32 2002
809.3'8762—dc21   2001033507

Cover Photo: Circa Art
Circa Art, 135
Library of Congress, 75

Copyright © 2002 by Greenhaven Press, Inc.
10911 Technology Place
San Diego, CA 92127
Printed in the U.S.A.

CONTENTS

Chapter 1: Within the Literary Tradition

Chapter 2: Movements Within the Genre

1. Verne and Wells: The Two Fathers of Modern Science Fiction
by Kingsley Amis

H.G. Wells and Jules Verne are considered by many to be the two creators of modern science fiction. A brief examination of their works demonstrates their contributions to the genre.

2. An Insider Remembers the Pulp Era
by Jack Williamson

The pulp era reflects the youth of modern science fiction: the early tales of outrageous adventure in its infancy, its growth to maturity under the guidance of innovators, and the shift to cynicism in its young adulthood.

3. *New Worlds* and the New Wave
by Brian W. Aldiss with David Wingrove

Britain's *New Worlds* magazine advocated radical experimentation with a genre that was growing stale in pulp formulas. Writers of this New Wave produced intellectually challenging and provocative works that greatly expanded the boundaries of science fiction.

4. A Cyberpunk Manifesto
by Bruce Sterling

Concentrating on themes of human nature, identity, and invasion, the cyberpunk movement gains inspiration from pop culture and the proliferation of modern technology.

Chapter 3: Genre Conventions

1. Negative Utopias and Orwell's Dark Vision
by Erich Fromm

1984 is a negative utopia that warns of the dangers of a predatory society and the oppressive conditioning of the individual.

2. The Paradoxes of Time Travel
by Paul A. Carter

Stories with time machines explore the opposition of individual will and predetermined destiny.

3. Understanding the Alien
by Gregory Benford

Encountering aliens in science fiction should present the reader with the unknown and unknowable. However, most science fiction depicts aliens in familiar terms, reflecting not the inhuman, but the human.

FOREWORD

The study of literature most often involves focusing on an individual work and uncovering its themes, stylistic conventions, and historical relevance. It is also enlightening to examine multiple works by a single author, identifying similarities and differences among texts and tracing the author's development as an artist.

While the study of individual works and authors is instructive, however, examining groups of authors who shared certain cultural or historical experiences adds a further richness to the study of literature. By focusing on literary movements and genres, readers gain a greater appreciation of influence of historical events and social circumstances on the development of particular literary forms and themes. For example, in the early twentieth century, rapid technological and industrial advances, mass urban migration, World War I, and other events contributed to the emergence of a movement known as American modernism. The dramatic social changes, and the uncertainty they created, were reflected in an increased use of free verse in poetry, the stream-of-consciousness technique in fiction, and a general sense of historical discontinuity and crisis of faith in most of the literature of the era. By focusing on these commonalities, readers attain a more comprehensive picture of the complex interplay of social, economic, political, aesthetic, and philosophical forces and ideas that create the tenor of any era. In the nineteenth-century American romanticism movement, for example, authors shared many ideas concerning the preeminence of the self-reliant individual, the infusion of nature with spiritual significance, and the potential of persons to achieve transcendence via communion with nature. However, despite their commonalities, American romantics often differed significantly in their thematic and stylistic approaches. Walt Whitman celebrated the communal nature of America's open democratic society, while Ralph Waldo Emerson expressed the need for individuals to pursue their own fulfillment regardless of their fellow citizens. Herman Melville wrote novels in a largely naturalistic style whereas Nathaniel Hawthorne's novels were gothic and allegorical.

Another valuable reason to investigate literary movements and genres lies in their potential to clarify the process of literary evolution. By examining groups of authors, literary trends across time become evident. The reader learns, for instance, how English romanticism was transformed as it crossed the Atlantic to America. The poetry of Lord Byron, William Wordsworth, and John Keats celebrated the restorative potential of rural scenes. The American romantics, writing later in the century, shared their English counterparts' faith in nature; but American authors were more likely to present an ambiguous view of nature as a source of liberation as well as the dwelling place of personal demons. The whale in Melville's *Moby-Dick* and the forests in Hawthorne's novels and stories bear little resemblance to the benign pastoral scenes in Wordsworth's lyric poems.

Each volume in Greenhaven Press's Companions to Literary Movements and Genres series begins with an introductory essay that places the topic in a historical and literary context. The essays that follow are carefully chosen and edited for ease of comprehension. These essays are arranged into clearly defined chapters that are outlined in a concise annotated table of contents. Finally, a thorough chronology maps out crucial literary milestones of the movement or genre as well as significant social and historical events. Readers will benefit from the structure and coherence that these features lend to material that is often challenging. With Greenhaven's Literary Movements and Genres in hand, readers will be better able to comprehend and appreciate the major literary works and their impact on society.

INTRODUCTION:
THE OTHERWORLDLY GENRE?

A study of science fiction literature reveals an impressive array of conventions and themes. As in all literature, the two are connected, but in science fiction the devices not only serve the fantastical world of the narrative but also reflect concerns of the real world. Navigating the unknown depths of space in a starship can be an expression of the frontier experience, or may represent a desire to escape the rigors of life on Earth. Ideal utopias and nightmare totalitarian regimes are used to contemplate political theory and criticize the faults of today's societies. Likewise, time travel considers the implications of history, or acts as a vehicle for social commentary on the present. Futures shaped by high technology may explore the direction of progress, the decline of civilization, or the alienation and dehumanization that results from life in an impersonal society. Extraterrestrial species on alien worlds may represent a xenophobic fear of the Other, or reflect humanity and life on this planet; similarly, artificial beings and intelligence represent an attempt to define and understand life, sentience, and consciousness. These science fiction devices may even serve as a catalyst for exploring spirituality and religion.

While this list represents a mere sampling of the multitude of possibilities within science fiction, a closer examination of the genre reveals a recurring effort to understand the universe, whether through a system of scientific thought, religious dogma, or metaphysical contemplation. And, to understand the universe, it is necessary to comprehend the relationship of human beings and the cosmos, another of science fiction's great quests. Many writers within the genre return to this issue, contemplating the collective human experience, as well as the place of the individual. A study of science fiction, therefore, is a search for the meaning of life and an understanding of existence.

Science fiction is itself subject to the laws of evolution it so frequently fictionalizes. Born to a literary heritage, the genre has awkwardly suffered adolescence and grown to maturity before admiring fans and harsh skeptics; it has been adopted by popular culture, and finally accepted, sometimes even canonized, by academics and literary critics. The forms of science fiction are always mutating as the genre develops in novels, novellas, short stories, films, television programs, animation, and other media. At once mysterious, imaginative, enjoyable, and entertaining, this unique living genre promises to help humanity understand itself and the universe for generations to come.

SCIENCE FICTION: AN OVERVIEW

Modern science fiction (known familiarly as sf) originates in the nineteenth century, its development roughly concurrent with the scientific discoveries and technological advances of the Industrial Revolution. However, older precedents certainly have influenced the genre. The otherworldliness of Homer's *Odyssey* and the utopic vision of Plato's *Republic* have been reflected in modern sf; Elizabethan playwrights William Shakespeare and Christopher Marlowe treated the Faustus legend, which contemplates obsession with knowledge that pervades many works of the genre. These themes and elements were adopted and explored by sf writers, but ultimately it would be the concerns and potential of science that would come to characterize the emerging genre.

ORIGINATORS OF THE GENRE

Some sf experts, like Brian W. Aldiss, argue that the British author Mary Shelley is the first sf writer precisely because she brought science into a Romantic narrative. To Aldiss, her novel *Frankenstein: or, The Modern Prometheus* (1818) marks the birth of the genre through its hybrid storytelling:

> Mary had imbibed the scientific ideas of [physician and poet Erasmus] Darwin and [poet Percy] Shelley; had heard what they had to say about the future; and . . . set about applying her findings within the loose framework of a Gothic novel.[1]

It is Shelley's attention to science in relation to a philosophical exploration of humanity that qualifies *Frankenstein* as the first sf novel. Her apparent moral that "there are some things in nature that humans are not meant to know" is an often repeated sf theme, though sometimes contested by those writers and readers who hope to construe a more optimistic view of science and its possibilities, rather than admit to the negative potential of those who would practice science irresponsibly. This debate over the positive and negative potentials of progress has even produced a sort of Frankenstein stigma within the genre.

Another nineteenth-century writer often cited as an early influence on the genre is the American Romantic Edgar Allan Poe. Much of Poe's fiction is Gothic in nature, but sometimes it crosses into sf territory, especially when Poe incorporates scientific principles in his stories, as he does in "Hans Phaall—A Tale" and "Mesmeric Revelation." Sometimes he engages in imaginative speculation that only loosely draws from science; for example, "The Narrative of Arthur Gordon Pym of Nantucket," with its incredible voyage and strange cultures, rides the line between fantasy and sf, while "A Tale of the Ragged Mountains" features time travel. Although most of Poe's work is outside sf, he remains to many the father of genre fiction, having written some of the first tales of mystery, detective fiction, and Gothic horror in addition to his sf and fantasy.

VERNE, WELLS, AND THE LATE NINETEENTH CENTURY

Besides Shelley and Poe, other nineteenth-century authors were developing themes that would be incorporated in science fiction. Stories modeled on Sir Thomas More's *Utopia* explored sociopolitical theory in a search for building a perfect nation-state. Among the most popular were Samuel Butler's *Erewhon* and Edward Bellamy's *Looking Backward.* Robert Louis Stevenson's novel *The Strange Case of Dr. Jekyll and Mr. Hyde* contemplated the rational and irrational sides of a man, or more specifically a man of science. Even genre-specific motifs such as future wars and subterranean societies worked their way into other nineteenth-century writings.

Despite all these dabblings with science fiction themes, none of the aforementioned authors would be considered true science fiction writers as recognized today. The first author to create stories within the vein of modern science fiction was Jules Verne. A Frenchman who published dozens of novels, including *Journey to the Center of the Earth* and *Twenty Thousand Leagues Under the Sea,* Verne consciously drew on what science seemed capable of offering humans. An admirer of Poe, Verne adopted the American author's technique of incorporating nineteenth-century science into his stories. Inventions such as Captain Nemo's remarkable submarine in *Twenty Thousand Leagues* predicted modern technology that the world had not yet seen. This fascination with future science has influenced many succeeding generations of writers, especially those whose work could be classified as "hard" sf—that is, writing that incorporates realistic science into a projected future.

At least of equal importance to the development of modern sf is English author H.G. Wells. Also a prolific writer, Wells penned most of his classic sf early in his career, beginning in the 1890s with *The Time Machine, The Island of Dr. Moreau, The War of the Worlds,* and *The Invisible Man.* Like Verne, Wells had some concerns for the science of his era, having studied with T.H. Huxley, who introduced Wells to the theories of Erasmus and Charles Darwin. With his broad vision, Wells linked scientific notions with other imaginative ideas that departed from his era's theories; examples include the time travel into the far future of *The Time Machine,* the grotesque Martians of *The War of the Worlds,* and the ambiguous mechanisms shaping the beast men of *Dr. Moreau.* Through such imaginative speculation, not always bound by realistic science, Wells could create whatever mechanisms necessary to explore and critique social issues. Wells is arguably the single most influential science fiction author; his blend of science and social commentary has inspired many generations of sf writers of every variety. Aldiss states that "Wells is the Prospero of all the brave new worlds of the mind, and the Shakespeare of science fiction."[2]

THE PULP ERA: FROM BURROUGHS TO GERNSBACK

Once authors began writing in the early vein of science fiction, the genre needed a vehicle to reach a large audience. Starting in the 1890s, pulp magazines were a very popular and inexpensive form of entertainment in America. Named after the cheap paper on which they were printed, the pulps appealed to a mass audience, and many genres began to develop in specialized magazines. No titles, however, were devoted exclusively to sf until Hugo Gernsback founded *Amazing Stories* in 1926. Before that time, the earliest sf writers of the pulp era published their work in nongenre-specific pulp titles, such as *Argosy.*

The first notable sf writer of the American pulp era was Edgar Rice Burroughs. Outside the genre, he is known as the creator of Tarzan; within sf, however, Burroughs is known for his Mars series, which began with the serialization of his first novel in 1912 (later published as *A Princess of Mars*).

Numerous sequels followed. The saga featured the able John Carter, an Earthman mysteriously transported to Mars who engages in a series of wild adventures among the inhabitants of that planet's civilizations. In two other series, Burroughs set his adventures in Pellucidar (a subterranean world) and on Venus. Emphasizing fantastic adventure over science, Burroughs's works are often called science fantasy. Aldiss designates him as a writer near the "dreaming pole" of science fiction, which stands opposite to the "thinking pole"[3] represented by H.G. Wells and other authors more interested in maintaining social commentary and a level of realism in science. On the heels of Burroughs, other writers published early sf stories in the pulps, including Abraham Merrit and H.P. Lovecraft, who are situated even closer than Burroughs to Aldiss's "dreaming pole," so much so that most of their works are more easily classified as fantasy (or in Lovecraft's case, horror), although both writers sometimes ride the blurry line between the genres.

Hugo Gernsback's *Amazing Stories* was the first pulp specializing in an all-sf content. Originally from Luxembourg, Gernsback came to America to be an inventor; after writing some sf, he soon detected a market for the budding new genre. He founded *Amazing* to publish the writings of a new generation of pulp writers who grew to maturity under the influence of Verne, Wells, and Burroughs. Some of these writers would earn much recognition within the newly forming sf community, including Jack Williamson, Murray Leinster, "Doc" E.E. Smith, David H. Keller, Edmond Hamilton, and Philip Francis Nowlan. In *Amazing,* Gernsback emphasized accurate technological prediction and invention. Imitators of Gernsback quickly appeared, starting many new sf pulp titles that drew in authors of adventure fantasy, realistic future science, and even the otherwordly horror akin to Lovecraft. Soon, according to sf experts Robert Scholes and Eric S. Rabkin, "These three strands of pulp fiction—adventure, hardware, and weird—dominated American science fiction in the twenties and thirties."[4]

Some credit Gernsback for inventing the term *science fiction* around the time that he launched his second sf magazine, *Science Wonder Stories* (after losing control of *Amazing* in 1929). Sf now assumed an identity; fans and aspiring writers mobilized into a community the likes of which had never been associated with any other genre. It was the beginning of the insular, vociferous community known as sf fandom. For his part in furthering the readership of science fiction, Gernsback was honored in 1953 when the Hugo Award was first given to designate the fan community's favorite sf works.

Despite the growing audience for sf pulps, the grouping of writers into specialized forums of cheap entertainment perpetuated the perception that the genre was substandard literature. The stigma has haunted the field to some degree ever since. Jack Williamson, a prominent writer of the era, describes the sf pulp tradition:

> Certainly [sf of the pulp era] was unliterary, if not anti-literary. . . . It was part of the popular culture. With its narrowness, its violence, its prudery, its strong male heroes, its innocent good women and wildly wicked bad ones, and its themes of material success, I think it reflects the Puritan heritage and the frontier experience. . . . The pulp story was written from the viewpoint of a pure-minded male who was successful in a conflict with powerful antagonists. Good and evil were clearly defined. Characters were simple, and action was paramount. The ending was happy. . . . The whole tradition assumed a rational moral order in the universe. The good guys won.[5]

Fantastically adventurous space operas with bug-eyed monsters, fast spaceships, and wild inventions began to proliferate, but the structured, often hackneyed, narratives displayed little literary merit. Still, the strong imaginative qualities of the genre helped pulp sf flourish, at least until World War II, by which time, transformed, it would enter the so-called golden age.

SCIENCE FICTION IN EUROPE

Contemporaneous to the growth of sf in the pulp magazines was the development of the genre in Europe. What the Europeans brought to science fiction in the 1930s and 1940s was a more literary tone and storylines that dealt with more sophisticated topics than high adventure. The Czech playwright Karel Căpek is credited with creating the term *robot* and introducing this device into sf with his most famous work, *R.U.R.*, which depicts the struggle of a slave-labor class of artificial beings. The social commentary was apparent, lending greater depth to Căpek's work.

Also significant at this time are the works of British writers, including Aldous Huxley. Huxley's *Brave New World* offers a dystopic vision of the future. Responding to the previous century's preoccupation with utopian fiction, the new dystopic form envisioned dark futures that served as powerful vehicles of social criticism. Huxley's novel features a society controlled by rigid genetic engineering, mental conditioning, drugs, and sensual pleasure. A respected intellectual with an influential philosophical discourse, Huxley wrote other sf works, including *Ape and Essence* and *Island.*

Huxley's famous contemporary C.S. Lewis, who resided as a professor at Oxford and Cambridge, heavily laced his novels with Christian symbolism, elevating sf with his trilogy *Out of the Silent Planet, Perelandra,* and *That Hideous Strength.* These works, set against an interplanetary backdrop, depict an allegorical spiritual journey in the vein of Milton's *Paradise Lost.* According to Scholes and Rabkin, Lewis challenged "science and science fiction to produce an ethic that might contend upon a footing of equality with his own Christian faith."[6]

Another important British author of the time was Olaf Stapledon. A name still obscure in literary circles, Stapledon has influenced many subsequent generations of sf writers with his poetically imaginative novels *Last and First Men,* which depicts the last species of man 2 billion years in the future, and *The Star Maker,* the account of an epic spiritual journey and a tour of the universe.

THE GOLDEN AGE OF *ASTOUNDING*

In the United States sf's golden age is linked to the significant shift that occurred after John W. Campbell Jr. began his tenure as the editor of *Astounding Science Fiction* in 1937. Previously a notable sf writer of the pulps, it was as the editor of *Astounding* that Campbell made his indelible mark on the genre. According to Aldiss, "Campbell [drew] on the first generation of young writers raised on magazine sf,"[7] assembling one of sf's elite stables, which included Isaac Asimov, Ray Bradbury, Robert Heinlein, Hal Clement, A.E. van Vogt, Lester del Rey, L. Sprague de Camp, and Theodore Sturgeon, as well as established pulp authors, such as E.E. Smith and Jack Williamson, who refocused their writing to adapt to Campbell's guidelines.

Like Gernsback, Campbell emphasized accurate science and the plausible extrapolation of technological progress, but also insisted on a greater degree of skill and quality in the writing. He was successful at eliciting both of these aspects from his writers, who would make insightful predictions that would soon be proven correct, such as the development of the atomic bomb. (*Astounding* was even investigated by the FBI because of its prophetic content in this area.) Asimov has noted that Campbell's *Astounding* marked the end of the adventure-dominant period of the pulp era, signaling a new period of technology-dominant (hard) sf. Jack Williamson further describes Campbell's influence in the field:

> When John Campbell became the editor [of *Astounding*] he soon made it the creative center of modern science fiction. . . . He brought a unique combination of gifts to . . . the whole field. He understood science, and he had a vivid sense of its impact on the future. He understood story construction—he had learned the use of form that came from the pulp tradition. . . . Richest gift of all, he had a well of invention that never ran dry. His generosity in planting new ideas was limitless. . . . As a creative editor, he had no equal.[8]

Indeed, many prominent writers of the era freely credit Campbell with helping them develop some of their best ideas, often resulting in their most successful works. For example, Asimov credits Campbell for helping inspire his famous Foundation series and his early robot stories (later collected in the book *I, Robot*), and recognizes Campbell as a collaborator in the development of Asimov's influential Three Laws of Robotics.

ASIMOV AND HEINLEIN

Two of the brightest stars of the *Astounding* constellation are Isaac Asimov and Robert A. Heinlein. First appearing in the July 1939 issue, both writers developed innovations that informed the work of their contemporaries and future generations of sf writers. As Aldiss explains: "In 1941, Heinlein revealed the plans of his scheme for a Future History series, while Asimov began his long series of stories about robots with positronic brains whose behaviour is guided by three laws of robotics which prevent them from harming men."[9] Future histories became a vogue for the Campbellian and later writers, as did stories about robots and androids, and other authors would even adopt Asimov's laws to use in their own stories. Asimov's own future history began as a serial in the magazine, eventually evolving into the Foundation novels, which have long been cherished by sf readers (a new generation of writers has even continued the series since Asimov's death).

Heinlein was one of Campbell's favorite writers for *Astounding,* dazzling sf audiences with his stories. His first novel, *If This Goes On . . . ,* which featured a dystopic dictatorship with religious authority, was serialized in 1940. A prolific writer for decades, Heinlein published many titles, including *Starship Troopers* and *Stranger in a Strange Land,* his most successful novel.

Despite the innovations of Asimov and Heinlein, the hard science of the golden age and the rough-and-tumble bravado of the pulp era led to sf's reputation as a masculinized genre. Although a few women writers were also part of the pulp era and golden age, they were the exceptions. Often they published under asexual pseudonyms or by-lines, like C.L. Moore and Leigh Brackett, keeping a low profile from the legions of male fans who expected their tales of adventure to be written by men.

VISIONS OF A DARK FUTURE

For several decades, magazine sf had displayed a positive attitude toward the power of science and technological progress, but America's involvement in World War II precipitated a shift to a more cynical outlook. Jack Williamson, who noted the optimism and naivete of the pulp age, observed this shift in tone:

> When I settled back to writing after the war, I found that the whole field had changed, as I had. . . . People who had seldom read the pulps began taking science fiction a little more seriously, perhaps because rockets and atomic bombs and all sorts of explosive changes had come off the old gray pages into reality. The shadow of the future was suddenly too dark to be ignored. . . . Definitions of evil had blurred. The old happy endings were lost in the mushroom clouds of atomic Armageddon.[10]

The postwar cynicism and the formation of a new cold war environment prompted many dark visions of the future, the most famous being the British intellectual George Orwell's dystopia, *1984.* It posits a world divided by three superpower nations, which subjugate their populations with thought control through propaganda and manipulation of language. Among other insights, *1984* prophesied the advent of the cold war, including the anxiety of mutually assured destruction. It serves as Orwell's warning to free-thinking people everywhere against totalitarian regimes that would suppress liberty through a variety of means, and the potential of despotism in any society. The novel anticipates what Asimov notes as a shift around 1950 to sociological-dominant science fiction, which presented a medium for "soft" sf, with its focus on social concerns.

The shift to cynicism could clearly be witnessed even in *Astounding*'s pages. Campbell, like Gernsback before him, had always had competitors, numerous magazines that lived off *Astounding*'s dregs; however, in the early fifties environment two new major magazines appeared: *Galaxy*, edited by Horace Gold, and the *Magazine of Fantasy and Science Fiction*, edited by Anthony Boucher. These two magazines provided a forum for the views of new writers with a social agenda, and sometimes a cynical streak and a satirical edge as well. Writers such as Ray Bradbury, Arthur C. Clarke, Damon Knight, Robert Sheckley, Alfred Bester, and Kurt Vonnegut Jr. came into prominence.

Ray Bradbury's popularity has persisted through the decades. Some of his landmark sf titles include *The Martian Chronicles*, a collection of stories set on Mars, which in Bradbury's imagination becomes an environment for the exploration of humankind's moral and social habits; *The Illustrated Man*, another story collection, connected through a unique framing device in which the narrator sports numerous tattoos, each representing a separate tale; and the dystopia *Fahrenheit 451*, which depicts an establishment that suppresses freedom of thought by outlawing books and proliferating television. These and numerous other Bradbury titles have elevated the prodigious writer to literary status in the minds of many readers.

ARTHUR C. CLARKE AND THE UNFATHOMABLE COSMOS

Arthur C. Clarke, a British writer whose stories, published in the sf magazines, appealed to the American audience, is known for his revisionist attitude regarding the optimistic Campbellian vision of science and technology as the savior of humankind. Clarke depicted a cosmos that was unfathomably huge compared with the individual, an approach that contradicted the earlier predominant treatment by other writers in which the human individual was usually the ultimate competitor for success in a universe ruled by the mechanisms of evolution. In contrast, Clarke's view is more ambivalent than that of many of his contemporaries and predecessors. Often writing in a hard sf mode, blending cynicism and optimism, Clarke contemplates the evolutionary worthiness of the human race and tests whether or not humans are mature enough to properly handle their scientific discoveries and technological advances. In addition to writing such classics as *Childhood's End, Rendezvous with Rama,* and story collections like *The Nine Billion Names of God,* Clarke coauthored (with Stanley Kubrick) the influential film *2001: A Space Odyssey,* which was released in 1968, well after the golden age. This film, according to many the best sf film ever, clearly illustrates the prevalent Clarkean themes, and stands as one of the greatest achievements in science fiction.

THE NEW WAVE

Another turning point in science fiction literature also occurred in the 1960s. This was the advent of the so-called New Wave, a sf movement that impressed audiences on both sides of the Atlantic. The focus of this movement was a British magazine called *New Worlds,* which had existed since the 1940s, but became revitalized in 1964 under the guidance of writer Michael Moorcock. Moorcock not only provided an excellent medium for British sf authors, but brought a conscious agenda to the magazine and the genre: It was his contention that science fiction should meet the standards applied to all literature. In the editorial to his first issue of *New Worlds,* Moorcock declares the magazine's intent: "[*New Worlds* would champion] a kind of SF which is unconventional in every sense. . . . A popular literary renaissance . . . is around the corner. Together, we can accelerate that renaissance."[11]

Consequently, a stable of formidable writers organized around Moorcock, including J.G. Ballard, Brian Aldiss, John Brunner, and the Americans Thomas Disch and Norman Spinrad. Striving for aesthetic merit, especially through literary experimentation, these writers often concentrated on social issues, emphasizing sociology, politics, anthropology, and philosophy over the hard science that informed Campbellian sf. The writers also raised subjects that had been relatively taboo in this genre embraced by so many young readers. Exploring or attacking religion and depicting sex and drug use were radical, provocative ideas at the time, and these motifs characterized the New Wave period. In fact, *New Worlds* stirred up controversy when it serialized Norman Spinrad's novel *Bug Jack Barron* in 1968. The explicit and disturbing content, centered around political and media corruption, prompted a member of the House of Commons to label Spinrad a degenerate, and the magazine barely held onto its government funding.

For Moorcock, the exemplar of the new movement was J.G. Ballard, whose avant-garde style was bizarre and surreal, influenced by American beat author William Burroughs (who himself had experimented with sf in *The Ticket That Exploded* and other titles), and similarly experimental. Ballard would forgo conventional narrative in order to present a prose rich in imagery and atmosphere, but often challenging for the reader. His novels and stories demonstrate how far the *New Worlds* writers pushed the envelope when it came to literary experimentation. Brian W. Aldiss garnered British and American awards for such titles as *Barefoot in the Head;* he has also enhanced sf as an astute critic. John Brunner's *Stand on Zanzibar,* a novel about overpopulation written in an innovative, postmodern narrative style, anticipates the hypertext of the computer age and is cited as a chief influence by the later cyberpunk writers. Moorcock himself wrote popular fantasy, as well as a number of acclaimed sf titles, including *Behold the Man,* a time travel novel that deposits the protagonist in Jesus' time.

American writers associated with *New Worlds,* such as Judith Merril and Harry Harrison, who published on both sides of the Atlantic, helped import the New Wave renaissance to America. Meanwhile, critic and writer Damon Knight, insisting on quality in the genre, founded the Science Fiction Writers of America, an elite guild that has bestowed the much-coveted Nebula Award annually to the best sf works since 1965. Harlan Ellison, a master of the "speculative fiction" short story who holds numerous Hugos and Nebulas, declared a revolution on sf's old guard in 1967 with *Dangerous Visions,* which anthologized a number of stories by bold new writers, such as Samuel Delaney and Roger Zelazny, as well as stories by older writers who thrived under the new style. The book, then the largest anthology of sf stories yet published, became the definitive statement of the American branch of the New Wave.

By this time, sf had traveled along a vast trajectory from the space opera adventures of the pulp era (with an emphasis on power and conquest) and the technological fixations of the Campbellian stable (which celebrated humanity and progress), through postwar disillusionment and cynicism, to a new literary awareness and an emphasis on social concerns and lifestyles. The stage was set for writers with previously unheard views, as well as writers who had been publishing before the New Wave but defied categorization, to express themselves to a wider, and more aware audience.

SCIENCE FICTION ENTERS ACADEMIA

Sf's expansion of themes provided a niche for social commentary and satire. Kurt Vonnegut Jr. was particularly successful at writing in this mode, gaining widespread popularity and critical recognition with such novels as *Slaughterhouse-Five, Player Piano,* and *Cat's Cradle,* which were written in a sf vein but whose appeal extended beyond the confines of sf fandom. This attention earned Vonnegut the much-envied respect of the literary establishment (a rare feat in the genre). Vonnegut has continued to mix satire and absurd humor with more traditional tropes of sf, as he does in *Galapagos* and other more recent works.

Another major writer associated with the New Wave is Philip K. Dick. Dick started publishing in the fifties, but, ahead of his time, earned little recognition and appreciation until the sixties. From the midfifties throughout the sixties, he published hundreds of short stories and dozens of novels, including the highly regarded titles *The Man in the High Castle, Ubik, The Three Stigmata of Palmer Eldrich,* and *Do Androids Dream of Electric Sheep?* (the basis of the film *Blade Runner*). Using many traditional sf elements, Dick was concerned with philosophy and the quality of existence, and he earned a reputation as an inspired master of metaphysics and alternate states of reality. The real presence of good and evil and the exploration of humanity, as well as a strong mysticism, pervade his fiction. By the time Dick's breakneck pace of production slowed in the early seventies, he claimed to experience an actual mystic connection to the divine. While many thought him insane, Dick struggled to reconcile his personal experiences for the last decade of his life, finally expressing his insights in a trilogy of books published shortly before his death: *Valis, The Di-*

vine Invasion, and *The Transmigration of Timothy Archer.* These novels, all with a dense philosophical and religious emphasis, are among the most difficult and dizzying of the works of this author. He is at present perhaps the sf author most studied by academics.

Another writer whose career was revitalized during this period was Robert Silverberg. Like Dick, Vonnegut, and Ellison, Silverberg had published as early as the fifties, although he had not yet earned a great reputation. However, during the New Wave period, Silverberg wrote under a different muse, penning a number of novels with a previously unseen depth that appropriately earned him the admiration and respect of his peers and fans. From the late sixties throughout the seventies, Silverberg fixated on issues of mortality, belief, religion and communion, love, relationships, and sex. He would become well known for his frank treatment of these themes, which are illustrated in novels like *The Masks of Time, Downward to the Earth, A Time of Changes, The Book of Skulls,* and *Dying Inside.* Also a thoughtful editor and anthologist, Silverberg has helped to make the work of many other sf authors available.

NEW BARRIERS BROKEN

The New Wave also broke down the often-noted gender barrier constructed during the decades of pulp and magazine sf. Writers like Ursula K. Le Guin, Joanna Russ, and James Tiptree Jr. (the pseudonym of Alice Sheldon) brought themes of gender to the foreground and helped overcome many assumptions regarding sf and the marginalization of women. These writers are often credited with introducing feminism into the genre. Sheldon, writing as Tiptree, was a scientist before starting her sf career in 1968. Her stories often concentrate on themes of gender and love and death, sometimes with a murder-and-mating motif. These themes permeate her acclaimed work, including the stories "Love Is the Plan, the Plan Is Death," "The Girl Who Was Plugged In," and "The Women Men Don't See." Like Philip K. Dick, Sheldon's reality was as extraordinary as the fiction she devised, and biographical research reveals that she enacted many of her fictional themes in her personal life.

Ursula K. Le Guin is one of the most academically minded and literary writers to contribute to the genre. Often categorized as a feminist, Le Guin's works also prescribe humanist values. She began writing sf in the sixties, and continued to produce popular and acclaimed works of both sf and fantasy throughout the seventies. She has received numerous awards for titles in both genres, including the sf novels *The Left Hand of Darkness* and *The Dispossessed*, each earning both the Hugo and Nebula Awards. Much of her fiction concentrates on utopian and dystopian themes in the tradition of such prestigious writers as More, Huxley, and Orwell. Also prevalent in Le Guin's writing is an abiding admiration for philosophy, especially Taoism and Jungian theory, as well as an aversion for the practices of Western science, and a concern for the environment (a popular sf theme since the sixties). Recently, Le Guin has not produced much sf, but has been a prolific poet, essayist, and academic in the areas of literary criticism and gender studies.

The New Wave was a time of great expansion for sf. The literary experimentation and attention to new themes shifted the predominant tone of the genre, not only from an emphasis on the hard to the social sciences, but also to an awareness of lifestyle and the consequences of irresponsible science. For many, the New Wave was the greatest period in sf history, challenging former assumptions, overturning traditional boundaries, and increasing the possibilities of the genre.

Although many of these themes carried on into the 1980s and beyond, it is popularly believed that George Lucas's film *Star Wars* (1977) sounded the death knell for the New Wave. While the film explored themes of mysticism and the struggle between good and evil, it influenced the sf market, creating a demand for the fast-paced wild adventures of science-fantasy space operas that had been so popular in the pulp era. Over the next few decades movie and television science fiction seemed to guide the genre. Serialized versions of movie and television storylines crowded the science fiction sections of bookstores. It appeared as if the literary genre had been set back to midcentury. Still, worthy authors kept critics entertained with more thought-provoking works. The mass influence of television, movies, and other media and information sources like the newly devised Internet even became subjects of study and debate in the more socially aware sf. The changing face of society as well as the so-called information revolution led the way to the next great movement within science fiction literature.

CYBERPUNK AND OTHER CONTEMPORARY SCIENCE FICTION

Contending with issues plaguing a media saturated society, sf authors created a new form dubbed cyberpunk. This on-going subgenre was initiated by William Gibson's *Neuromancer*, a novel that depicts a world overrun by the proliferation of technology, in which human life becomes devalued and characters often despise or reject their bodies in favor of cybernetics and interaction within the consensual hallucination known as cyberspace. This novel sparked a cyberpunk revolution in sf, influencing many of Gibson's contemporaries, like John Shirley, author of *Eclipse,* and Bruce Sterling, the author of numerous short stories and novels. It was Sterling who assembled the subgenre's definitive anthology, *Mirrorshades,* which includes stories by many of the movement's popular authors. Often with a cynical edge, cyberpunk fiction explores themes of invasion of the body and mind, as well as the dehumanization and alienation that accompanies life in an impersonal, high-tech society. The cyberpunk movement continues, exerting a pervasive influence on numerous works of television and film, and its tropes (especially the use of computers, cyberspace, and artificial intelligences) are widely treated in those media as well as in the writings of many contemporary, noncyberpunk sf authors.

REVAMPING AND EXPANDING

Much contemporary sf, however, still comes from authors unassociated with the cyberpunk movement. Alternate histories, which have long been a sf form, have again become popular, as witnessed by the success of authors like Harry Turtledove, a historical expert who specializes in creating alternate realities in which history deviates from this world's at some crucial point, as it does in his novels *The Guns of the South* and *How Few Remain,* both set in a world where the Confederacy won the American Civil War.

The past twenty years have also seen the reign of sf's "Killer B's": David Brin, Gregory Benford, and Greg Bear, all of whom have won the major awards in the field. Their works are often perceived as a new kind of hard sf, which also takes into account some of the concerns of the New Wave, including Brin's *Earth,* Benford's *Timescape,* and Bear's *Blood Music,* all three of which posit ecological disaster as a result of humanity's use of technology and science (although technology itself is not the culprit, and sometimes has the potential to avert the disaster). The Killer B's have also continued Asimov's famous Foundation series.

One of the most acclaimed contemporary writers of sf literature is Octavia Butler. Not only recognized for her award-winning sf, Butler has also contributed to the African American literary community, often concentrating on themes of gender, race, and the social disparities between groups and classes. She is noted for works like her Xenogenesis series (*Dawn, Adulthood Rights,* and *Imago*), which utilizes the sf device of an alien takeover to explore issues of gender and sexuality, and the *Parable of the Sower,* a dystopia through which Butler contemplates her social concerns.

Another writer who has achieved similar status is Margaret Atwood. She displays a feminist perspective in *The Handmaid's Tale,* which depicts a future in which women are horribly oppressed. Atwood's is a dystopic vision of the magnitude of Orwell's, and her dark visions are among the most significant demonstrated in contemporary literature.

Science fiction, unlike many other literary movements that are the subject of academic study, is a living, ongoing genre, persisting with irrepressible strength and generating the enthusiastic response of readers and fans. Beyond the traditional written media, sf has manifested an increasing presence in film and television. Programs like *Star Trek* and films such as Lucas's *Star Wars* series, as well as the growing Japanese sf tradition (exemplified by the Anime genre), have appealed to wide audiences and enlisted many new fans; they have won a mainstream appreciation and reflect the multi-faceted nature of the genre. Much loved, often misunderstood, and sometimes despised, science fiction remains one of the most diverse and imaginative of literary genres.

NOTES

1. Brian W. Aldiss, *Billion Year Spree: The True History of Science Fiction.* Garden City, NY: Doubleday, 1973, pp. 21–23.

2. Aldiss, *Billion Year Spree,* p. 132.

3. Aldiss, *Billion Year Spree,* p. 159.

4. Robert Scholes and Eric S. Rabkin, *Science Fiction: History, Science, Vision.* New York: Oxford University Press, 1977, p. 36.

5. Jack Williamson, "The Years of Wonder," in Thomas D. Clareson, ed., *Voices for the Future: Essays on Major Science Fiction*

Writers. Bowling Green, OH: Bowling Green University Popular Press, 1976, pp. 5–6.

6. Scholes and Rabkin, *Science Fiction,* p. 51.
7. Aldiss, *Billion Year Spree,* pp. 226–27.
8. Williamson, "The Years of Wonder," pp. 7–9.
9. Aldiss, *Billion Year Spree,* p. 229.
10. Williamson, "The Years of Wonder," pp. 11–12.
11. Quoted in Colin Greenland, *The Entropy Exhibition: Michael Moorcock and the British 'New Wave' in Science Fiction.* London: Routledge & Kegan Paul, 1983, p. 17.

CHAPTER 1

Within the Literary Tradition

Science Fiction

Science Fiction as a Literary Movement

William Atheling Jr.

William Atheling Jr. is the pseudonym for the critical persona of science fiction author James Blish, whose many popular works include the novels *A Case of Conscience, And All the Stars a Stage, The Star Dwellers, The Night Shapes,* and a number of titles in the *Star Trek* series. In this selection Blish addresses the difficulty inherent in trying to define the elusive genre of science fiction. Blish suggests that the difficulty may stem from the nature of science fiction itself, which requires that its authors create universes from the private visions of their own minds and then display them for all to see (like metaphorical tattoos). Instead of defining the genre by the characteristic of accurate extrapolation, Blish emphasizes the human quality of science fiction, claiming that the genre's value is in its exploration of human problems. Finally, even from this early vantage point of 1970, Blish declares the emergence of science fiction as a literary movement, illustrating how the genre fulfills the characteristics of literature.

Writers who attempt to define science fiction inevitably suffer the fate decreed by Archibald MacLeish (who was caught by it) for poets who follow armies: their bones are subsequently found under old newspapers. I was reminded of the melancholy fact some years ago when I was set to constructing such a definition for the *Grolier Encyclopedia*. At that time I could do no better than repeat the usual routine of defining the thing by its trappings—the far journey, the future, extrapolation—but I could not help but feel that when I was done, the emperor had no more clothes than before.

Though I can feel in anticipation the rustling over my bones, I am about to attempt it again, for I've since come to think that the question is a simpler one—O fatal gambit!— than it is usually made to appear. At least there do seem to me to be certain basic assumptions which stand under inspection, and pass the test by which so many definitions fall: that of remaining applicable to practitioners as apparently incompatible as Ray Bradbury and Hal Clement, yet at the same time clearly excluding the whole category—which everyone *feels* ought to be excluded, however difficult that proves—of fiction about science, as exemplified by *Arrowsmith* or the novels of C. P. Snow. If the assumptions are a little bizarre, I will have to plead that so is the subject-matter; but the argument is reasonably straightforward.

THE TATTOOS OF PRIVATE VISION

Short stories of any kind are like tattoos: though they are on public display, they come into being to identify the self to the self. The commonest and hence the most stereotyped were undertaken to prove that the subject/object is grown up, with a flourish of brightly colored but non-functional women, guns, cars and other machinery. Another kind attempts to seal an identification with some stronger and more stable entity—Mother, Mamie, Semper Fidelis or Free Enterprise; or make real some pigeon-hole into which the personality is trying to cram itself—Lover, Killer, Mighty Hunter.

The most interesting kinds, however, are those cryptic symbols which the mentally ill inflict upon themselves. Here the vision of the outside world which the story or tattoo tries to make real is almost as private as the psyche which so stigmatizes itself. Only the necessity to adopt some sort of artistic convention, and to limit the message to something less than the whole of the mystery, makes the end-product even partially intelligible—and, to some part of the audience, holds out the hope that the mystery might be solved.

There is at least a little of the private vision in every work of fiction, but it is in fantasy that the distance between the real world—that is, the agreed-upon world, the consensus we call reality—and the private vision becomes marked and disturbing. The science-fiction writer chooses, to symbolize *his* real world, the trappings of science and technology, and in so far as the reader is unfamiliar with these, so will the story seem *outré* [foreign] to him. It is commonplace for outsiders to ask science-fiction writers, "Where do you get those crazy ideas?" and to regard the habitual readers of science fiction also as rather far off the common ground. Yet it is not really the ideas that are "crazy" but the trappings; not the assumptions, but the scenery. Instead of Main Street—in itself only a symbol—we are given Mars, or the future.

The reason for this choice is put succinctly by Brian Aldiss:

"I am a surrealist at heart; that is, I'm none too sure whether the reality of the world agrees with its appearance. Only in sf, or near sf, can you express this feeling in words."

Of course, this is not entirely true; neither Kafka nor Beckford had any difficulty in expressing the same feeling in quite different trappings, in sporting quite different tattoos. But for any writer who knows how surrealistic are the assumptions of our modern metaphysics, the science-tattoo is not only attractive but compelling.

It is not even essential that the symbols be used correctly, although most conscientious science-fiction writers try to get them right in order to lure the reader into the necessary suspension of disbelief. There is no such place as Ray Bradbury's Mars—to use the most frequently cited complaint—but his readers have justly brushed the complaint aside, recognizing the feeling as authentic even though the facts are not. This is probably what Mr. Aldiss means by "near-sf," as it is what I mean by fantasy. The essential difference lies only in how close to the consensus the writer wants his private tattoo to appear.

HONESTY TO THE ASSUMPTIONS

In this matter of correctness, the reader also has preferences, so that it is rare to find someone who is drawn to a Hal Clement who relishes Mr. Bradbury too, and vice versa. . . . However, there are other kinds of accuracy than the factual which are important to poetry (*Dichtung* = any work of art), chief among which is faithfulness to the language of symbol. As precisely this point is pursued at enormous length by Robert Graves in *The White Goddess,* I will rest content with a bare mention of it here.

The absolutely essential honesty, however, must lie where it has to lie in all fiction: honesty to the assumptions, not to the trappings. This brings us back, inevitably, to the often quoted definition by Theodore Sturgeon:

"A good science-fiction story is a story about human beings, with a human problem, and a human solution, which would not have happened at all without its science content."

This is a laudable and workable rule of thumb, it seems to me, as long as the writer is aware that the "science content" is only another form of tattoo design, differing in detail but not in nature from those adopted by the writers of all other kinds of fiction.

Viewed in this light, the writing of science fiction is an activity which cannot usefully be divorced by the critic from the mainstream of fiction writing, or from artistic creation as a whole. It does not even differ from them in being idiosyncratic in its choice of a symbol-system, since every artist must be odd in this respect, choosing from the real world (has anyone seen it lately?) those parts which make the best fit with the universe inside his skull. The science-fiction writer centers his universe-of-discourse in the myths of Twentieth Century metaphysics, as other writers found their intellectual homes and furniture on Olympus or the Mount of Olives. . . .

SCIENCE FICTION BECOMES A LITERARY MOVEMENT

The process of gradual re-assimilation of science fiction into the mainstream of literature—which was where it started out, with such figures as Wells and Conan Doyle—is bound to be painful for fans who want to claim some special superiority for the genre (as well as for writers who would much prefer *not* to have the usual standards of criticism applied to what they do), but growing up always has its twinges.

The field will *always* remain to some extent a separate, self-conscious branch of letters; that change, which began in 1926, is not in my judgment reversible now. But there is another such change of character now in the making. Science fiction is now in the process of emerging from the status of a small category of commercial fiction, and taking on the characteristics of a literary movement.

It is too early to attempt a history of this change, but some already quite familiar events tend to change proportions and relationships when viewed in this light. Primarily, the change is the work of such magazine editors as John W. Campbell, who whatever his side-hobbies has always insisted that stories written for him have something to say and that the characters in them act and talk like flesh-and-blood human beings, and like Horace L. Gold and Anthony Boucher, who demanded stylistic distinction and who flensed away many of the pulp taboos with which the field was encumbered; of anthologists like William Sloane and Fletcher Pratt, who gave some of the best early stories the relative permanence of book format; of critics like Kingsley Amis and Damon Knight, who saw nothing unreasonable in applying the same standards of judgment to science fiction as are customarily applied to any fiction of serious intentions; and of publishers like Ballantine Books and Faber and Faber, who looked for distinguished work and offered it to the public without either apologies or appeals to special cults of readers. (These citations are intended to be representative, not inclusive, but an inclusive list would not be much longer.)

But the main responsibility for the change, as you would expect, must be assigned to that small but potent group of writers to whom science fiction was not just a meal-ticket but an art form, demanding the broadest vision, the deepest insights, and the best craftsmanship of which each man was capable. The roster of such men is gratifyingly long for its age; and although until recently science fiction has been primarily an American phenomenon, it is gratifyingly international, too. Again, an inclusive list would be impossible without the benefit of greater hindsight than time has yet allowed, but any such list would have to cite Algis Budrys and Theodore Sturgeon in the United States, Brian Aldiss and C. S. Lewis in England, and Gérard Klein in France. Some of the major editors, anthologists and critics have also contributed as writers.

CHARACTERISTICS OF A MOVEMENT

What are the characteristics of a literary movement? Everyone will have his own list of distinguishing features—the scholar, for example, will demand that the movement exert some influence on literature as a whole, and this is certainly demonstrable here, all the way from firmly popular writers like Nevil Shute to iconoclasts like William Burroughs—but I think they can all be summed up under the heading of self-consciousness. Among the symptoms of this awareness might be listed the emergence of histories and bibliographies of the field, such as those by Sam Moskowitz and Donald B. Day; of works of criticism such as those by Messrs Amis and Knight . . . of specialized literary quarterlies such as *SF Horizons*, the late international journal edited by Mr. Aldiss and Harry Harrison; of professional organizations such as Science Fiction Writers of America, recently revived by Mr. Knight; and perhaps of such forms of articulate reader support as the "Hugo" and "Nebula" awards (given each year for the best work of the previous year), and publishing houses such as Advent (Chicago) which specialize in works *about* science fiction.

But these remain symptoms. A literary genre cannot also become a movement until a significant number of its primary practitioners, the writers, begin to think of themselves as artists, not just journeymen, working in what to them seems to be the most important and rewarding field of the many they might have chosen. (Note that many of the major science-fiction writers have contributed to other fields as well, particularly the detective story and the historical novel.)

Detecting a writer thinking about himself in this way must remain mostly a matter of reading between the lines. A few—Mr. Heinlein is an example—may come right out and say that science fiction is for them worthy of more attention than anything else being written today, but such statements are often construed as bids for special attention, or pleas for special exemptions from critical attention. In any event, most science-fiction writers still tend to shy away from making such public claims. One place where the claim may be implicit, James Blish has suggested, may be in those stories where they turn to speculating on the future of the arts other than their own. Considering how belligerently defensive science-fiction people often are, there is a notable lack of narcissism in these stories; self-conscious though these artists are, they are unprecedentedly more interested in their subjects than they are in themselves.

This freedom from involution among these writers . . . may indeed indicate that they are speaking for a movement, of which they are proud. If that is the case (and necessarily I agree that it is), the movement will have every reason to speak well of them hereafter.

The Literature of Human Possibility

Ben Bova

Ben Bova is the author of such science fiction novels as *Star Watchmen* and *The Weathermakers*. He has also served as one of the genre's influential editors, having succeeded John W. Campbell Jr. as the mind behind *Analog Science Fiction-Science Fact* magazine. Bova sees science fiction as a bridge between science and art. To him the potential of technology in science fiction is always tempered by the qualities of the humans who oversee that technology. In this way what readers often perceive as the cold, unemotional world of science is merged with humanity's heroism and tragedy. The effect not only emphasizes human capabilities but also highlights the wonder and beauty of science. The task of good science fiction writers, then, is the same as that of all fiction writers: to help humanity understand itself.

Science fiction writers are not in the business of predicting *the* future. They do something much more important. They try to show the many possible futures that lie open to us. If the history of the human race can be thought of as an enormous migration through time, with thousands of millions of people wandering through the centuries, then the writers of science fiction are the scouts, the explorers, the adventurers who send back stories that warn of the harsh desert up ahead, or tales that dazzle us with reports of the beautiful mountains that lie just over the horizon.

For there is not simply *a* future, a time to come that's preordained and inexorable. Our future is built, bit by bit, minute by minute, by the actions of human beings. One vital role of science fiction is to show what kinds of future might result from certain kinds of human actions.

Excerpted from "The Role of Science Fiction," by Ben Bova, in *Science Fiction Today and Tomorrow*, edited by Reginald Bretnor. Copyright © 1974 by Reginald Bretnor. Reprinted by permission of HarperCollins Publishers, Inc.

Have you ever stood on a flat, sandy beach, at the edge of the water, and watched the little wavelets that play at your feet? After the breakers have dumped their energy and the water rushes as far up the beach as it can, there's a criss-cross pattern of wavelets that mottle the beach. If the sun's at the proper angle, you can clearly see what physicists call *interference patterns.* The wavelets interact with one another, sometimes adding together to form a stronger wave, sometimes canceling each other to form a blank spot in the pattern.

The myriads of ideas that parade across the pages of science fiction magazines and books each month form such a pattern in the minds of readers and writers. Some ideas get reinforced, added to, strengthened by repetition and enlargement. Other ideas get canceled, fall out of favor, are found lacking in one way or another. Thus, for more than a generation now, science fiction people have been worrying about problems such as pollution, nuclear warfare, overpopulation, genetic manipulation, runaway technology, thought control, and other threats that burst on the general public as shocking surprises.

Other potential problems have been examined and dropped. Today there are few stories about invisible men seized by dreams of power. Or plagues of "space germs" infecting Earth. When Michael Crichton's *Andromeda Strain* became a vastly popular book and movie, most science fiction people groaned. "But it's an old idea!" they chorused, meaning that it's no longer a valid idea: the problem does not and probably will not exist. But this old idea was shatteringly new and exciting to the general public.

THE ART OF SCIENCE FICTION

To communicate the ideas, the fears and hopes, the shape and feel of all the infinite possible futures, science fiction writers lean heavily on another of their advantages: the art of fiction.

For while a scientist's job has largely ended when he's reduced his data to tabular or graph form, the work of a science fiction writer is just beginning. His task is to convey the human story: the scientific basis for the possible future of his story is merely the background. Perhaps "merely" is too limiting a word. Much of science fiction consists of precious little except the background, the basic idea, the gimmick.

But the best of science fiction, the stories that make a lasting impact on generations of readers, are stories about *people.* The people may be nonhuman. They may be robots or other types of machines. But they will be people, in the sense that human readers can feel for them, share their joys and sorrows, their dangers and their ultimate successes.

The art of fiction has not changed much since prehistoric times, mainly because man's nervous system and the culture he's built out of it have not basically changed.

From the earliest Biblical times, through Homer to Shakespeare, Goethe, and right down to today's commercial fiction industry, the formula for telling a powerful story has remained the same: create a strong character, a person of great strengths, capable of deep emotions and decisive action. Give him a weakness. Set him in conflict with another powerful character—or perhaps with nature. Let this exterior conflict be the mirror of the protagonist's own interior conflict, the clash of his desires, his own strength against his own weakness. And there you have a story. Whether it's Abraham offering his only son to God, or Paris bringing ruin to Troy over a woman, or Hamlet and Claudius playing their deadly game, Faust seeking the world's knowledge and power, Gully Foyle, D. D. Harriman, Montag the Fireman, Michael Valentine Smith, Muad'Dib—the stories that stand out in the minds of the readers are those that are made incandescent by characters—people—who are unforgettable.

To show other worlds, to describe possible future societies and the problems lurking ahead, is not enough. The writer of science fiction *must show how these worlds and these futures affect human beings.* And something much more important: *he must show how human beings can and do literally create these future worlds.* For our future is largely in our own hands. It doesn't come blindly rolling out of the heavens; it is the joint product of the actions of billions of human beings. This is a point that's easily forgotten in the rush of headlines and the hectic badgering of everyday life. But it's a point that science fiction makes constantly: the future belongs to us—whatever it is. We make it, our actions shape tomorrow. We have the brains and guts to build paradise (or at least try). Tragedy is when we fail, and the greatest crime of all is when we fail even to try.

SCIENCE FICTION BRIDGES SCIENCE AND ART

Thus science fiction stands as a bridge between science and art, between the engineers of technology and the poets of humanity. Never has such a bridge been more desperately needed.

Writing in the British journal *New Scientist*, the famed poet and historian Robert Graves said in 1972, "Technology is now warring openly against the crafts, and science covertly against poetry."

What Graves is expressing is the fear that many people have: technology has already allowed machines to replace human muscle power; now it seems that machines such as electronic computers might replace human brainpower. And he goes even further, pointing a shaking finger at science as the well-spring of technology, and criticizing science on the mystical grounds that science works only in our usual four dimensions of space/time, while truly human endeavors such as poetry have a power that scientists can't recognize "because, at its most intense, [poetry] works in the Fifth Dimension, independent of time."

Graves explains that poetry is usually the product of intuitive thinking, and grants that some mathematical theories have also sprung from intuition. Then he says, "Yet scientists would dismiss a similar process . . . as 'illogical.' "

Apparently Graves sees scientists as a sober, plodding phalanx of soulless thinking machines, never making a step that hasn't been carefully thought out in advance. He should try working with a few scientists, or even reading James D. Watson's *The Double Helix*.

As a historian, Graves should be aware that James Clerk Maxwell's brilliant insight about electromagnetism—the guess that visible light is only one small slice of the spectrum of electromagnetic energy, a guess that forms the basis for electronics technology—was an intuitive leap into the unknown. Maxwell had precious little evidence to back up his guess. The evidence came later. Max Planck's original concept of the quantum theory was also mainly intuition. The list of wild jumps of intuition made by these supposedly stolid, humorless scientists is long indeed.

Scientists are human beings! They are just as human, intuitive, and emotional as anyone else. But most people don't realize this. They don't know scientists, any more than they know much about science.

C. P. Snow pointed out . . . decades ago that there is a gap between the Two Cultures, and Graves's remarks show that the gap is widening into a painful chasm. Graves is a scholar who should know better. He's justly renowned for his work in ancient mythology, where he's combined his gifts of poetry and historical research in a truly original and beautiful way.

But he doesn't seem to understand that scientists do precisely the same thing. Because he doesn't understand scientists.

Since the prehistoric days of tribal shamans, most people have held a highly ambivalent attitude toward the medicine man-astrologer-wizard-scientist. On the one hand they envied his abilities and sought to use his power for their own gain. On the other hand, they feared his power, hated his seeming superiority, and knew damned well that he was in league with dark forces of evil.

There has been little change in this double-edged attitude over the centuries. Today most people still tend to hold scientists in awe. After all, scientists have brought us nuclear weapons, modern medicines, space flight, and underarm deodorants. Yet at the same time, we see scientists derided as fuzzy-brained eggheads or as coldly ruthless, emotionless makers of monsters. Scientists are a minority group, and like most minorities they're largely hidden from the public's sight, tucked away in ghettos—laboratories, campuses, field sites out in the desert or on Pacific atolls.

Before the public can understand and appreciate what science can and cannot do, the people must get to see and understand the scientists themselves. Get to know their work, their aims, their dreams, and their fears.

SCIENCE FICTION AS MYTHOLOGY

A possible answer to this problem of humanizing science and scientists comes from the field in which Graves made his major contribution: mythology.

Joseph Campbell, professor of literature at Sarah Lawrence College, has spent a good deal of his life studying humankind's mythology and writing books on the subject, such as the four-volume *The Masks of God,* and *Hero with a Thousand Faces.* He has pointed out that modern man has no real mythology to turn to. The old myths are dead, and no new mythology has arisen to take their place.

And man needs a mythology, Campbell insists, to give a sort of emotional meaning and stability to the world in which he lives. Myths are a sort of codification on an emotional level of man's attitudes toward life, death, and the whole vast and sometimes frightening universe.

An example. Almost every primitive culture has a Prometheus myth. In our Western culture, the Greek version is the one most quoted. Prometheus was a demigod who saw man as a weak, starving, freezing creature, barely able to survive among the animals of the fields and woods. Taking pity on man, Prometheus stole fire from the heavens and gave it to man, at the cost of a horrible punishment to himself. But man, with fire, became master of the Earth and even a challenge to the gods.

A typical myth, fantastic in detail yet absolutely correct in spirit. One of man's early ancestors "discovered" fire about half a million years ago, according to anthropological evidence. Most likely these primitive *Homo erectus* creatures saw lightning turn shrubbery into flame; hence the legend of the gift from the heavens. Before fire, our ancestors were merely another marginal anthropoid, most of whom died out. With fire, we've become the dominant species on this planet.

The Prometheus myth "explains" this titanic event in terms that primitive people can understand and accept. The myth gives an emotional underpinning to the bald facts, ties reality into an all-encompassing structure that explains both the known and the incomprehensible parts of man's experience.

Much of today's emotion-charged, slightly irrational urge toward astrology and the occult is really a groping for a new mythology, a mythology that can explain the modern world on a gut level to people who are frightened that they're too small and weak to cope with this universe.

FULFILLING THE TENETS OF MYTHOLOGY

Joseph Campbell's work has shown that there are at least four major functions that any mythology must accomplish.

First: a mythology must induce a feeling of awe and majesty in people. This is what science fictionists call "a sense of wonder."

Second: a mythology must define and uphold a system of the universe, a pattern of self-consistent explanation for both the known and incomprehensible parts of man's existence. A modern mythology would have a ready-made system of the universe in the continuously expanding body of knowledge that we call science.

Third: a mythology must usually support the social establishment. For example, what we today call Greek mythology apparently originated with the Achaean conquerors of the earlier Mycenaean civilization. Zeus was a barbarian sky god who conquered the local deities of the matriarchal Mycenaean agricultural cities. Most of the lovely legends about Zeus's romantic entanglements with local goddesses are explanations of the barbarian, patriarchal people overwhelming the farmers' matriarchies.

Fourth: a mythology must serve as an emotional crutch to help the individual member of society through the inevitable crises of life, such as the transition from childhood into adulthood, the adjustments of the individual to his society, the inescapable prospect of death.

Science fiction, when it's at its very best, serves the functions of a modern mythology.

Certainly science fiction tries to induce a sense of wonder about the physical universe and man's own interior private universe. Science fiction depends heavily on known scientific understanding as the basic underpinning of a universal order. Science fiction does not tend to support a given political establishment, but on a deeper level it almost invariably backs the basic tenet of Western civilization: that is, the concept that the individual man is worth more than the organization—whatever it may be—and that nothing is more important than human freedom.

Whether or not science fiction helps people through emotional crises is more difficult to tell, and probably the only remaining test to the genre's claim to mythological stature. It is interesting that science fiction has a huge readership among the young, the adolescents who are trying to figure out their own individual places in the universe. And how many science fiction stories about superheroes and time travel and interstellar flights are really an attempt to deny the inevitability of death?

On this emotional level, science fiction can—and does— serve the functions of mythology. On a more cerebral level, science fiction helps to explain what science and scientists are all about to the non-scientists. It is no accident that sev-

eral hundred universities and public schools are now offering science fiction courses and discovering that these classes
are a meeting ground for the scientist-engineers and the hu-
manists. Science *and* fiction. Reason *and* emotion.

Science fiction can also blend reason with emotion in another way: to show the true beauty and grandeur of the universe, whether it's a galaxy full of stars or a drop of water
teeming with delicate, invisible life.

How many young students have been "turned on" to science by reading science fiction? Most of the men who have
walked on the Moon's surface trace their careers back to
early readings in science fiction. For, in addition to examining the problems of the future, science fiction opens the door
to the widest of all possible worlds. The bone chess cities of
Ray Bradbury's Mars, the galaxy-spanning adventures of
E. E. Smith, the quietly extra-ordinary pastorals that Zenna
Henderson writes, Asimov's robots, Dickson's droll aliens—
the canvas available to science fictionists is as wide as the
universe and as long as time itself. And by showing this marvelous, varied, puzzling, colorful universe—and humanity's
role in it—science fiction stories give their readers the kind
of excitement that simply does not exist elsewhere.

THE BEAUTY OF SCIENCE

And there's more. By showing the wonders of the physical
universe, science fiction also tends to show the beauty of this
system of thought that is called science.

The essence of the scientific attitude is that the human
mind can succeed in understanding the universe. By taking
thought, men can move mountains—and have. In this sense,
science is an utterly humanistic pursuit, the glorification of
human intellect over the puzzling, chaotic, and often frightening darkness of ignorance.

Much of science fiction celebrates this spirit. Although
there are plenty of science fiction stories that warn of the
dangers of science and technology—the Frankenstein,
dystopia stories—there are even more that look to science
and technology for the leverage by which human beings can
move the world. Even in the dystopia stories, where the basic message is usually, "There are some things that man was
not meant to know, Doctor," there is still an aura of striving,
an attempt to achieve greatness. Very few science fiction stories picture humanity as a passive species, allowing the tidal

forces of nature to flow unperturbed. The heroes of science fiction stories—the gods of the new mythology—struggle manfully against the darkness, whether it's geological doom for the whole planet or the evil of grasping politicians. They may not always win, these Kimball Kinnisons and Charlie Gordons and James Retiefs. But they always *try*.

This attitude may stem from science fiction's long ghetto existence in the pulp magazines. But it is very much the same attitude that motivates scientists. As Einstein once said, when struggling with a particularly difficult problem in theoretical physics, "God may be subtle, but He isn't perverse." The problem may be tough, unsolvable even; but men still try, through the application of human thought.

That's what is behind this elusive quality that science fictionists call "the sense of wonder." When a Larry Niven hero detours his spaceship so that he can take a look at the complex beauty of the double star Beta Lyrae, when James Blish creates a detailed and marvelous world of intelligent creatures of microscopic size whose world is a tiny pond, when A. E. van Vogt's time traveler swings across the aeons to trigger the creation of the universe—the sense of wonder inspired in the reader is twofold. First is the sheer stupendous audacity of the writer in attempting to create such exciting settings, and getting away with it! But at a deeper, perhaps unconscious, level is the thrill of realizing that the human mind can reach this far, can encompass such ideas, can both produce and appreciate such beauty.

Understanding and appreciation: two more words that help define the role of science fiction.

SCIENCE FICTION IS THE LITERATURE OF CHANGE

But perhaps the most important aspect of science fiction's role in the modern world is summed up in a single word: *change.*

After all, science fiction is the literature of change. Each and every story preaches from the same gospel: tomorrow will be different from today, violently different perhaps.

For aeons, humankind accepted and expected that tomorrow would be very much the same as today. Change was something to worry over, to consult priests and oracles about, to fear and dread. Today we talk about "future shock" and long for the Good Old Days when everything was known and in its proper place.

Science fiction very clearly shows that changes—whether good or bad—are an inherent part of the universe. Resistance to change is an archaic, and nowadays dangerous, habit of thought. The world will change. It is changing constantly. Humanity's most fruitful course of action is to determine how to shape these changes, how to influence them and produce an environment where the changes that occur are those we want.

Again, in this attitude, science fiction mirrors science itself. Lewis M. Branscomb, former director of the National Bureau of Standards, has said:

> Technology has brought us changes, most of which we should welcome, rather than reject. Wealth is the least important of these changes. Of greater importance is change itself. Those young humanists who think themselves revolutionaries are nothing compared to technology.

Perhaps this is the ultimate role of science fiction: to act as an interpreter of science to humanity. This is a two-edged weapon, of course. It is necessary to warn as well as evangelize. Science can kill as well as create; technology can deaden the human spirit or lift it to the farthermost corners of our imaginations. Only knowledgeable people can wisely decide how to use science and technology for humankind's benefit. In the end, this is the ultimate role of all art: to show ourselves to ourselves, to help us to understand our own humanity.

Science fiction, with its tremendous world view, with all of time and space to play with, gives its adherents a view that spans galaxies and aeons, a breadth of vision that exposes provincialism and prejudice for the petty concepts that they are. This is the world view that a modern mythology must have.

And this is what makes science fiction so much fun.

Science Fiction as Classic Romance

Janice Antczak

Janice Antczak analyzes the romantic aspect of science fiction and the genre's positive impact on young readers. For her discussion Antczak defines the term *romance* not by its modern associations of sentimentalized love stories, but rather by its medieval European roots that identifies a romantic tale as an incredible adventure with extraordinary heroes and deeds. Antczak points out the elements that science fiction shares with the romantic tradition, particularly the hero, the quest, and fantastic settings. She explains that the genre's often youthful audience readily identifies with these romantic qualities, enabling science fiction to inspire and educate young readers.

Science fiction is a romance form of the technological age. This category of "romance" is not the constellation of moonlight, flowers, whispered words, and caresses the word evokes in the common imagination. The heroes of science fiction may find themselves falling in love, but this idea of romance does not play a major role in the genre. In science fiction novels for children, it constitutes only a minor component, for the characters are most often young children themselves.

The romance meant here springs from the medieval European tale, often in verse, which tells of marvelous heroic deeds from history and legend, and has come to identify any tale or novel of extraordinary adventure filled with mysterious or even supernatural occurrences. The unknown, the possibilities, and the probabilities of the future in science fiction possess an aura of the mysterious which beckons those who ponder them. The heroes of science fiction venture forth on quests which, in this sense, can be called romantic.

THE SCIENCE FICTION HERO

Although the idea of the romantic adventure full of extraordinary and mysterious events characterizes science fiction
in a broad fashion, a more detailed examination of the nature of romance reveals pervasive patterns of imagery and
structure in the science fiction novel for children. In this
structural pattern, the hero (here the term "hero" applies to
either male or female protagonists) is an ideal one who
manifests some virtue or power to a degree greater than that
seen in the average person. The hero is not a deity, but
rather a person with a marked attribute which will aid him
or her in the course of the story.

The hero may possess any number of attributes. He or she
may exhibit multiple talents and abilities and appear as the
all-around hero who is strong and brave, kind and good,
honest and just. Or, the hero may possess only a single attribute, for instance, superior intelligence or a perfect memory; which will work to his or her advantage while pursuing
the goal. Whatever the number of abilities or degree of
power he or she possesses, the hero must utilize these
strengths when engaging a foe in tests of power; and the
hero's attributes ultimately work to defeat the foe who poses
a threat to the hero and the hero's world—good overcomes
evil. The hero's victory over evil constitutes one of the hall-
marks of the romance, and in triumph, the hero remains
true to his or her ideals and does not fall prey to the lures of
corrupting power. Other characters of the romance recognize the hero's innate goodness and steadfast virtue. Often
the hero is befriended by the neutral spirits of nature. Plants,
animals, and even the weather develop a rapport with the
hero and offer aid at a crucial point.

The child reader, like the neutral spirits of nature, recognizes the hero's innate goodness. The child also responds to
the hero's marvelous abilities. Whether the hero possesses
telekinetic powers or the ability to fly, the child reader's response and recognition may lead to identification with this
character and a closer sharing of the adventure and ideals of
the story. Within the structure of the science fiction novel,
the seemingly marvelous and mysterious join with the possible and probable as the child looks toward his or her own
future through the exploits of the hero.

The romance structure requires that this idealized hero

engage in the quest within an unusual setting. In the traditional fashion of romance, such a setting is usually an idyllic one—a lush green meadow at the height of summer or a magical kingdom. It need not be completely a fantasy world, but the setting must be a place that is in some way different from everyday reality. This distance from the mundane world allows the unusual or mysterious to play a role in the quest. Science fiction takes the reader at least one step beyond the present and places him or her in the brave new world with the hero, where the hero's attributes and the unique features of the environment and society are "actualities." The many worlds of the future provide seemingly infinite variations of time and place for the hero's exploits.

This idealized world of the romance often conjoins upper and lower realms. The hero journeys to the mountaintop or descends into the dark spaces of the underworld in order to pursue the quest. Often these periods of ascent or descent accompany points of epiphany or revelation for the hero. Such aspects of setting foster a sense of a place apart. Once more, science fiction's many worlds provide for new images of ascent and descent, especially the many forms of rocket and starships, or the submersibles which traverse the underworld of the ocean floor. In such vehicles, the reader can journey with the hero to the unusual world of strange powers and possibilities. The increasingly sophisticated technological and environmental detail of science fiction forms a unique hybrid of the actual and the imaginable which the child reader finds particularly compelling. These are worlds which the reader may someday inhabit as the hero of his or her own quest.

THE ROMANTIC QUEST OF SCIENCE FICTION

The marvelous setting provides the stage for the primary component of the story—the quest. Within the structure of the romance, adventure becomes the central aspect of the tale. The adventure assumes a quality of wish-fulfillment or dream of deeds performed for the hero and vicariously for the reader. The innocent hero is called to a dangerous mission by fate or by choice. This mission often involves a journey to a distant land or to a time filled with hardship and struggle and enemies. The hero, with comrades, encounters obstacles placed by the foe along the path to successful completion of the quest. The minor adversities pave the way to a final and furious confrontation between the hero and the adversary. This ultimate test of the hero's powers results in the defeat of the antagonist and in the triumph and recognition of the hero.

The three stages of adventure in the romance, the minor struggles of the quest, the ultimate confrontation with the opponent, and the hero's final triumph, reflect the structure of the hero myths of ages past, such as the death-resurrection myths of Attis or Christ, who faced conflict, died in their major test, and rose in triumph and glory from the dead. The science fiction hero who descends into a lunar cave and emerges three days later with an answer concerning the survival of the colonists on a new world follows the pattern set in these ancient myths, and the reader recognizes and responds to this mythic form on conscious or unconscious levels. This structure in traditional story or contemporary science fiction houses the classic battle between good and evil.

An even closer examination of the structure of the romance reveals that within the adventurous framework of the narrative lies an even more important aspect of the quest. At the heart of the quest, the hero is engaged in a deep, inner struggle. Whether the hero slays a dragon or searches for a lost treasure, or conquers hostile aliens or settles a Martian colony, he or she is participating in an almost primal quest for self, for identity, for knowledge. The mythic quest for self of the character mirrors the lifelong quest for self of the reader.

The classic hero of myth and legend has served as the ideal for people over centuries in many lands. The hero of science fiction stands as a direct descendant or as a new form of this eternal character. Often the hero has mysterious origins; his or her true parents may be unknown. The child hero may have been abandoned, set adrift like Moses, or raised in a foster home or by an animal, as were Romulus and Remus. There may be a search for the child, as Herod searched for the infant Christ. The unusual birth or mysterious parentage of the hero has been a common theme in romance over the centuries. The hero of science fiction is also often orphaned or abandoned, but the mysterious parentage may be the experiment in the genetics laboratory or the aliens who once visited earth.

The supporting characters align themselves for or against the quest. They are the comrades and traitors to the cause. Their portrayal of some virtue or vice is often one-dimensional. The comrades and traitors frequently play roles in direct opposition to each other. A wise old man, or a woman akin to a fairy godmother, appears to offer the hero guidance on the quest. There appear in juxtaposition evil witches, sorcerers, or scientists who work to foil the quest and bring the hero to ruin. The male hero may encounter a fair damsel or may find it necessary to resist the temptations of a siren. The faithful comrades of the hero must help to counter the force of the traitors and lackeys of the foe. Even animal characters adhere to this pattern of opposites as they too take sides for and against the quest. Once more, although such characters may be mutants or aliens, in keeping with the nature of science fiction, they perform in roles which have been part of the structure of the romance story in all ages.

Among the exceptions to this dialectical configuration are the neutral spirits of nature. They are drawn to the innate goodness of the hero and realize the importance of the successful completion of the quest. These beings represent the impartiality of nature. Their ancient lore and law are far removed from the petty wars of mankind, but the spirits understand that all things are related and they are moved to work toward and support the common good as identified by the hero.

One other character-role stands apart from the quest itself, that is the clown or fool who enters the scene to warn the hero of the perils of following the quest. The classic character of the wise fool in more traditional literature is frequently assumed by a parental or authority figure in juvenile science fiction. The sage counsel of one not involved in the quest, but who cautions the hero on the hardships and obstacles to be encountered, is a counterpoint to what might be the idealistic foolhardiness of the hero.

Setting is another literary element of primary importance in science fiction. Much of an author's creativity in this genre is seen in the development and description of the wonders of the universe. New worlds with strange plants and rock formations or earth much changed by earthquakes, floods, or nuclear devastation provide dramatic imagery in science fiction. Nevertheless, the manner in which exotic planets or a dramatically different earth are set forth conforms to the pattern of the romance and contributes to the success or failure of the hero's quest.

Characterization and setting provide much of the glamour and color of the romance. The seemingly infinite possibilities of portrayal of such imagery within science fiction are part of the genre's richness. Still, in the romantic quest the focus is on adventure. The hero must face the challenge of the many obstacles as he or she attempts to attain the goal. In the ultimate confrontation with the archenemy which determines the outcome of the quest, either the hero, the adversary, or both may die; but the hero's cause is triumphant and the hero is exalted. In our age of cynicism, when many ask where have all the heroes gone, science fiction supplies heroes who are the stuff of dreams, especially youthful dreams of great deeds to come in the future.

SCIENCE FICTION INSPIRES AND EDUCATES

Science fiction is a literature which has seen many dreams come true. To some the genre is a prophetic tool. After centuries of fabulous stories recounting it, man walked on the moon. This prophetic aspect has been a topic of debate and discussion, with many well-known voices clearly claiming that science fiction does not foretell the future. While such debates generate interest, whether or not the genre serves this function absolutely is not as significant to our age as the ability of the genre to provide children with a new perspective by presenting a vast array of alternative futures. Such diverse visions of the future may contain warnings of dire consequences resulting from present practices, such as poisoned seas, fouled air, and nuclear disaster. Yet within these doomsday images, the stories may offer the reader confidence in the adaptability and resourcefulness of humanity in coping with such problems. Such speculation can provide the child with a better understanding of the present state of society.

In recent years, science fiction has moved beyond the glorification of scientific and technological invention to an investigation of the effects of science and technology on the individual and the universe. This change of perspective may assist the child in dealing with the emotional, intellectual, and social demands of the future. Science fiction is a literature concerned with change, and for contemporary youth in confrontation with the future, such a perspective can be of greater importance than the security of the past.

Science fiction author Sylvia Louise Engdahl says, "Many

of today's children feel a closer kinship with the future than with the past . . . Only through speculation about the future as related to the past can these readers gain the sense of continuity that their elders acquired through the study of history." This is perhaps due to the rapid rate of change, both technological and societal, which characterizes contemporary life. The child in the age of "future shock" may see more of value in contemplation and speculation of the future. To such a child the lessons of history may seem especially far removed and ancient. The recognition by educators of this relationship between the child, history, and the future has wrought change in the status and use of science fiction with young people. Viewpoints such as Engdahl's now play an essential role in the education of the child.

Although many educators have, in the past, looked askance or even condemned the reading of science fiction by youth, future studies and other learning programs now in schools may be centered about or at least include aspects of this literature. Adults who understand and respect the changing role and reputation of science fiction may be able to communicate more effectively with children about literature and society. Science fiction is entertaining, romantic adventure, but it is adventure served up with history, social comment, and serious speculation about what may be. It is a literature in which past, present, and future are inextricably linked for the reader, and it is a literature whose own past, present, and future reveal much about its role as the myth and romance of the technological age.

The Potential for Social Criticism

Robert Bloch

Robert Bloch (1917–1994), the author of *Psycho*, is also known for his contributions to science fiction, both as a writer and as a critic. In this selection he examines the function of science fiction as a vehicle for modern social criticism. Concentrating particularly on the early science fiction of the golden age, Bloch feels that the genre's project to critique society has met with mixed success; he asserts that many authors only reinforce the status quo in their attempts to challenge the social order. Identifying popular motifs in the genre, Bloch feels that too many works of science fiction rely on the traditional conceptions of good and evil, and, more dangerously, on unfair notions of power and hierarchy. Nevertheless, Bloch suggests that these works are valid as social criticism in that they are unconscious reflections of the problems of society.

Modern social criticism—adverse, that is—seems just about dead. There's just one place where you're still likely to run into it; and in a form of writing so minor that most serious literary reviewers aren't even aware of it.

I refer, of course, to the field of science fiction. Now when I was a child, science fiction was different, too. Back in the late twenties and early thirties, science fiction was a field in which stories about Bug-Eyed Monsters were read by bug-eyed boys. It was full of crazy stuff about airplanes going faster than the speed of sound . . . and splitting the atom to harness its energy . . . and space-platforms hanging out in the middle of nowhere above the Earth. Just pulp trash, the product of diseased imaginations. Of course, nobody took it seriously.

Excerpted from "Imagination and Modern Social Criticism," by Robert Bloch, in *The Science Fiction Novel: Imagination and Social Criticism*, edited by Earl Kemp. Copyright © 1959, Advent:Publishers. Reprinted with permission from the publisher.

But something happened, along about the time of World War II. Maybe it was the atomic bomb; maybe there is something to this idea that radiation and fallout can affect people in mysterious ways. At any rate, it affected our main-stream writers and caused them to begin producing wonderful new stories in praise of the status quo. And at the same time, it seemingly caused science fiction writers to suddenly emerge as rebels and prophets. Science fiction became the vehicle for social criticism. . . .

RECOGNIZABLE WORLDS

Ignoring the extra-terrestrial invaders, ignoring the gadgetry, ignoring the universal-disaster backgrounds, one encounters a fundamental dramatic premise known to all eminent critics who are six years old or over. The world is plainly divided into "cops and robbers," "cowboys and Indians" or "good guys and bad guys."

There's a reason, of course. People who have come to revere science almost as a religion place great faith in the ability of technologists to safeguard our future. Many of these people had that faith literally exploded with the explosion of the atomic bomb. Science fiction has attempted to shore up that faith once more with something called the "upbeat" story—one in which science, despite the danger of thermonuclear destruction, triumphs in the end and restores a brave new world. Sometimes these stories are quite deceptively satirical and begin in an atmosphere of tyranny. But if you read further, you're apt to encounter the same old hero, learning the error of his ways and overthrowing the tyrants. There are minor variations, of course: in *Brave New World* and *1984,* for example, the heroes fail—and the point is, you can't beat the system. In one or two books the authors, seeking for novelty, invert the premise at the end and we discover that the system is right after all—whereupon the hero wisely concludes that if you can't lick 'em, join 'em.

No wonder so many adolescents are attracted to this form of fiction; here, in a transparent disguise, is the story of revolt against organized society. The hero—with whom the adolescent identifies—defies the rules and the taboos and the authorities.

In an era where "escape fiction" cannot serve up a convincing trip to the Wild West or an exploration of Darkest Africa as a refuge against social constraints, our adolescents revel in spaceships breaking free to seek the stars, and in contradictions of supposedly immutable order. There's a vicarious thrill in breaking the law, even if it's the law of gravity. . . .

CHALLENGING AND REINFORCING THE STATUS QUO

While main-stream fiction glorifies the status quo, science fiction seemingly singles it out as the villain. And at the same time it presents us with the reassuring Father-Image of the all-wise scientist and psychotherapist. With his aid, the hero triumphs. Science fiction thus reassures people that they are the masters of their fate, and that every mushroom cloud has a silver lining.

Now this is admittedly a generalization, and there are notable exceptions. One can pick out . . . such memorable character-delineations as Tucker's *The Long Loud Silence*, Vidal's *Messiah* and Moore's *Greener Than You Think*, for example.

But by far the majority adhere to that stereotyped concept—the Hero Who Saves the World.

Here is Doctor Martine, hero of *Limbo:* the brilliant scientist incarnate, who single-handedly seeks to rescue the world from a social order he himself unwittingly imposed upon it. Here is Doctor Paul Proteus of *Player Piano*, not too different in his attitude from those other famous medicos, Doctor Kildare, Doctor Christian and Young Doctor Malone.

Mitch Courtenay of *The Space Merchants* is no M.D., but a willing conformist—until the scales are stripped from his eyes and he takes a good look at the society around him—whereupon he realizes that it is his mission in life, too, to Fight Tyranny. Does this begin to sound familiar? Have you read about this hero before—in Edson McCann's *Preferred Risk*, in Damon Knight's *Hell's Pavement* and heaven knows how many other books?

But note this well: I'm not decrying such heroes, as such. I'm not ridiculing lofty motives, or the device of allowing a conformist character to rebel against what he discovers to be a false system of values. The device of casting down the mighty and making them realize how conditions are under slavery was good enough for Mark Twain in *A Connecticut Yankee in King Arthur's Court;* this is sound plotting, and the result, properly handled, can be a realistic and convincing story.

IGNORING THE GENRE'S POTENTIAL

Yet in many of these novels, something is off-key. Can it be—I wonder—that the heroes are too important?

That's where some of these books destroy the illusion of reality for me. I'm transported right back to the days of Hugo Gernsback where, in many instances, the handsome but brilliant young fullback landed on Mars and immediately found himself involved with the Princess, the High Priest and the Emperor. By the time you reached the fourth page of such epics, Our Boy was always tangling with the highest figures in the Hierarchy, and he and he alone eventually decided the fate and future of the planet, the galaxy or the entire universe.

And here we are again today. Sophisticated superimpositions of satire, sophistry, sociology and psychiatry notwithstanding, there's one basic plot—Boy Meets Big Wheel, and overturns the world.

Now the thing that made *1984* a convincing tour-de-force was its depiction of an average citizen against an average background. It was not necessary for Orwell to pit his commonplace hero against the Top Dogs in order to make a plot and a point. Indeed, the strength and the conviction of his book lies in the way he deliberately offers a "slice of life" rather than an orgy of name-dropping.

Is there a sound sociological reason why so much of science fiction must concern itself with so-called Key Figures? It is certainly not a criminal offense to do so, but to some extent I believe it is a literary offense. Because in science fiction novels which are deliberately presented as glimpses of our possible society of tomorrow, the writer is in effect offering a promise to the reader. He is saying, "Come with me and I'll show you how the world of the future will be—the kind of people who live there, what they think, and what effect tomorrow's social order will have upon them."

In *1984*, Orwell did just that. But in the average tale of tomorrow, the author goes straight to the top. He may make grudging mention of the lower classes or even present picturesque (and usually criminal) specimens in one or two chapters—but the greater part of his book usually offers glimpses of Important Officials Guiding Destiny and Revealing Their Philosophy. The heroes and their peers seem just a bit larger than life-sized, and you seldom come away from your reading with the feeling of, "Yes, this is how it really could be."

You may, if the author is skillful—and many of them are— enjoy sharing the experience and the danger, and revel in the hero's eventual triumph. But your attention has been directed away from the theme and centered upon the gaudy melodrama of Intrigue in High Places. . . .

Science fiction as a vehicle for social criticism is stalled when one of those super-heroes climbs into the driver's seat and insists on racing full-speed-ahead right down the center of the main highway. You're so busy watching for the possibility of accidents and smashups that you never really see the scenery. Thrilling? Yes. Contemplative? Hardly. . . .

Our science fiction novelists, by and large, agree that dictators are bad—that a world run by and for Big Business is

THE MALE HERO AND THE PROBLEM OF POWER

In this excerpt from a university lecture, Joanna Russ, an award-winning science fiction writer associated with the New Wave, addresses one of the criticisms of traditional science fiction: namely, the male hero's problematic relationship with power.

The only real He-Man is the Master of the Universe.

Which, of course, leaves out a great many people.

If you believe this but are a little less extreme about stating it, it comes out something like this:

The real He-Man is invulnerable. He has no weaknesses. Sexually, he is super-potent. He does exactly what he pleases, everywhere and at all times. He is absolutely self-sufficient. He depends on nobody, for this would be a weakness. Toward women he is possessive, protective and patronizing; to men he gives orders. He is never frightened by anything or for any reason; he is never indecisive; and he always wins.

In short, he is an alien monster. . . .

This leads to trouble. The trouble with making masculinity equal to power—especially the sort of absolute, ultimate power that s.f. writers like to write about—is that you can't look at either power or masculinity clearly. This is bad enough when you can't think clearly about masculinity, but when you can't think clearly about power, it's godawful. In politics, for instance, power is simply real—it exists—it's like the electricity in the lights of this room; and if you look at a real political situation or a real moral situation, and instead of seeing what's really there, you see Virility—Manhood at Stake—goodness knows what—everything gets all mucked up. Of course, this sort of problem isn't confined to science fiction; you can see it happening all over the place. But sci-

subject to false value-orientation—that religious bigotry or military fanaticism or criminal ethics are to be deplored as the basis of governmental philosophy. As social critics, then, they serve a function by showing how an extension of these tendencies in present-day society could bring about undesirable results in the future.

But there they seem, by and large, to stop. In presenting the dangers of possible future societies, they seem to be saying we need better government. Yet very few of them suggest that we need better citizens. . . .

ence fiction has a unique chance to deal with these things in the chemically pure form, so to speak, to really speculate about them. But so often we don't.

One of the strangest things in s.f., when you meet this concern with power, is that s.f. writers seem pretty much to insist on an either-or situation. That is, people in stories tend to be either all-powerful (this is the Ruler of the Universe again) or absolutely powerless. Either the hero is conquering the world or the world is returning the compliment by conquering *him.* In any case, it's a completely black-and-white situation with nothing in between. Alexei Panshin once complained about characters who are strangled by their vacuum cleaners. Well, I think this idea of megalithic, absolute power has a lot to do with being strangled by your vacuum cleaner. If the real man is absolutely invulnerable, then if you're not absolutely invulnerable, you're not a real man, and if you're not a real man, you're absolutely weak and absolutely vulnerable, so even a vacuum cleaner can get you. You even sometimes get this weird hybrid, who is at the same time a superman (utterly powerful) and is being persecuted by the whole world (i.e., he is utterly powerless). In fact, he's being persecuted *because* he's a superman, that is, because he's powerful. But if he's persecuted, he's powerless. That is, he's powerless because he's powerful. Or vice versa. Sometimes the brain just reels.

Also, you get something else very bad in science fiction from this confusion of maleness—masculinity—with power. You get what's been called pornoviolence, that is, violence for the sake of violence.

Excerpted from Joanna Russ, "Alien Monsters," *Turning Points: Essays on the Art of Science Fiction.* New York: Harper & Row, 1977.

They go to marvelously clever lengths to paint a convincing picture of a complex, intricately-ordered future society; complete, in many instances, with every technological advantage, and with the addition of super-psychotherapy, extrasensory perception, even teleportation powers.

But when it comes to a question of personal ethics, when it comes to a question of social justice—again and again we run right smack into our old friend Mike Hammer in disguise.

How, in this marvelous world of the future, does one go about settling an argument?

With the same old punch in the jaw . . . the same old kick in the guts . . . the same old bullet in the same old belly. . . .

Isaac Asimov recently pointed out that science fiction heroes are permitted to be intelligent. This is admirable. And yet, emotionally, most of them are primitive and immature.

Where is the science fiction novel with the ordinary family man as hero . . . or the teacher . . . or the creative artist . . . or the philosopher? Where is the science fiction novel that contents itself with showing us the everyday world of the future, devoid of Master Spies and Master Technicians and Master Psychologists and Master Criminals? . . .

EFFECTIVE CRITICISM

Remember that I am not discussing these novels in terms of literary craftsmanship or entertainment. If so, I'd be the first to tell you how very much I enjoyed reading Damon Knight's vivid *Hell's Pavement*, Alfred Bester's *The Demolished Man* and Fritz Leiber's powerful *Gather, Darkness!*—the latter utilizing the standard picture of an authoritarian state but going far beyond the ordinary work in its criticism of Science as Religion. Here is fine writing, here are clever concepts, here is enthralling escape-fiction.

There are other exceptions which should be noted. *Brave New World*, of course—with social criticism as its primary and well-realized objective. We do get a touch of Big-Name dropping here, but by and large, Huxley presents a panoramic approach. Orwell's *1984* sticks to the common fate of the common man, with uncommon results. The common man also figures in Wilson Tucker's *The Long Loud Silence*. His hero's struggle to survive in the bomb-wasted and plague-infested wilderness is a moving, memorable and utterly logical adventure; what it has to say about man and motivations under conditions of stress is far more eloquent than a dozen science-fictional sermons served up with surrealistic shock-sequences. The same holds true for C. M. Kornbluth's *Not This August;* the old theme of totalitarian conquest takes on new meaning and new impact when told in terms of everyday living. In Frank M. Robinson's *The Power,* the author wisely adheres to familiar surroundings to stress the terrors of the unfamiliar. Damon Knight says that the novel is actually "anti-science fiction." This point is debatable, but even if we concede it, I'm sure that Knight admits Robinson's right to present this viewpoint as his own form of social criticism—and that he succeeded in producing a powerful, suspenseful book. There is fine theological philosophy to be found in Vercors' *You Shall Know Them.*

In Fredric Brown's *The Lights in the Sky Are Stars,* our hero is a 57-year-old rocket mechanic with an artificial leg. He and the heroine dedicate themselves to furthering a rocket flight to Jupiter. The heroine dies and the hero never makes the flight himself, but the thinking reader comes away from this book with at least a partial feeling of, "Yes, this is the way it will be—or could be." I repeat, the thinking reader; not the adolescent who wants to identify with a hero who is intent solely on smashing in the face of Authority.

At the other extreme, that of almost pure fantasy, we find such efforts as *Fahrenheit 451, War With the Newts* and *Doctor Arnoldi.* In *Fahrenheit 451,* Ray Bradbury has something to say about book-burning. Whether you agree with him or not, find his treatment convincing or unconvincing, or admire his highly personalized style (I do), there is nevertheless not the slightest doubt but that he has written a novel of social criticism in the science fiction field. In *War With the Newts* Karel Capek produced a remarkable satire, which fell flat on its face in this country twenty years ago, but has since been re-issued as a pocket-book. Here again is witty and perceptive social criticism. Such is also the case in Tiffany Thayer's early *Doctor Arnoldi*—in which the problems of overpopulation were discussed some twenty-five years before our learned ecologists and social scientists got around to becoming alarmed. And finally we have Theodore Sturgeon's *More Than Human*—a book that stands virtually alone in its consideration of empathy, the basic problem of

MAN AGAINST HIMSELF, and even more important, MAN *FOR* HIMSELF and MAN *FOR* MANKIND.

Against the more popularly-held notions in the science fiction field that technology will save the world, or mass-psychological conditioning will save the world, these few dissenters stand, affirming that only man's spirit avails to save himself. They preach evolution rather than revolution, evaluation rather than revelation, individual right rather than individual might. . . .

When a literature of imaginative speculation steadfastly adheres to the conventional outlook of the community regarding heroes and standards of values, it is indeed offering the most important kind of social criticism—unconscious social criticism.

With its totalitarian societies, its repudiation of individual activity in every role save that of the self-appointed leader and avenger, science fiction dramatizes the dilemma which torments modern man. It provides a very accurate mirror of our own problems, and of our own beliefs which fail to solve these problems.

Gazing into that mirror, we all might find it profitable to indulge in a bit of reflection.

The Feminist Struggle in Science Fiction

Debra Benita Shaw

Debra Benita Shaw examines the history of the science fiction genre from a feminist perspective. Shaw believes that the scientific realm has traditionally excluded women, and that many female science fiction writers have had to assimilate themselves into a masculine genre. Sometimes these writers concealed their identities with androgynous initials (like C.L. Moore) or male pseudonyms (James Tiptree Jr., for example); others adhered to the macho subject matter of the genre in order to continue writing. To Shaw however, the unique position of writing within a genre that has alienated women has given some female science fiction authors the chance to explore this sense of alienation in their work. By being both "part of" and "excluded from" the science fiction tradition, these authors can effectively critique the genre and the society that created it.

[Science fiction] can have a socially or politically critical purpose and indeed, as Patrick Parrinder has written, "[a]dmirers of science fiction have always pointed to its role in questioning social assumptions, and today there is widespread recognition of this." However, as he points out, "[i]n modern literature the terms 'social fable' and 'moral fable' may be applied to almost any fiction in which the author's didactic intentions override his [sic] impulses towards artistic . . . detachment." Where sf differs is that it is concerned with imagining how scientific theory, if that theory is applied and assimilated into society, may affect the future development of that society. It is fiction "concerned with the impact of contemporary knowledge and its extension into the future on human behaviour."

Excerpted from *Women, Science, and Fiction: The* Frankenstein *Inheritance*, by Debra Benita Shaw (London: Palgrave, 2000). Copyright 2000 Debra Benita Shaw. Reprinted by permission of Macmillan Ltd.

What John Griffiths is referring to here is the technique of "extrapolation", which describes the way in which sf narratives develop their themes by projecting onto a future, or other, world a scenario that can plausibly be imagined, given that a current scientific theory, or discovery, is provided as the basis. But, unlike Griffiths, I do not want to take issue with "the extrapolists" over whether this term merely "equate[s] sf with no more than technological forecasting" but rather make clear my intention to use the term to describe the way in which sf offers potential futures whose most important function is to distance the reader from, and thus offer a critical perspective on, her present. The scientific sub-text thus roots the text in the time and place of its production, while the extrapolation is not so much a forecast of the future but rather a statement about the political implications of scientific theories and new technologies. Writers are free to imagine worlds other than our own, with different historical and biological evolutions, different geographies and hence radically different forms of social relations. This, I would argue, has been the particular appeal of sf for feminists. As Jen Green and Sarah Lefanu put it:

> Science fiction . . . allows us to take the present position of women and use the metaphors of science fiction to illuminate it. We may be writing *about* the future, but we are writing *in* the present.

But what is now recognised as feminist sf is a relatively recent phenomenon, a phenomenon consolidated by Sarah Lefanu in her authoritative overview of the genre *In the Chinks of the World Machine* (1988). For Lefanu, "Feminist SF . . . is part of science fiction while struggling against it," and she states her intention to "chart that extraordinary relationship between feminism and science fiction that flowered in the 1970s and that continues to the present day."

THE FEMINIST STRUGGLE WITHIN SCIENCE FICTION

However, the particular nature of the genre makes it difficult to ascertain by precisely what conventions the site of struggle is marked. Since Hugo Gernsback first named sf in 1929, a succession of struggles over what exactly its form might be has ensured a plethora of sub-genres and re-definitions. As Patrick Parrinder has pointed out, "Definitions of science fiction are not so much a series of logical approximations to an elusive ideal, as a small, parasitic sub-genre in themselves," and, since the growth of academic interest in sf, the net has widened to include earlier works that fall within the terms of various definitions that have been offered to distinguish "true" sf from fantasy or space opera. So it is perhaps more accurate to suggest, as Jenny Wolmark has done, that, since the 1970s, "Feminist science fiction has brought the politics of feminism into a genre with a solid tradition of ignoring or excluding women writers." However, I would disagree with Lefanu's assertion that the "struggle" necessarily began in the 1970s. . . .

Serious critical analysis of sf, along with its inclusion in university English Literature courses, can probably be traced to the first publication of the critical journal *Extrapolation* in 1959. Two years later, as Parrinder writes, "Kingsley Amis's widely-read and controversial survey *New Maps of Hell* (1961) did much to make sf intellectually fashionable." Since this time, Mary Shelley's *Frankenstein* (1818) has been acknowledged as the first sf novel, and H. G. Wells and Jules Verne have been drawn into the net along with individual novels by such writers as Aldous Huxley (*Brave New World*, 1932) and George Orwell (*Nineteen Eighty-Four*, 1949). Brian Aldiss and David Wingrove's comprehensive history of the genre, *Trillion Year Spree* (1988), also includes, among others, Edgar Allan Poe. Despite the proliferation of definitions, conditions for inclusion in this new literary canon generally required the presence of a plausible extrapolation and what Darko Suvin has called "estrangement and cognition." The familiar is de-familiarised to facilitate a critical reflection on the writers' and readers' perceived reality.

Although Shelley is the acknowledged "mother" of the genre, most historical analyses do not dwell at any length on a single woman writer until the publication, in 1969, of Ursula Le Guin's *The Left Hand of Darkness*. As Patricia Monk points out, women in the intervening years have often written "under the cover of initials or ambisexual pseudonyms" so that "women writers of science fiction have often tended to be invisible, even when they did exist." Monk has identified what she calls the "androcentric mystique" of sf, "a literary mystique characterised by gadgetry, adventure and androcentric thinking," and finds it unsurprising that "women writers who have broken into the genre have, on finding it dominated by this androcentric mystique, shown a tendency to succumb and to incorporate the mystique into

their own writing." I would argue here that, in the very macho early days of magazine sf, it would have been virtually
impossible for a woman who did not appear to succumb to
find publication. These women were engaged in a struggle
of their own. What, then, made the likes of Katharine Bur-
dekin, Judith Merril, C. L. Moore, Catherine Maclean, Margaret St Clair, Leigh Brackett, C. J. Cherryh and Marion Zim-
mer Bradley, among others, wish to involve themselves in
the androcentric mystique? I believe this is an important
question which can be answered by returning to Suvin's definition of the genre as requiring the presence of "estrangement and cognition."

EXPRESSING AND EXPLORING ALIENATION

Recent discussions of sf in the context of postmodernism
have emphasised the way in which extrapolation has now
necessarily become disconnected from what it attempts to
refer to. Jean Baudrillard, for instance, considers sf to be
now less concerned with presenting potential futures than
with attempting to represent what Istvan Csicsery-Ronay Jr
has called "the problematic autonomy of reality". In other
words, the imaginary space that was once held to exist between the extrapolation and its origin has collapsed amid
postmodern uncertainty about the concept of originality.

As Baudrillard has (now famously) claimed, "sf . . . is no
longer an elsewhere, it is an everywhere." "Classic sf", according to Baudrillard, concerned with colonisation dreams
and the conquest of space, was able to function in the imaginary space opened up by the concept of progress. It has, in
this sense, a historical specificity and is no longer relevant
to a world where, as he says, "the map covers all the territory". . . . So, as Jenny Wolmark explains it, "it becomes the
task of contemporary SF to present us with the fiction that is
our own world."

But, if sf *is* lived reality, estrangement can no longer function as a distancing technique. Science fiction can only function as a long series of re-presentations in which the pleasure is, perhaps, one of re-cognition. And, if this is the case,
what happens to the socially critical function of sf, and of
feminist sf in particular? As Wolmark has pointed out, "as
the specificity of human experience is displaced by simula-
tion, then the lived realities of oppression and subordination
experienced by women have no way of being expressed." To

return to the allure of the "androcentric mystique", I think it is clear that the "decentred situations" that Baudrillard prescribes for contemporary sf were always to be found among the fictions of women writers for whom centrality was never a position that they themselves could claim. We need, perhaps, to return to the days of "classic" sf in order to discover a continuity in women's sf writing that can re-establish the connection between gender conditioning and the practice and application of science, a connection that much postmodern theory has too readily effaced in favour of the claim that all categories of the "human" are de-centred in the postmodernist scenario. The (female) scientist, Alice Sheldon, posing as the (male) sf writer, James Tiptree Jr and taking part in a symposium on feminist sf is, for me, a suitably ironic "fiction" with which to illustrate this point. It is my belief that the appeal of sf for women has always been that it allows opportunities both to express and explore alienation as well as to offer a fictional description of the kind of world that a gender-free or differently gendered science might produce. . . .

Women's Relationship to Scientific Knowledge

As Evelyn Fox Keller has pointed out, "the breach which separates women from science is very deep." The mythology which surrounds the practice and application of science is, as Keller reminds us, inseparable from the cultural construction of gender. The frame of mind thought necessary to the production of scientific research, uninfected with affective bias, is thus thought impossible for women, who are invested with the emotional and affective qualities not permitted to the masculine type. The practice of science can be seen as confirming masculinity and thus jealously guarded as a panacea to male gender insecurity. The problem for feminists in attacking this ground is that science comes to be regarded as monolithic; as so essentially a male invention that nothing less than the stripping away of the entire cultural tradition of scientific practice and technological production will do. . . .

What I believe is needed is a more comprehensive understanding of how women perceive themselves in relation to scientific knowledge and the use of technology. In other words, as Sandra Harding says, it is imperative that any dialogue should be informed "by the voices of the majority of the world's women who are not involved in criticising the sciences at all, but simply in surviving." If we recognise that science is determined by its social context and that women provide part of that context, whether as consumers of technological products, production line workers affected by science-based working practices, users (not always willingly) of reproductive and medical technology, or simply as excluded from the knowledge that allows individual autonomy in a technological world, then we must also acknowledge a hidden social and philosophical history which can be revealed by the study of women's forays into a literature that explicitly engages with science, its products and producers. . . .

THE NEARLY SILENT LISTENER

In her introduction to the 1831 edition of *Frankenstein*, Mary Shelley described how she was motivated to write the novel. In the summer of 1816, she and Shelley 'visited Switzerland, and became the neighbours of Lord Byron'. Also present was Byron's secretary, Polidari. The weather being particularly bad, they spent much of their time reading ghost stories and agreed that each would attempt a story of their own. Mary was lost for ideas until a particular night when a discussion between Byron and Shelley fired her imagination:

> Many and long were the conversations between Lord Byron and Shelley, to which I was a devout but nearly silent, listener. During one of these, various philosophical doctrines were discussed and among others the nature of the principle of life, and whether there was any possibility of its ever being discovered and communicated. They talked of the experiments of Dr [Erasmus] Darwin . . . who preserved a piece of vermicelli in a glass case, till by some extraordinary means it began to move with voluntary motion. Not thus, after all, would life be given. Perhaps a corpse would be re-animated; galvanism had given token of such things; perhaps the component parts of a creature might be manufactured, brought together and endued with vital warmth.

Shelley then goes on to describe how, once in bed, she "did not sleep, nor could I be said to think. My imagination, unbidden, possessed and guided me, gifting the successive images that arose in my mind with a vividness far beyond the normal bounds of reverie."

This, for me, is a potent description of the feminist imagination at work in creating sf. The "nearly silent" listener, excluded from, but affected by, scientific discourse, finds a voice through an imaginative medium in which she can express her own hopes and fears about the potential for science to transform her life. . . . Attention to that voice can reveal a powerful and insistent dialogue which argues for a recognition of women's unique relationship to how knowledge of the world and ourselves is understood.

CHAPTER 2

Movements Within the Genre

Science Fiction

Verne and Wells: The Two Fathers of Modern Science Fiction

Kingsley Amis

Writer Kingsley Amis is one of the sf field's esteemed scholars, having written an often-cited history and overview of the genre, *New Maps of Hell: A Survey of Science Fiction.* In this selection Amis discusses the works of the French writer Jules Verne and the British writer H.G. Wells. These two writers, both from the nineteenth century, are credited by Amis as the creators of science fiction in its modern form. In a survey of their work Amis illustrates how both writers introduced many ideas and conventions that persist in the genre to this day.

A definition of science fiction, though attempted with enormous and significant frequency by commentators inside the field, is bound to be cumbersome rather than memorable. With the "fiction" part we are on reasonably secure ground; the "science" part raises several kinds of difficulty, one of which is that science fiction is not necessarily fiction about science or scientists, nor is science necessarily important in it. Prolonged cogitation, however, would lead one to something like this: Science fiction is that class of prose narrative treating of a situation that could not arise in the world we know, but which is hypothesised on the basis of some innovation in science or technology, or pseudo-science or pseudo-technology, whether human or extra-terrestrial in origin. . . .

JULES VERNE AND SCIENCE PROPHECY

With Verne we reach the first great progenitor of modern science fiction. In its literary aspect his work is, of course, of

Excerpted from "Starting Points," in *New Maps of Hell: A Survey of Science Fiction*, by Kingsley Amis (New York: Harcourt, 1960). Copyright © 1960 Kingsley Amis. Reprinted by kind permission of Jonathan Clowes Ltd., London, on behalf of the Literary Estate of Sir Kingsley Amis.

poor quality, a feature certainly reproduced with great fidelity by most of his successors. Although interspersed on occasion with fast and exciting narrative, for instance in the episode [in *20,000 Leagues Under the Sea*] where Captain Nemo and his associates find their twenty-thousand-league voyage interrupted by the Antarctic ice pack, the story line is cluttered up again and again by long explanatory lectures and bald undramatised flashbacks. Even the more active passages are full of comically bad writing:

> What a scene! The unhappy man, seized by the tentacle and fastened to its blowholes, was balanced in the air according to the caprice of this enormous trunk. He was choking, and cried out, *"A moi! à moi!"* (Help! help!). Those French words caused me a profound stupor. Then I had a countryman aboard, perhaps several! I shall hear that heartrending cry all my life!
>
> The unfortunate man was lost. Who would rescue him from that powerful grasp? Captain Nemo threw himself on the poulp, and with his hatchet cut off another arm. His first officer was fighting with rage against other monsters that were climbing the sides of the *Nautilus*. The crew were fighting with hatchets.
>
> The Canadian, Conseil, and I dug our arms into the fleshy masses. A violent smell of musk pervaded the atmosphere. It was horrible.

One would have to blame Verne's translator for some of those ineptitudes, but such was the form in which the novels reached English-speaking readers, none of whom, to my knowledge, has bothered to complain. The story and the ideas were the thing. These ideas, the scientific ones at least, have naturally got a bit dated: the helicopter with seventy-four horizontal screws, the tunnel to the centre of the Earth, the moon-ship shot out of a gun at a speed that would have pulped the travellers before they were clear of the barrel. But these errors hardly matter, any more than Swift's Brobdingnagians cease to be impressive when we reason that they would have broken most of their bones whenever they tried to stand up. It matters hardly more that Verne did successfully foretell the guided missile, nor that this extract from *Five Weeks in a Balloon* (1862) has a bearing on events of eighty years later:

> "Besides," said Kennedy, "the time when industry gets a grip on everything and uses it to its own advantage may not be particularly amusing. If men go on inventing machinery they'll end by being swallowed up by their own inventions.

I've often thought that the last day will be brought about by some colossal boiler heated to three thousand atmospheres blowing up the world."

"And I bet the Yankees will have a hand in it," said Joe.

The general prophecy about invention overreaching itself is clearly far more interesting than the particular glimpse of something like the nuclear bomb, or rather of its possible outcome. Verne's importance is that, while usually wrong or implausible or simply boring in detail, his themes foreshadow a great deal of contemporary thinking, both inside and outside science fiction.

As regards the mode itself, Verne developed the tradition of the technological utopia, presenting in *The Begum's Fortune* a rival pair of these, the one enlightened and paternalistic, the other totalitarian and warlike. This was published in 1879, so it is no surprise to find that the nice utopia is French and the nasty one German. There are also several novels virtually initiating what has become a basic category of science fiction, the satire that is also a warning, and it is here that Verne is of some general interest. Thus in *Round the Moon,* after the projectile has fallen back into the sea— at a speed of 115,200 miles an hour, incidentally, and without hurting anyone inside—we find a company being founded to "develop" the moon after a fashion that anticipates *The Space Merchants.* The sequel to *Round the Moon, The Purchase of the North Pole,* involves not only the said purchase on the part of the Baltimore Gun Club, the people who set up the cannon to fire the moon-projectile, but a scheme whereby a monstrous explosion shall alter the inclination of the Earth's axis and so bring the polar region into the temperate zone. Since parts of the civilised world would correspondingly be shifted into new polar regions, the response of officialdom is unfavourable. However, the explosion takes place, and only an error in the calculations preserves the *status quo.* The notion of an advancing technology increasing the destructive power of unscrupulousness reappears on a smaller scale in *The Floating Island,* where the huge artifact breaks up in mid-ocean as a result of rivalry between two financial cliques. The book closes with a straightforward Vernean sermon on the dangers of scientific progress considered as an embodiment of human arrogance. The heavy moral tone of this and many passages in the other books is among the less fortunate of Verne's legacies to modern science fiction, and some of his other anticipations, if they are properly that, give no cause for congratulation. In particular, his sexual interest is very thin: Phileas Fogg, the hero of *Around the World in Eighty Days*, does pick up an Indian princess in the course of his travels, but we discover almost nothing about her, and Fogg treats her with an inflexible courtesy which goes beyond mere Victorianism and which any girl of spirit might find subtly unflattering. Even the villains rarely do so much as aspire to lechery. It is in his political tone, which, however vague and eccentric, is nearly always progressive, and even more in his attitude to technology, fascinated but sceptical and at times tinged with pessimism, that Verne's heritage is most interesting and valuable: his last book, *The Eternal Adam*, is a kind of proleptic elegy for the collapse of Western civilisation. These are the considerations which go some way to override his ineptitude and pomposity, his nineteenth-century boys'-story stuffiness, and make him, not only in a science-fiction sense, recognisably modern.

H. G. WELLS AND THE SCIENCE ADVENTURE

Whatever else he may or may not have been, Jules Verne is certainly to be regarded as one of the two creators of modern science fiction; the other, inevitably enough, is H. G. Wells. To treat Wells as such, rather than as the first important practitioner in an existing mode, is no denigration. Rather, it takes account of the fact that all his best and most influential stories appeared between 1895 and 1907, before science fiction had separated itself from the main stream of literature, and so were written, published, reviewed, and read as "romances" or even adventure stories. The expected comparison with Verne, made often enough at the time (though repudiated by both), now shows not only a huge disparity in literary merit but certain differences in the direction of interest. A main preoccupation of Verne's, as I said, was technology itself, "actual possibilities," as Wells put it, "of invention and discovery," and this holds true equally when what were possibilities to Verne are impossibilities or grotesque improbabilities to us. The long scientific lectures interpolated in his stories—"If I created a temperature of 18°, the hydrogen in the balloon will increase by 18/480s, or 1,614 cubic feet" and so on—these lectures, however tedious, are highly germane to what Verne was do-

H. G. Wells

ing. Wells, on the other hand, is nearly always concerned only to fire off a few phrases of pseudo-scientific patter and bundle his characters away to the moon or the 803rd century with despatch. Verne himself saw this point all right, and complained after reading (rather cursorily, it seems) *The First Men in the Moon:*

I make use of physics. He fabricates. I go to the moon in a cannon-ball discharged from a gun. There is no fabrication here. He goes to Mars [*sic*] in an airship [*sic*], which he constructs of a metal that does away with the law of gravitation. That's all very fine, but show me this metal. Let him produce it.

It is often said that Wells's main interest was not in scientific advance as such but in its effect on human life. Although this is true of some of his works, as we shall see in a moment, it is patently not true of the ones which had the most immediate effect on the growth of science fiction. Indeed, in this respect the Verne of *The Floating Island* or *The Purchase of the North Pole* seems distinctly more contemporary than the Wells of *The Time Machine* or *The Invisible Man.* The real importance of these stories is that they liberated the medium from dependence on extrapolation and in so doing initiated some of its basic categories. The time machine itself, the Martians and their strange irresistible weapons in *The War of the Worlds,* the monsters in the first half of *The Food of the Gods,* the other world coterminous with ours in "The Plattner Story," the carnivorous plant in "The Flowering of the Strange Orchid," all these have had an innumerable progeny. What is noticeable about them is that they are used to arouse wonder, terror, and excitement, rather than for any allegorical or satirical end. When the Time Traveller finds that mankind will have become separated into two races, the gentle ineffectual Eloi and the savage Morlocks, the idea that these are descended respectively from our own leisured classes and manual workers comes as a mere explanation, a solution to the puzzle; it is not transformed, as it inevitably would be in a modern writer, into a warning about some current trend in society. *The Invisible Man* is only very incidentally concerned with the notion that a scientific discovery may be dangerously two-edged; the novel is about the problems, firstly of being, secondly of catching, an invisible man. "The Country of the Blind," which is science fiction of the physical-change variety, is about what it would be like for a sighted person in a country of the blind: the proverb about the one-eyed man being king there doubtless inspired the story, but its theme is a concretisation, not a daring imaginative statement, of the untruthful aspect of that proverb. A contemporary writer, again, would have used the proposed blinding of the hero as a climactic point for the enfilading of our intolerance towards exceptional talents; Wells throws this away in an aside, giving us the hero of an adventure story in danger, not the representative of anything being threatened with anything representative. Dr. Moreau's beast-men are beast-men, not symbolic puppets enacting a view of beasts and men, or of men. *The First Men in the Moon* admittedly has some satirical discussions of war and human irrationality, together with one of several early anticipations of the conditioning-during-sleep idea Huxley developed in *Brave New World,* but Wells's main drive here is simple delight in invention, in working out an alien ecology, typical of what I might call primitive science fiction.

Despite the fluent imaginativeness of the stories mentioned, the most forceful of Wells's romances is the strongly Verne-like *The War in the Air* of 1907. This curious synthesis of World Wars I, II, and III, with Germany attacking the United States before both are overwhelmed by a Chinese-Japanese coalition, is certainly concerned with the effect of technology on mankind, since the one is made to reduce the other to barbarism, and being both satire and warning, it has, in the science-fiction context at any rate, an unmistakably modern ring. *The War in the Air,* however, rates comparatively little attention from the commentators, as do Wells's utopian romances and their not-so-remote ancestor of the early Fabian period, William Morris's *News From Nowhere. Men Like Gods,* with its nudism, or *In the Days of the Comet,* where a strange gas so fills humanity with loving-kindness that everyone gets started on companionate marriage, have none of the fire of the early Wells, and give a soporific whiff of left-wing crankiness, but their virtual exclusion from the modern science-fiction canon is surprising. This part of Wells's output anticipated, but evidently did not influence, later developments. Even "A Story of the Days to Come," an early and lively piece, never gets a mention, and yet it forecasts the modern satirical utopia with fantastic exactness: advertising matter is everywhere bawled out of loudspeakers, phonographs have replaced books, mankind is urbanized to the point where agriculturalists commute in reverse, huge trusts reign supreme, an army of unemployables is maintained by a kind of international poorhouse called the Labour Company, all children are brought up in State crèches, deviates get their antisocial traits removed by hypnosis, dreams can be obtained to order, and as a last detail, a prophecy so universal nowadays as to justify panic in razor-blade circles, men don't shave any more, they use depilatories. Quite likely Wells will soon get all, instead of part, of the recognition as pioneer he clearly deserves.

An Insider Remembers the Pulp Era

Jack Williamson

Jack Williamson, author of *The Humanoids* and *The Legion of Space*, made his mark in science fiction's pulp era, which preceded World War II and the genre's golden age. Here Williamson remembers the early days of science fiction writing: its humble beginnings among the voluminous generic pulps; the advent of *Amazing Stories* in 1926, edited by Hugo Gernsback, who invented the term *science fiction*; and especially the contribution of John W. Campbell Jr., who revolutionized science fiction as the editor of *Astounding Stories* by requiring his authors to develop well-written fiction with responsible science. As an insider, Williamson describes in detail the environment of the age, the rise of the science fiction pulp magazines, the value of writing in that "anti-literary" medium, and his experiences with various influential editors. Williamson reveals many of the tools of the trade. Conventions of story-telling in that era included a predominance of adventure, male heroes, and happy endings that often displayed an optimistic view of science. Finally, Williamson notes the shift within the genre to a cynical view of science and its impact on humanity that occurred after the war.

The mental excursion back to 1930 is a trip into another culture. Copies of the old *Amazing Stories, Wonder Stories,* and *Astounding Stories of Super-Science* still exist, the pulp paper gone brown and brittle and the monster-haunted covers often detached, but their world is gone forever.

Those were the days of the "sense of wonder" Sam Moskowitz has celebrated. The world had not yet been satu-

Excerpted from "The Years of Wonder," by Jack Williamson, in *Voices for the Future: Essays on Major Science Fiction Writers*, vol. 1, edited by Thomas D. Clareson (Bowling Green, OH: Bowling Green State University Popular Press, 1976). Reprinted with permission from the publisher.

rated with science fiction in kiddie cartoons, in *Star Trek* re-runs, and in comic books, *Playboy*, and paperbacks—even in college classes. It still seemed dazzlingly new.

Before I discovered *Amazing Stories*, late in 1926, I had come across no science fiction except for the tales of Poe and Hawthorne and a few such books as Bulwer-Lytton's *The Coming Race*. I recall very vividly my first encounters with the enchantment of the bright . . . covers and the excitement of travel in space and time, of strange beings and powers and inventions. By 1930 I was selling stories of my own, but the exhilaration of exploring the future had not worn dull.

Of course there were times when writing for the maga-zines—at least for me—was rather lonely and poorly paid. For most people, it had nothing to do with reality. My parents felt that my preoccupation with such fiction was not quite healthy. The term *science fiction*—invented by Hugo Gerns-back when he launched *Science Wonder Stories*—was only a year old in 1930, and still bewildering to most outsiders. I used to explain that I was writing adventure stories with a science background. . . .

In an odd way, our poverty was not only material but also intellectual. Of course our capital was new ideas, and our in-spiration came from science. But the magazines were pulps. Not yet welcome in libraries, they were part of the popular culture, scorned by the academic establishment. Our intel-lectual ghetto was narrow and very real.

THE RUNTS OF THE LITTER

Science fiction does have honorable literary origins, though I think our critical defenders sometimes try to trace them too far back. *Amazing Stories* was certainly well enough born. Originally a reprint magazine, it carried the classic fiction of Poe and Verne and Wells. But down in the ghetto that noble birth was soon forgotten.

Outside the pulps, in the respectable world of books and libraries and critical reviews, literary science fiction lived on through those decades. Aldous Huxley was writing *Brave New World* and *After Many a Summer*. C. S. Lewis was be-ginning his great allegoric trilogy with *Out of the Silent Planet*. Stapledon was publishing *Last and First Men*. Kafka was being discovered. With never a ripple in the magazines.

Science fiction had been submerged in the pulp tradition. Since the pulps are gone, perhaps they need explaining.

They were called pulps because they were printed on cheap gray woodpulp paper. In the days before radio and TV, they were a major medium of popular entertainment.

The pulp tradition had been growing since before the turn of the century. Through the 1930's and the early 1940's the newsstands were still stacked with pulp fiction magazines, at prices from a dime to a quarter. A few, such as *Argosy,* offered a variety, but most were specialized. There were Western pulps, detective pulps, sports pulps, love pulps, air-war pulps, and any others that could find a public. The great pulp houses, like Clayton, Street and Smith, and Standard Magazines, were always putting out new titles, to keep the presses rolling and keep the circulation totals up to the advertising guarantees. One overworked editor often had single-handed charge of several books.

When science fiction magazines were added to these groups during the 1930's, they were commonly the runts of the litter. . . .

THE PULP INFLUENCE

The Gernsback magazines, mixing classic reprints with German and French translations and amateurish new stories, were not quite real pulps. The first actual impact of the pulp tradition on the magazines came with Harry Bates, the busy editor who added *Astounding Stories of Super-Science* to the Clayton chain with the issue for January, 1930.

This pulp influence has been deplored, but it was not altogether bad. Certainly it was unliterary, if not anti-literary. It was scorned by the intellectual establishment. But, in the long run, it was probably good for science fiction. The pulp tradition is worth a closer look. It was part of the popular culture. With its narrowness, its violence, its prudery, its strong male heroes, its innocent good women and wildly wicked bad ones, and its themes of material success, I think it reflects the Puritan heritage and the frontier experience.

The pulp story was written from the viewpoint of a pure-minded male who was successful in a conflict with powerful antagonists. Good and evil were clearly defined. Characters were simple, and action was paramount. The ending was happy. Though incidental satire was sometimes permitted, the whole tradition assumed a rational moral order in the universe. The good guys won. Plot itself, of course, has thematic implications. Every story ending reflects an ethical judgment. Logical order in the story implies a reasonable order in the world outside.

Though Huxley was using science fiction to challenge these venerable beliefs, as Wells before him had done, the pulp tradition still supported the convictions of the mass audience in 1930. Evil was still definable and beatable, success still possible and meaningful. Applied science still held more promise than menace; the possible future still looked more pleasant than the past. By the late 1940's, those cheerful assumptions had begun to crumble, and the pulp empires with them.

As part of the popular culture, the pulp tradition was almost anti-academic. Certainly the craft of pulp writing was not taught or learned in college. My burning desire in those days was to join Merritt and Burroughs and Max Brand among the writers for *Argosy*, and I used to study the weekly biographical page about "Men Who Make the *Argosy*." What the writers had in common, so far as I could discover, was a rich experience of life and very little school.

I'm convinced, in fact, that the pulp tradition is more oral than literary. When I came to study the folk epics and the theories of oral transmission, it struck me that Max Brand's Westerns had a good deal in common with Homer. The language was rhythmic, rich with figures of speech. The field of action was vast, the characters above life-size, the values simple and sharply defined. It also brought form.

Except for some of the reprints, *Amazing* and *Wonder* had been pretty formless. Gernsback emphasized science above fiction, and he printed stories stuffed with long educational lectures. Bates demanded strongly plotted action stories with a bare minimum of science.

Though not many stories from the Bates era are remembered, the sense of form is still alive. The old pulps were better schools for writers than the universities, because they required the expression of character, setting, and theme in well-motivated action. . . .

THE SCIENCE FICTION PULPS

Argosy and *Blue Book*, another great adventure pulp, were also still running occasional science fiction through the 1930's and the 1940's, though their circulations and rates of pay were falling. *Weird Tales* still mixed science and fantasy. Other science fiction magazines appeared and often quickly died. But the major markets, through those two decades, were *Amazing, Wonder,* and *Astounding.*

Even these had their crises: all three changed owners, editors, policies, and titles. *Amazing,* by 1930, had already run through its wealth of classic reprints and settled into something like suspended animation. *Wonder,* under any name, was never very influential. *Astounding* soon overshadowed both. When John Campbell became the editor in 1938, he soon made it the creative center of modern science fiction.

Though Gernsback bought my first stories—and I felt duly thankful—I met him only briefly. He was shrewd enough to see the potential appeal of science fiction, when he launched *Amazing Stories* in 1926 and *Science Wonder Stories* three years later, but my own experiences with him were not very happy. Most of the actual editorial work on his magazines was done by poorly paid subordinates who were cramped by a narrow editorial policy and by his reluctance to pay for published stories—even at rates of only a quarter to half a cent a word—except under threat of legal action. . . .

In 1938, *Amazing* was bought by the Ziff-Davis group and moved to Chicago, with Ray Palmer as editor. I tried a couple of stories for them, but Davis didn't like them, and the transformed magazine never appealed to me. Though it published some good action fiction by Edgar Rice Burroughs, for example, it was slanted in a rather cynical way at people not enlightened enough to tell the difference between crude fiction and actual fact.

Wonder, after years of decline under Gernsback, was sold in 1936 to Standard Magazines, a pulp chain owned by Ned Pines and edited by Leo Margulies. As *Thrilling Wonder Stories,* it became a livelier magazine and a more attractive market. I rather liked writing for it, and its new companion, *Startling Stories.* . . .

Stories for them had to fit a very narrow action pattern. . . . Good or bad, the writing simply didn't matter. What did matter was fast melodramatic action, a sort of novelty that didn't go beyond the limits of the formula, and a kind of superficial cleverness. The essential thing was to file off every rough spot that might make the reader stop reading.

When the Clayton chain went bankrupt, *Astounding* was taken over by Street and Smith, under another able pulp editor, F. Orlin Tremaine. Though the rate of pay fell to a cent a word, the intellectual content of the magazine soon went up. What Tremaine added to the pulp formula was an interest in ideas. He wasn't critical of these, in any scientific way—he serialized Charles Fort's *Lo*, which was a challenge to the whole scientific orthodoxy. He featured "thought-variant" stories, for which almost any far-out idea would do.

In one "thought-variant" of my own, the sun is a living being and the planets are its eggs; in the course of the story, the earth hatches. . . .

THE *ASTOUNDING* AGE

The great age of *Astounding* began in 1938, when John Campbell replaced Tremaine as editor. Campbell had earned a degree in science from Duke University, after flunking out of MIT. He had begun his career by challenging Doc Smith in the field of space opera. Later, writing as Don A. Stuart, he had learned to put more character, meaning, and style into his fiction. He brought a unique combination of gifts to *Astounding* and the whole field. He understood science, and he had a vivid sense of its impact on the future. He understood story construction—he had learned the use of form that came from the pulp tradition. He had a healthy skepticism of all sorts of orthodoxy, along with perhaps a little too much credulity for such notions as dianetics and psionics and the Dean drive. Richest gift of all, he had a well of invention that never ran dry. His generosity in planting new ideas was limitless.

Under his editorial direction, *Astounding* dominated the magazine field all through the 1940's, with no real rivals until *Galaxy* and the *Magazine of Fantasy and Science Fiction* appeared in 1950.

Campbell soon began gathering and inspiring the group of new or rejuvenated writers who made *Astounding's* Golden Age. One measure of his success is the contents page of *Adventures in Time and Space*, the first of the great science fiction anthologies, edited in 1946 by Raymond J. Healy and J. Francis McComas. Out of thirty-five stories, all but three had first appeared in *Astounding*.

As a creative editor, he had no equal. I received his long letters, saw him in his office hidden behind huge rolls of pulp paper in the old Street and Smith building, had lunch with him, was invited to his home in New Jersey. His ideas flowed as steadily in his talk, and sometimes as dogmatically, as in his editorials.

When I was in a stale period, he suggested that I do what he had done when he found a new name and a new style for the Don Stuart stories. I had gone to him with the idea for a series about the planetary engineers, who were to terraform new worlds to fit them for human use. He suggested that some of these new worlds might offer special problems because they were contraterrene—or what is now called antimatter. The result was a series of stories about "seetee"—for contraterrene—by Will Stewart. When I wrote a novelette about robots which suffocate humanity with too much solicitude, he suggested a sequel in which men with folded hands are forced to develop paranormal powers. The outcome was my most successful novel, *The Humanoids*.

The quality of Campbell's mind shows up clearly in *Unknown*, his great fantasy magazine, which was born in 1939 and killed during the war-time paper shortage. He borrowed the classic fantasy formula, first stated I think by H. G. Wells, which requires just one new assumption per story, with everything else as convincing as possible. In science fiction, this assumption should be possible; in *Unknown*, it could be drawn from magic or pure imagination. The sort of thinking involved in which logic challenges reality was Campbell's special delight.

WEIRD TALES AND OTHER MAGAZINES

Another pulp fantasy magazine I liked writing for was Farnsworth Wright's *Weird Tales*. As different as possible from *Unknown*, it offered a far richer variety with no trace of Campbell's sometimes too-insistent formula. The stories were sometimes polished, sometimes barely literate. Though the magazine lacked sophistication, it had a tone of its own—it really was, as it styled itself, "unique." . . .

Though its staple was the supernatural, *Weird Tales* did publish "weird-scientific" fiction. Edmond Hamilton was the most prolific producer of this, and I think the most popular writer for the magazine. Wright never rejected any of his stories. The most outstanding, perhaps, were his tales of the Interstellar Patrol. Though they all had the same simple save-the-universe plot, the action moved at a dizzy pace across a vast galactic canvas. They deserve to be remembered as pioneer steps in the creation of the splendid myth of man's coming future in space that has been picked up and elaborated by more recent writers as sophisticated as Ursula [K.] Le Guin.

There were other magazines, of course. I sold occasional stories to *Marvel Science Stories, Future Fiction, Super Science*, and *Comet*. A whole crop of new titles appeared in the late 1930's, but most of them died during the war. One worth mentioning is *Astonishing Stories*, edited by Fred Pohl for Popular Publications. Fred was just out of high school; he worked for nearly nothing and paid half a cent a word for stories. Twenty bi-monthly issues appeared between February 1940 and April 1943, selling for ten cents a copy. If the magazine itself was not very distinguished, it was at least a fine training ground for newcomers to the field. The first issue includes letters and features by Robert Lowndes, Richard Wilson, Donald A. Wollheim, and a story by Isaac Asimov.

Planet Stories, a Fiction House pulp, was born in 1939 and enjoyed a longer life. Edited by Malcolm Reiss, it was pitched in the beginning at about the same crowd who now watch the TV kiddie cartoons on Saturday morning, but later stories by such people as Leigh Brackett and Ray Bradbury had vitality and a memorable sense of exotic atmosphere. . . .

WHAT HAPPENED TO THE YEARS OF WONDER?

If the 1930's and the 1940's really were the years of wonder, we should ask what changed them. Most obviously, as people keep suggesting, readers and writers grew up. Beyond that, a lot of things happened to shake the world outside our little ghetto. The great depression. World War II. The hydrogen bomb. Such things killed the pulp tradition.

In the war, I was an Army Air Forces weather forecaster. It was another science fiction fan, on a Pacific island, who told me about Hiroshima. I was not delighted, but at least we knew what it meant. Outside science fiction, few people did. When I settled back to writing after the war, I found that the whole field had changed, as I had.

The suspended pulps were not revived; their junior readers, I suppose, were turning to the comics and a little later to TV. For the older readers, there were a thousand new and more elaborate ways of killing or filling time. At the same time, however, people who had seldom read the pulps began taking science fiction a little more seriously, perhaps because rockets and atomic bombs and all sorts of explosive changes had come off the old gray pages into reality. The shadow of the future was suddenly too dark to be ignored. The unbeatable epic heroes of 1930 science fiction were maybe still around, in sword and sorcery fiction, but no longer taken very seriously. Definitions of evil had blurred. The old happy endings were lost in the mushroom clouds of atomic Armageddon.

Outside science fiction, a great shift in the American mind had begun. In the 1930's the scientist and the technologist had been the people's hero. In school we learned about Ben Franklin taming lightning, Robert Fulton building the steamboat, and the Wright Brothers inventing the airplane. We venerated Louis Pasteur and Thomas Alva Edison, Alexander Graham Bell and Henry Ford, Luther Burbank and Albert Einstein. Suddenly, in the 1940's, the offspring of the Model T were choking us with fumes; the billions of people saved by Pasteur and his heirs were crowding us off the planet, the Wright Brothers' aircraft were dropping Einstein's bombs. Our heroes had betrayed us. The sense of wonder at the power of science had become a sense of terror.

I think the people in science fiction were a little more sensitive to all this a little earlier than anybody else. In fact, I think science fiction has spread the gospel of terror, perhaps most widely through the science horror films. The climax, I think, has been the notorious New Wave—which I think carries the panic somewhat too far.

If I may cite two stories of my own, I think they exemplify what happened to the years of wonder. *The Legion of Space* was written in 1932, within the canons of the pulp tradition. I tried to make it epic. The field of action was light-years wide. The heroes were the defenders of mankind, the villains were as bad as I could make them. Science was used to bring a happy ending. *The Humanoids* was written for John Campbell in 1947. Though it is an action story on the epic scale, it has neither hero nor villain. The viewpoint character is more victim than victor. The busy little machines that suffocate mankind with too much benevolence were designed to end all war, to serve, obey, and save man from himself. Progress leads to nightmare. Science, used even by the best of men, produces appalling evil.

New Worlds and the New Wave

Brian W. Aldiss with David Wingrove

Brian W. Aldiss is a prominent writer associated with science fiction's New Wave. The author of many titles, including *The Dark Light Years* and *Barefoot in the Head*, Aldiss is the recipient of both the Hugo and Nebula awards. Aldiss is also awarded for his literary scholarship in the field of science fiction; his *Trillion Year Spree*, written with David Wingrove, is a celebrated comprehensive overview of the genre. In this excerpt Aldiss describes the importance of Britain's *New Worlds* magazine and the literary movement it spawned in the 1960s and 1970s, of which he was a primary figure. Aldiss contends that the New Wave movement in England, more than its American counterpart, represented a revolution within the genre. He credits Michael Moorcock, who became editor of *New Worlds* in 1964, for initiating and fomenting this revolution. Moorcock encouraged writers to experiment with form and controversial material. While creating financial and political difficulties for the magazine, the literary innovation of the *New Worlds* writers greatly developed the genre.

In Ladbroke Grove, in the heart of London, home of the Swinging Sixties, a British SF magazine was reshaping the materials and attitudes of the genre by producing work that was both genuinely radical and, within the larger context of the mainstream, literary.

New Worlds was founded by British fans. It made its first appearance in 1946 and, for the first eighteen years and 141 issues of its life, was a small circulation, fairly traditional British science fiction magazine, operating like an outpost of the American pulp tradition. It published the early works of

Excerpted from *The Trillion Year Spree: The History of Science Fiction*, by Brian W. Aldiss with David Wingrove. Copyright © 1973, 1986 by Brian W. Aldiss. Reprinted by permission of the author and his agent, Robin Straus Agency, Inc., New York, N.Y.

British authors such as Arthur C. Clarke (his "The Sentinel", basis for *2001,* appeared there in no. 22 back in 1953); E. C. "Ted" Tubb (for many years the great producer of British SF and in recent years prolific author of the yet-multiplying *Dumarest* series, with about 30 titles to date); James White; John Rackham; Kenneth Bulmer; Philip E. High; Arthur Sellings; John Brunner (who was selling SF to *Astounding* at the age of seventeen); Brian Aldiss (a stalwart of *New World*'s pages since 1955); and J. G. Ballard; as well as a number of American writers.

Under E. J. "Ted" Carnell's editorship, anything experimental or new got in along with the hack work. But from issue 142, May–June 1964, all that changed. Carnell retired. Michael Moorcock took over the editorship of the magazine. Moorcock was twenty-four and the veteran of ten years' magazine editing and, in what was tantamount to a manifesto, began to alter radically the contents and direction of the magazine. The new god was not Edgar Rice but William Burroughs, of whom Moorcock wrote:

> And in a sense his work is the SF we've all been waiting for—
> it is highly readable, combines satire with splendid imagery,
> discusses the philosophy of science, has insight into human
> experience, uses advanced and effective literary techniques,
> and so on.

Moorcock (and Ballard) saw Burroughs as the perfect mirror of "our ad-saturated, Bomb-dominated, power-corrupted times" and viewed him as the archetype for a new kind of unconventional SF which did not neglect the demands of entertainment. In the later sixties many could question whether the demands of entertainment *were* considered by the magazine at its most excessive. Yet Moorcock did not merely stick to his ideal of a new form of science fiction, one that wasn't simply a mimicry of Burroughs, but offered a variety of experimentation and themes; he also encouraged a good number of American as well as British writers. He was to prove the most dedicated and generous of editors.

In the mid-sixties, metamorphosis was necessary. England was *swinging* by then, with Beatlemania gripping the country, hair lengthening, consumerism thriving, and miniskirts shortening; a new mood of hedonism was in the air. The British Empire had dissolved; the Romans were becoming Italians.

MOORCOCK INITIATES THE *NEW WORLDS* MOVEMENT

Moorcock's *New Worlds* had few taboos—something that often got it into trouble with distributors. It encouraged rather than rejected literary experimentation and steadily became the focus for a re-evaluation of genre standards and a crucible for new attitudes. The very first Moorcock issue contained the beginning of a two-part Ballard serial and an article by Ballard on William Burroughs.

> In *The Naked Lunch*, Burroughs compares organized society with that of its most extreme opposite, the invisible society of drug addicts. His implicit conclusion is that the two are not very different, certainly at the points where they make the closest contact—in prisons and psychiatric institutions . . .

It was to these extreme points that Ballard instinctively journeyed, the poles of mental inaccessibility, where normal and abnormal met on apotropaic neutral ground.

Moorcock's energy and the imagery of Ballard and Aldiss attracted a new audience to science fiction. It was, in fact, an audience already around, grokking the more way-out strata of the life of their time, but not at all tuned to the old pulp idiom, of which the Carnell magazines had been the tired inheritors.

The new *New Worlds* seized on an essential truth: that the speculative body of work contained in the SF of the past had been directed towards just such a future as the mid-sixties: the Sunday colour mags, proliferating LPs, drugs, promiscuity, cheap jet flights, colour TV, pop music that suddenly spoke with a living mouth—and the constant threat that the Middle East or Vietnam or South Africa or Somewhere would suddenly blow up and end the whole fantastic charade forever and ever amen—this actually *was* the Brave New World, nor were we out of it!

By 1967, while Harlan Ellison was trumpeting about how dangerous his anthology was, Moorcock was busy publishing Disch's *Camp Concentration*, Aldiss's *Report on Probability A* and *Barefoot in the Head*, Pamela Zoline's "The Heat Death of the Universe" and parts of John Brunner's *Stand on Zanzibar*, not to mention the more extreme experimentation of writers like Ballard, Michael Butterworth, Giles Gordon and Barrington Bayley.

Around *New Worlds* and the flamboyant figure of Moorcock gathered a staff who often doubled as writers, among them the redoubtable Charles Platt, Langdon Jones, Hilary

Bailey, Mal Dean, M. John Harrison, Diane Lambert, and the anthologist (and subsequently children's writer) Douglas Hill. Word got about. By 1967, however, matters were getting slightly out of hand. Anarchy collided with its creditors.

New Worlds had been in financial trouble but had been bailed out by a generous Arts Council grant, an appeal for which had been supported by such eminent figures as Edmund Crispin, Anthony Burgess, Roy Fuller, Kenneth Allsop, Angus Wilson (for years a staunch friend of science fiction and whose *Old Men at the Zoo* is peripherally SF), J. B. Priestley, and Marghanita Laski.

The magazine was never far from trouble with officialdom, however. When Moorcock published American writer Norman Spinrad's thumping novel about cryogenics, the politics of power and the power of TV, *Bug Jack Barron*—serialized throughout most of 1968—its four-letter words and eleven-letter activities like cunnilingus, led to Spinrad's being referred to as a "degenerate" in the House of Commons—a notable if not singular honour—and to the magazine being dropped by W. H. Smith, the biggest distributor and retail outlet in Britain. Paradoxically, all this happened at the same time that the Arts Council—government funded—extended its grant for a further period.

THE INNOVATIVE WRITING OF J. G. BALLARD

As important as the medium, however, were the writers with the new message. Ballard—perhaps made slightly frenzied by having been so firmly nailed to the masthead of Moorcock's pirate ship—rejected linear fiction and was writing "condensed novels", impacted visions of a timeless, dimensionless world, lacerated by anguish, desiccated by knowledge, and illustrative of William Burroughs's dictum, "A psychotic is a guy who's just discovered what's going on."

> *Pentax Zoom.* In these equations, the gestures and postures of the young woman, Trabert explored the faulty dimensions of the space capsule, the lost geometry and volumetric time of the dead astronauts.
>
> (1) Lateral section through the left axillary fossa of Karen Novotny, the elbow raised in a gesture of pique: the transliterated pudenda of Ralph Nader.
>
> (2) A series of paintings of imaginary sexual organs. As he walked around the exhibition, conscious of Karen's hand gripping his wrist, Trabert searched for some valid point of junction. These obscene images, the headless creatures of a

nightmare, grimaced at him like the exposed corpses in the Apollo capsule, the victims of a thousand auto-crashes.

(3) *The Stolen Mirror* (Max Ernst). In the eroded causeways and porous rock towers of this spinal landscape Trabert saw the blistered epithelium of the astronauts, the time-invaded skin of Karen Novotny.

One "chapter" from "The Death Module", powerfully conveying some of the dislocation and unexpressed connections of its time. It is principally a question of style, once more, but style complementing its austere and haunting subject matter.

As a novelist, Ballard was less successful. *The Wind from Nowhere* has already been mentioned as a cosy catastrophe. The purest draught is contained in *The Drowned World* (1962), a picture of a landscape glowing in flood and heat, in which man is an amphibious thing, a native of disaster lured towards some ultimate nemesis.

The Drowned World sets the pattern for other Ballard novels of the sixties, all of which are novels of catastrophe, and in form—if form only—owing a good deal to John Wyndham; which may be why Ballard has cutting things to say about Wyndham. *The Crystal World* (1966) shows Ballard's style glittering darkly and reduplicating itself like the jewels encasing his saturnine forests. But the central problem of writing a novel without having the characters pursue any purposeful course of action—even more acute in *The Drought* (1965)—is not resolved. Ballard resolved it only in his novels of the seventies, *Crash!* (1973) and *Concrete Island* (1974) for instance, where obsession has usurped more normal plot criteria, or in his non-SF novel of the eighties, *Empire of the Sun* (1984), where the strength of autobiographical reminiscence powers the recasting of images familiar to the reader from Ballard's science fiction.

Ballard's short stories are *sui generis* [unique]. They hinge upon inaction, their world is the world of loss and surrender, their drama the drama of a limbo beyond despair where action is irrelevant. Early novels coin colourful doom-worlds; the best short stories stick (as do the seventies novels) to regions on the outskirts of London or Los Angeles only too bleakly familiar. Ballard's singular gift has been to identify this urban wilderness and give it a voice.

Some of Ballard's condensed novels were published together as *The Atrocity Exhibition* in England in 1970. American publishers took longer to bite and retitled the book *Love and Napalm: Export USA* (1972). Read together, the condensed novels become repetitive, and Ballard's habit of pushing jargon as others push dope becomes distracting. So is a repetitive use of what may almost be termed "Ballardian" imagery, setting and characterization. Indeed, in the last case *The Atrocity Exhibition* tends to illustrate the facelessness and colourlessness of a typical Ballard character. Interchangeable and anonymous in name and identity, he has no more significance than anything else in the obnubilated landscape.

Taken singly, as was originally intended, the condensed novels are more impressive; but it is perhaps the stories of Ballard's "Terminal Beach" period which will last the longest. His ferocious intelligence, his wit, his cantankerousness, and, in particular, his single-minded rendering of the perverse pleasures of today's paranoia, make Ballard one of the grand magicians of modern fiction. His is an uncertain spell, and not to all tastes, but it spreads—as Moorcock was among the first to perceive—far beyond the stockades of ordinary science fiction. Ballard may have his weaknesses but his strengths are inimitable. . . .

MOORCOCK AS A *NEW WORLDS* WRITER

If some of *New Worlds*'s writing was deliberately difficult, Moorcock's campaign converted a lot of fans and won new readers. Another major writer working regularly within the magazine's pages was Michael Moorcock himself.

Moorcock is a great, vital, generous figure, full of vigour and creative juice. He is also an awesome producer, though he over-produced throughout the late sixties and the first few years of the seventies. Much of that earliest work is hastily written sword-and-sorcery adventure (Hawkmoon, Elric and the Eternal Champion), which has proved durable in the popularity stakes. It was written in response to financial necessity—but of a kind different from the needs of most SF writers of the period. Moorcock had a towering, passionate disinterest in money for its own sake. He wanted money only to keep *New Worlds* going. Subscriptions and the Arts Council grant covered production costs, but Moorcock was often left with the problem of finding money to pay the contributors. His solution was to conjure a fantasy out of a bottle of whisky in three days flat.

Saying so much doesn't explain enough. Moorcock's sword-and-sorcery, for all its hasty construction, is not of the usual stereotyped kind. Edgar Rice Burroughs may have been an early hero of Moorcock's, but the young English writer switched Burroughs's formulae. Burroughs's swaggering heroes became Moorcock's uncertain, tormented victims-as-heroes, like Elric with his vampiric broadsword, Stormbringer. Blood and gore a-plenty flowed about Elric's saddle, but Moorcock's anti-heroes lived and breathed and had more personal problems than Conan would ever have dreamed of. As critic Colin Greenland has remarked, "Moorcock is the first sword-and-sorcery writer to build the psychological function of reading fantasy into the work itself."

Moorcock did not confine himself to sword-and-sorcery. Perhaps his best known work from the *New Worlds* era chronicled the adventures of sixties' anti-hero Jerry Cornelius. The Cornelius books were loosely structured and baroque, owing something to Bester's two fifties' novels as well as to Burroughs (William, this time), Ballard and Wells. In a sense it was the same contemporary world coldly glimpsed in Ballard's work, but a world in which warm pastiche breathed, a world with far greater animation and personality. Cornelius himself was an attractive anti-hero, almost the hedonistic, amoral Everyman of his time. The novels themselves, cluttered with images and objects—vibrators, Sikorsky helicopters, Mars bars among them—are deliberately less meaningful. Of course, this was a kind of fictional in-joke amongst the writers of *New Worlds*: consequently, a comic book quality often pervades much of the writing.

Moorcock seems not to have taken his subject matter too seriously; the Cornelius adventures were a dark comedy set not just in space and time, but in all spaces and all times (though essentially *here* and *now* . . . Portobello Road, London, circa 1966)—in Moorcock's all-connecting "Multiverse", that realm of infinite possibilities:

> It was a world ruled these days by the gun, the guitar, and the needle, sexier than sex, where the good right hand had become the male's primary sexual organ, which was just as well considering the world population had been due to double before the year 2000.
>
> This wasn't the world Jerry had known, he felt, but he could only vaguely remember a different one, so similar to

this that it was immaterial which was which. The dates
checked roughly, that was all he cared about, and the mood
was much the same. (*The Final Programme,* Chapter 6)

Perhaps ultimately more lasting was a novella Moorcock
wrote for *New Worlds* 166 (September 1966) and subsequently revised for novel publication. *Behold the Man* won
that year's Nebula for Best Novella and is the strongest argument against the view that Moorcock failed to practise what
he so vehemently preached in the pulpit of *New Worlds.*

HERE COMES THE REVOLUTION

While Moorcock and the New Worlds *writers were
launching the New Wave in Britain, the multiple award-
winning science fiction author, Harlan Ellison, was simultaneously editing the definitive New Wave anthology,* Dangerous
Visions, *in America. In this excerpt from his introduction, Ellison announces the arrival of the New Wave revolution.*

But even *more* heinous is the entrance on the scene of writers
who won't accept the old ways. The smartass kids who write
"all that literary stuff," who take the accepted and hoary ideas
of the speculative arena and stand them right on their noses.
Them guys are blasphemers. God will send down lightning to
strike *them* in their spleens.

Yet speculative fiction (notice how I cleverly avoid using
the misnomer "science fiction"? getting the message, friends?
you've bought one of those s—e f—n anthologies and didn't
even know it! well, you've blown your bread, so you might as
well hang around and get educated) is the most fertile ground
for the growth of a writing talent without boundaries, with
horizons that seem never to get any closer. And all them
smartass punks keep emerging, driving the old guard out of
their jugs with frenzy. And lord! how the mighty have fallen;
for most of the "big names" in the field, who dominated the
covers and top rates of the magazines for more years than
they deserved, can no longer cut it, they no longer produce.
Or they have moved on to other fields. Leaving it to the
newer, brighter ones, and the ones who were new and bright
once, and were passed by because they weren't "big names."

But despite the new interest in speculative fiction by the
mainstream, despite the enlarged and variant styles of the
new writers, despite the enormity and expansion of topics
open to these writers, despite what is outwardly a booming,

Behold the Man is *The Time Machine* as Wells would never have dreamed it. Part of the novel concerns the childhood and adult experiences of a young sixties male, Karl Glogauer. In its psychological portrait of Glogauer, *Behold the Man* is a superbly written mainstream novel concerned with how character is determined by event and vice versa. It was definitely *new* in this respect—in that it was concerned more with inner space than outer, with the effects of drugs on human life more than alien encounters, with psychology

healthy market . . . there is a constricting narrowness of mind on the part of many editors in the field. Because many of the editors were once simply fans, and they retain that specialized prejudice for the s-f of their youth. Writer after writer is finding his work precensored even before he writes it, because he knows this editor won't allow discussions of politics in his pages, and that one shies away from stories exploring sex in the future, and this one down here in the baseboard doesn't pay except in red beans and rice, so why bother burning up all those gray cells on a daring concept when the tenant in the baseboard will buy the old madman-in-the-time-machine *shtick.*

This is called a taboo. And there isn't an editor in the field who won't swear under threat of the water torture that he hasn't got them, that he even sprays the office with insecticide on the off-chance there's a taboo nesting in the files like a silverfish. They've said it at conventions, they've said it in print, but there are over a dozen writers in this book [*Dangerous Visions*] alone who will, upon slight nudging, relate stories of horror and censorship that include every editor in the field, even the one who lives in the baseboard.

Oh, there are challenges in the field, and truly controversial, eye-opening pieces get published; but there are so many more that go a-begging.

And no one has ever told the speculative writer, "Pull out all the stops, no holds barred, get it said!" Until this book came along.

Don't look now, but you're on the firing line in the big revolution.

Harlan Ellison, "Introduction: Thirty-Two Soothsayers," *Dangerous Visions.* New York: Signet, 1967.

and not technology. But it is a science fiction novel, and an excellent vehicle for its ideas at that. For Karl Glogauer finds himself travelling back in time—in an experimental machine—to 28 AD. Back to the time of Jesus Christ, whom he finally meets:

> The figure was misshapen.
>
> It had a pronounced hunched back and a cast in its left eye. The face was vacant and foolish. There was a little spittle on the lips.
>
> "Jesus?"
>
> It giggled as its name was repeated. It took a crooked, lurching step forward.
>
> "Jesus," it said. The word was slurred and thick. "Jesus."
>
> "That's all he can say," said the woman. "He's always been like that."
>
> "God's judgement," said Joseph. (Chapter 12)

Glogauer's discovery that the "real" Christ is a congenital idiot results in his taking on the Christ role, recreating the life of Christ he remembers from his childhood scriptures—resulting, of course, in the crucifixion. Though the novel itself is a serious enough investigation of all the implications of this event and not a sensationalized account, the obvious blasphemy of the theme was attuned to the *New Worlds* experiment and did in reality what Ellison, in his introduction to *Dangerous Visions*, claimed to be doing. It is important to note also Moorcock's editorial presentation of *New Worlds* 166, which also contained the controversial "The Atrocity Exhibition" by Ballard:

> So, though we anticipate a certain response to some of the stories we publish in this issue, we hope that they will be accepted on their merits, on their own terms, and not regarded as "breakthrough stories" or "controversial" stories, or stories written to be sensational and to shock. They are seriously intentioned and deal with subjects that the authors felt deeply about. They are trying to cope with the job of analysing and interpreting various aspects of human existence, and they hope that in the process they succeed in entertaining you.

A wide gulf separates this from Ellison's "Them guys are blasphemous". And yet, for all the mumblings and grumblings of the "Golden Age" writers, Ellison's fake revolution was accepted without too much fuss, while most of what *New Worlds* attempted was—at least in immediate terms—rejected out of hand. Put it all down to showbiz razzamatazz, perhaps, but the emergent fact was clear—experiments with style were fine, perhaps even fun. Experiments with a style that reflected content matter was . . . well, it was different, unacceptable to most of the traditional readership.

OTHER WRITERS PARTICIPATE IN THE MOVEMENT

Ironically, Ellison, Delany and Zelazny wrote some of their best material for publication in *New Worlds*. Bright new American writers, sensing the importance of Moorcock's experiment, actually upped and moved to London. But we'll come to them in just a while.

Among the home-grown British talent were several names which deserve all-too-brief mention. Michael Butterworth, a fiercely intelligent writer, challenged *New Worlds*'s readers to untangle his literary conundrums, while Barrington Bayley—perhaps the most underrated short story writer in the genre—explored unconventional concepts with a remarkable ingenuity. His 1973 story, "An Overload", where future political constructs (named Sinatra, Bogart, Reagan!) control a multi-levelled city, is typical of his dark insights. Poets George Macbeth and D. M. Thomas were also drawn into the experiment. The latter extended the *New Worlds* lessons in his own novels, with great commercial success, *The White Hotel* (1981) becoming an international bestseller, while Macbeth's flamboyant novels seem to owe something to Jerry Cornelius. Pamela Zoline, with her exceptional "The Heat Death of the Universe", Langdon Jones ("Eye of the Lens"), Giles Gordon and M. John Harrison (to whom we shall return when talking of the seventies), all added to the flavour of *New Worlds*.

Before passing to those emigrés who graced the magazine's pages, brief mention must be made of David I. Masson, whose clutch of stories in the mid-sixties greatly enriched the *New Worlds* brew. He began spectacularly, in issue 154 (September 1965) with the story "Traveller's Rest", where H travels home from the war zone, the Frontier, and returns a few seconds later after his replacement has been killed. In the interim he has journeyed far south, away from the Frontier and its time-acceleration. The further he goes, the more slowly time passes. He has time enough to marry and have three children before he returns; time enough for normality before returning to the madness. Life as a long dream lived between moments of impacted madness. It suited the *New Worlds* idiom perfectly.

Masson's second venture was the powerfully evocative "Mouth of Hell" in January 1966, where atmosphere and idea are large enough to swallow any reader whole. It was science fiction of the most imaginative kind—metaphysical statements that touched one personally. Masson wrote only five more stories for *New Worlds* and wrote little fiction after 1967. His work, collected as *The Caltraps of Time* (1968), awaits rediscovery.

Two other writers, both Americans who moved to London in the sixties to be closer to the crucible of *New Worlds*, deserve more than a passing mention: Tom Disch and John Sladek.

Thomas M. Disch's science fiction rarely, if ever, left Earth. His first two novels, *The Genocides* (1965) and *The Puppies of Terra* (1966, also as *Mankind Under the Leash*) dealt with alien invasions in a far from conventional manner. People and their strange, alien ways mattered more to Disch than the aliens themselves. When Disch came to London and started contributing to *New Worlds* in September 1966, he was still very much an unknown commodity in terms of the SF audience. In the space of five years he produced a series of short stories—"The Squirrel Cage", "Casablanca", "The Asian Shore" and "Angoulême" foremost among them—and two novels, *Echo Round his Bones* (1967) and *Camp Concentration* (serialized 1967, book form 1968) which established him as one of the most intelligent and innovative of science fiction writers. With the intensity of a lapsed catholic he tailored science fiction's metaphoric richness to an investigation of the "human condition". Never more so, perhaps, than in *Camp Concentration:*

> Enough of heaven, enough of God! They neither exist. What *we* want to hear of now is hell and devils. Not Power, Knowledge, and Love—but Impotence, Ignorance, and Hate, the three faces of Satan. You're surprised at my candour? You think I betray my hand? Not at all. All values melt imperceptibly into their opposites. Any good Hegelian knows that. War is peace, ignorance is strength and freedom is slavery. Add to that, that love is hate, as Freud has so exhaustively demonstrated. As for knowledge, it's the scandal of our age that philosophy has been whittled away to a barebones epistemology, and thence to an even barer agnoiology. Have I found a word you don't know, Louis? Agnoiology is the philosophy of ignorance, a philosophy for philosophers. (Book 2, Section 56)

The diarist of *Camp Concentration* is Louis Sacchetti, a minor poet and conscientious objector to the war in Vietnam. Transferred from a more regular prison to the deep caverns of Camp Archimedes, he is subjected to an experiment in intelligence raising. The "drug" used in the experiment, Palladine, is a derivative of syphilis; its effect is not merely to raise intelligence to new and giddy heights (some of which Disch strains to present in its own terms—a valiant if incomprehensible attempt!) but eventually to kill its subjects. Disch acknowledges his sources—Thomas Mann's study of syphilitic super intelligence, *Doctor Faustus*, undoubtedly lies behind the conception of Disch's novel—but shapes them to science fictional ends. It is a harrowing, difficult book, more an intellectual treat than a good read, which in its last twenty pages proves as gripping as the most garish traditional SF yarn, as revelation follows revelation.

If Disch was shaping science fiction's metaphors to his own metafictional ends, John Sladek took the same bag of tricks and, with an intelligent and darkly humorous eye, turned the genre on its head. Although America and its contemporary inanities were often the butt of Sladek's humour, the science fiction story itself was just as likely to be subjected to Sladek's mischievous attentions. Parody and logical conundrum, blended with intelligent insight into the real problems behind SF's thoughtlessly-utilized themes—particularly that of artificial intelligence—marked Sladek's work from the first. . . .

[Sladek's novel] *The Müller-Fokker Effect* (1970), tells the story of Bob Shairp, who is reduced to computer data and stored on tape in a newly-discovered process. Like much of Sladek's work, it is a deeply satirical book, homing in on the US Army, evangelism, newspapers and the like for its targets, with an overall sense of fun reminiscent of the work of Kurt Vonnegut, Philip K. Dick and Sheckley. In recent years Sladek's stories of Roderick, a young, almost-human machine have, in their thoughtful and funny way, provided an answer to the previous mechanistic views of robots.

THE IMPACT OF *NEW WORLDS* AND THE NEW WAVE

In many ways *New Worlds* and its writers brought a cold sixties sophistication to the ideative content of the genre, together with some mere trendiness and a concern for a means of expression rather than simple stylistic showmanship.

Delany and Zelazny gave you the icing but no cake; the *New Worlds* writers to a large degree provided both. In the States any writer with a freaky style became an honourable member of the New Wave—as Judith Merril publicized it—but the mistake was in assuming that style was all and meaning nothing. At the heart of *New Worlds's* New Wave—never mind the froth at the edges—was a hard and unpalatable core of message, an attitude to life, a scepticism about the benefits of society or any future society. Merril demonstrated this in an early issue of *Extrapolation.*

Alarmed by the new hoo-ha (and it was, perhaps, pretty tiring unless you were young, high and living in Ladbroke Grove), Isaac Asimov said, "I hope that when the New Wave has deposited its froth and receded, the vast and solid shore of *science fiction* will appear once more."

What the New Wave deposited was much needed alluvial soil on that overtilled strip of shore. For the New Wave was but one of many tides and came much nearer to the source and impetus of creative writing than pulp formulae could. Its heroes did not swagger around in magnetized boots. They were generally anti-heroes, their destination more often bed than Mars.

To argue too strongly for either in such a controversy is a mistake. Failures and fatalities are thick on either hand, and good writers few. The new movement certainly widened both the scope of SF and its audience. For some years, at least, the image of SF was changed. It has become fashionable to write SF and even to read it.

The great mountain chains of old SF magazines, in which one may wander lost for a lifetime, may, in the perspectives of time, be seen as no more than a brief tectonic shrug of shoulders in the vaster plate movements of SF.

One should, nevertheless, recall the point that George Melly made about the Beatles in *Revolt into Style,* that "they destroyed Pop with their intelligence". The New Wave did the same to SF; intelligence and irreverence did it. Ballard's was not the sole perception of the world, nor Moorcock's the only approach to authorship, and it would be a myopic critical viewpoint which saw only the onset of the new and not the continuance of the old.

Shore and waves are inseparably linked in one function.

A Cyberpunk Manifesto

Bruce Sterling

Bruce Sterling is one of the seminal writers of science fiction's cyberpunk subgenre. He is the author of a number of science fiction novels and short stories, including *Islands in the Net, The Artificial Kid,* and the collection *Globalhead.* He is also an occasional collaborator and coauthor with William Gibson, whose *Neuromancer* Sterling cites as "the quintessential cyberpunk novel." In this selection Sterling defines the cyberpunk movement, which has its origins firmly within the 1980s, and clearly influences much of the science fiction produced at present. Sterling traces cyberpunk to its inception, acknowledging the influence of the New Wave writers and other science fiction visionaries, and identifying the subgenre's roots in pop culture and the technological revolution. Sterling states that the writers of the cyberpunk movement share an intense vision and address common themes, including concerns about human nature, identity, physical and mental invasion, and artificial intelligence.

Cyberpunk is a product of the Eighties milieu—in some sense, as I hope to show later, a definitive product. But its roots are deeply sunk in the sixty-year tradition of modern popular SF.

The cyberpunks as a group are steeped in the lore and tradition of the SF field. Their precursors are legion. Individual cyberpunk writers differ in their literary debts; but some older writers, ancestral cyberpunks perhaps, show a clear and striking influence.

From the New Wave: the streetwise edginess of Harlan Ellison. The visionary shimmer of Samuel Delany. The freewheeling zaniness of Norman Spinrad and the rock esthetic of Michael Moorcock; the intellectual daring of Brian Aldiss; and, always, J. G. Ballard.

Excerpted from the preface, by Bruce Sterling, *Mirrorshades: The Cyberpunk Anthology,* edited by Bruce Sterling (New York: Arbor House, 1986). Copyright © 1986 by Bruce Sterling. Reprinted by permission of Writers House LLC, as agent for the author.

From the harder tradition: the cosmic outlook of Olaf Stapledon; the science/politics of H. G. Wells; the steely extrapolation of Larry Niven, Poul Anderson, and Robert Heinlein.

And the cyberpunks treasure a special fondness for SF's native visionaries: the bubbling inventiveness of Philip José Farmer; the brio of John Varley, the reality games of Philip K. Dick; the soaring, skipping beatnik tech of Alfred Bester. With a special admiration for a writer whose integration of technology and literature stands unsurpassed: Thomas Pynchon.

Throughout the Sixties and Seventies, the impact of SF's last designated "movement," the New Wave, brought a new concern for literary craftsmanship to SF. Many of the cyberpunks write a quite accomplished and graceful prose; they are in love with style, and are (some say) fashion-conscious to a fault. But, like the punks of '77, they prize their garage-band esthetic. They love to grapple with the raw core of SF: its ideas. This links them strongly to the classic SF tradition. Some critics opine that cyberpunk is disentangling SF from mainstream influence, much as punk stripped rock and roll of the symphonic elegances of Seventies "progressive rock." (And others—hard-line SF traditionalists with a firm distrust of "artiness"—loudly disagree.)

THE CYBERPUNK GENERATION LIVES IN A SCIENCE-FICTIONAL WORLD

Like punk music, cyberpunk is in some sense a return to roots. The cyberpunks are perhaps the first SF generation to grow up not only within the literary tradition of science fiction but in a truly science-fictional world. For them, the techniques of classical "hard SF"—extrapolation, technological literacy—are not just literary tools but an aid to daily life. They are a means of understanding, and highly valued.

In pop culture, practice comes first; theory follows limping in its tracks. Before the era of labels, cyberpunk was simply "the Movement"—a loose generational nexus of ambitious young writers, who swapped letters, manuscripts, ideas, glowing praise, and blistering criticism. These writers—Gibson, Rucker, Shiner, Shirley, Sterling—found a friendly unity in their common outlook, common themes, even in certain oddly common symbols, which seemed to crop up in their work with a life of their own. Mirrorshades, for instance.

Mirrored sunglasses have been a Movement totem since the early days of '82. The reasons for this are not hard to grasp. By hiding the eyes, mirrorshades prevent the forces of normalcy from realizing that one is crazed and possibly dangerous. They are the symbol of the sun-staring visionary, the biker, the rocker, the policeman, and similar outlaws. Mirrorshades—preferably in chrome and matte black, the Movement's totem colors—appeared in story after story, as a kind of literary badge.

These proto-cyberpunks were briefly dubbed the Mirrorshades Group. . . . But other young writers, of equal talent and ambition, were soon producing work that linked them unmistakably to the new SF. They were independent explorers, whose work reflected something inherent in the decade, in the spirit of the times. Something loose in the 1980s.

Thus, "cyberpunk"—a label none of them chose. But the term now seems a fait accompli, and there is a certain justice in it. The term captures something crucial to the work of these writers, something crucial to the decade as a whole: a new kind of integration. The overlapping of worlds that were formerly separate: the realm of high tech, and the modern pop underground.

This integration has become our decade's crucial source of cultural energy. The work of the cyberpunks is paralleled throughout Eighties pop culture: in rock video; in the hacker underground; in the jarring street tech of hip-hop and scratch music; in the synthesizer rock of London and Tokyo. This phenomenon, this dynamic, has a global range; cyberpunk is its literary incarnation.

In another era this combination might have seemed farfetched and artificial. Traditionally there has been a yawning cultural gulf between the sciences and the humanities: a gulf between literary culture, the formal world of art and politics, and the culture of science, the world of engineering and industry.

But the gap is crumbling in unexpected fashion. Technical culture has gotten out of hand. The advances of the sciences are so deeply radical, so disturbing, upsetting, and revolutionary, that they can no longer be contained. They are surging into culture at large; they are invasive; they are everywhere. The traditional power structure, the traditional institutions, have lost control of the pace of change.

THE TECHNOLOGICAL REVOLUTION

And suddenly a new alliance is becoming evident: an integration of technology and the Eighties counterculture. An unholy alliance of the technical world and the world of organized dissent—the underground world of pop culture, visionary fluidity, and street-level anarchy.

The counterculture of the 1960s was rural, romanticized, anti-science, anti-tech. But there was always a lurking contradiction at its heart, symbolized by the electric guitar. Rock technology was the thin edge of the wedge. As the years have passed, rock tech has grown ever more accomplished, expanding into high-tech recording, satellite video, and computer graphics. Slowly it is turning rebel pop culture inside out, until the artists at pop's cutting edge are now, quite often, cutting-edge technicians in the bargain. They are special effects wizards, mixmasters, tape-effects techs, graphics hackers, emerging through new media to dazzle society with head-trip extravaganzas like FX cinema and the global Live Aid benefit. The contradiction has become an integration.

And now that technology has reached a fever pitch, its influence has slipped control and reached street level. As Alvin Toffler pointed out in *The Third Wave*—a bible to many cyberpunks—the technical revolution reshaping our society is based not in hierarchy but in decentralization, not in rigidity but in fluidity.

The hacker and the rocker are [the Eighties] pop-culture idols, and cyberpunk is very much a pop phenomenon: spontaneous, energetic, close to its roots. Cyberpunk comes from the realm where the computer hacker and the rocker overlap, a cultural Petri dish where writhing gene lines splice. Some find the results bizarre, even monstrous; for others this integration is a powerful source of hope.

Science fiction—at least according to its official dogma—has always been about the impact of technology. But times have changed since the comfortable era of Hugo Gernsback, when Science was safely enshrined—and confined—in an ivory tower. The careless technophilia of those days belongs to a vanished, sluggish era, when authority still had a comfortable margin of control.

For the cyberpunks, by stark contrast, technology is visceral. It is not the bottled genie of remote Big Science boffins; it is pervasive, utterly intimate. Not outside us, but next to us. Under our skin; often, inside our minds.

Technology itself has changed. Not for us the giant steam-snorting wonders of the past: the Hoover Dam, the Empire State Building, the nuclear power plant. Eighties tech sticks to the skin, responds to the touch: the personal computer, the Sony Walkman, the portable telephone, the soft contact lens.

CENTRAL THEMES IN CYBERPUNK FICTION

Certain central themes spring up repeatedly in cyberpunk. The theme of body invasion: prosthetic limbs, implanted circuitry, cosmetic surgery, genetic alteration. The even more powerful theme of mind invasion: brain-computer interfaces, artificial intelligence, neurochemistry—techniques radically redefining the nature of humanity, the nature of the self.

As Norman Spinrad pointed out in his essay on cyberpunk, many drugs, like rock and roll, are definitive high-tech products. No counterculture Earth Mother gave us lysergic acid—it came from a Sandoz lab, and when it escaped it ran through society like wildfire. It is not for nothing that Timothy Leary proclaimed personal computers "the LSD of the 1980s"—these are both technologies of frighteningly radical potential. And, as such, they are constant points of reference for cyberpunk.

The cyberpunks, being hybrids themselves, are fascinated by interzones: the areas where, in the words of William Gibson, "the street finds its own uses for things." Roiling, irrepressible street graffiti from that classic industrial artifact, the spray can. The subversive potential of the home printer and the photocopier. Scratch music, whose ghetto innovators turn the phonograph itself into an instrument, producing an archetypal Eighties music where funk meets the Burroughs cut-up method. "It's all in the mix"—this is true of much Eighties art and is as applicable to cyberpunk as it is to punk mix-and-match retro fashion and multitrack digital recording.

The Eighties [were] an era of reassessment, of integration, of hybridized influences, of old notions shaken loose and reinterpreted with a new sophistication, a broader perspective. The cyberpunks aim for a wide-ranging, global point of view.

William Gibson's *Neuromancer*, surely the quintessential cyberpunk novel, is set in Tokyo, Istanbul, Paris. Lewis

Shiner's *Frontera* features scenes in Russia and Mexico—as well as the surface of Mars. John Shirley's *Eclipse* describes Western Europe in turmoil. Greg Bear's *Blood Music* is global, even cosmic in scope.

The tools of global integration—the satellite media net, the multinational corporation—fascinate the cyberpunks and figure constantly in their work. Cyberpunk has little patience with borders. Tokyo's *Hayakawa's SF Magazine* was the first publication ever to produce an "all-cyberpunk" issue, in November 1986. Britain's innovative SF magazine *Interzone* has also been a hotbed of cyberpunk activity, publishing Shirley, Gibson, and Sterling as well as a series of groundbreaking editorials, interviews, and manifestos. Global awareness is more than an article of faith with cyberpunks; it is a deliberate pursuit.

CYBERPUNK'S INTENSE VISION

Cyberpunk work is marked by its visionary intensity. Its writers prize the bizarre, the surreal, the formerly unthinkable. They are willing—eager, even—to take an idea and unflinchingly push it past the limits. Like J. G. Ballard—an idolized role model to many cyberpunks—they often use an unblinking, almost clinical objectivity. It is a coldly objective analysis, a technique borrowed from science, then put to literary use for classically punk shock value.

With this intensity of vision comes strong imaginative concentration. Cyberpunk is widely known for its telling use of detail, its carefully constructed intricacy, its willingness to carry extrapolation into the fabric of daily life. It favors "crammed" prose: rapid, dizzying bursts of novel information, sensory overload that submerges the reader in the literary equivalent of the hard-rock "wall of sound."

Cyberpunk is a natural extension of elements already present in science fiction, elements sometimes buried but always seething with potential. Cyberpunk has risen from within the SF genre; it is not an invasion but a modern reform. Because of this, its effect within the genre has been rapid and powerful.

CHAPTER 3

Genre Conventions

Science
Fiction

Negative Utopias and Orwell's Dark Vision

Erich Fromm

Erich Fromm (1900–1980) was an important psycho-
analyst who emphasized the effect of social conditioning on behavior. In his afterword to George Orwell's novel, *1984*—a work that contends with the
notion of mass social conditioning, Fromm examines
the negative utopian vision. Although *1984* warns
against the threat of war and weapons of mass destruction, its most dire prophecy is of a society in
which individuals are dehumanized through social
conditioning to slavishly and unquestioningly serve a
totalitarian state. Fromm explores Orwell's themes
with attention to the Cold War perspective from
which the novel was written, noting how technology
and industrial production are beginning to serve the
political aims of the emerging superpowers. As their
power grows, these nations gain more control over
their citizens and soon are able to manufacture truths
to legitimize their own existence and the righteous-
ness of their political philosophy. For Fromm, Orwell's novel is a dark prediction of a future in which
these power structures continue unchecked.

George Orwell's *1984* is the expression of a mood, and it is a
warning. The mood it expresses is that of near despair about
the future of man, and the warning is that unless the course
of history changes, men all over the world will lose their
most human qualities, will become soulless automatons,
and will not even be aware of it.

The mood of hopelessness about the future of man is in
marked contrast to one of the most fundamental features of
Western thought: the faith in human progress and in man's

capacity to create a world of justice and peace. This hope has its roots both in Greek and in Roman thinking, as well as in the Messianic concept of the Old Testament prophets. The Old Testament philosophy of history assumes that man grows and unfolds in history and eventually becomes what he potentially is. It assumes that he develops his powers of reason and love fully, and thus is enabled to grasp the world, being one with his fellow man and nature, at the same time preserving his individuality and his integrity. Universal peace and justice are the goals of man, and the prophets have faith that in spite of all errors and sins, eventually this "end of days" will arrive, symbolized by the figure of the Messiah.

The prophetic concept was a historical one, a state of perfection to be realized by man within historical time. Christianity transformed this concept into a transhistorical, purely spiritual one, yet it did not give up the idea of the connection between moral norms and politics. The Christian thinkers of the late Middle Ages emphasized that although the "Kingdom of God" was not within historical time, the social order must correspond to and realize the spiritual principles of Christianity. The Christian sects before and after the Reformation emphasized these demands in more urgent, more active and revolutionary ways. With the breakup of the medieval world, man's sense of strength, and his hope, not only for individual but for social perfection, assumed new strength and took new ways.

The Birth of the Utopia Story

One of the most important ones is a new form of writing which developed since the Renaissance, the first expression of which was Thomas More's *Utopia* (literally: "Nowhere"), a name which was then generically applied to all other similar works. Thomas More's *Utopia* combined a most penetrating criticism of his own society, its irrationality and its injustice, with the picture of a society which, though perhaps not perfect, had solved most of the human problems which sounded insoluble to his own contemporaries. What characterizes Thomas More's *Utopia,* and all the others, is that they do not speak in general terms of principles, but give an imaginative picture of the concrete details of a society which corresponds to the deepest longings of man. In contrast to prophetic thought, these perfect societies are not at "the end of the days" but exist already—though in a geographic distance rather than in the distance of time.

Thomas More's *Utopia* was followed by two others, the Italian friar Campanella's *City of the Sun*, and the German humanist Andreae's *Christianopolis*, the latter being the most modern of the three. There are differences in viewpoint and in originality in this trilogy of utopias, yet the differences are minor in comparison with what they have in common. Utopias were written from then on for several hundred years, until the beginning of the twentieth century. The latest and most influential utopia was Edward Bellamy's *Looking Backward*, published in 1888. . . .

This hope for man's individual and social perfectibility, which in philosophical and anthropological terms was clearly expressed in the writings of the Enlightenment philosophers of the eighteenth century and of the socialist thinkers of the nineteenth, remained unchanged until after the First World War. This war, in which millions died for the territorial ambitions of the European powers, although under the illusion of fighting for peace and democracy, was the beginning of that development which tended in a relatively short time to destroy a two-thousand-year-old Western tradition of hope and to transform it into a mood of despair. The moral callousness of the First World War was only the beginning. Other events followed: the betrayal of the socialist hopes by Stalin's reactionary state capitalism; the severe economic crisis at the end of the twenties; the victory of barbarism in one of the oldest centers of culture in the world—Germany; the insanity of Stalinist terror during the thirties; the Second World War, in which all the fighting nations lost some of the moral considerations which had still existed in the First World War; the unlimited destruction of civilian populations, started by Hitler and continued by the even more complete destruction of cities such as Hamburg and Dresden and Tokyo, and eventually by the use of atomic bombs against Japan. Since then the human race has been confronted with an even greater danger—that of the destruction of our civilization, if not of all mankind, by thermonuclear weapons as they exist today and as they are being developed in increasingly frightful proportions. . . . It is precisely the significance of Orwell's book that it expresses the new mood of hopelessness which pervades our age before this mood has become manifest and taken hold of the consciousness of people.

NEGATIVE UTOPIAS

Orwell is not alone in this endeavor. Two other writers, the Russian Zamyatin in his book *We*, and Aldous Huxley in his *Brave New World*, have expressed the mood of the present, and a warning for the future, in ways very similar to Orwell's. This new trilogy of what may be called the "negative utopias" of the middle of the twentieth century is the counterpoint to the trilogy of the positive utopias mentioned before, written in the sixteenth and seventeenth centuries. The negative utopias express the mood of powerlessness and hopelessness of modern man just as the early utopias expressed the mood of self-confidence and hope of post-medieval man. There could be nothing more paradoxical in historical terms than this change: man, at the beginning of the industrial age, when in reality he did *not* possess the means for a world in which the table was set for all who wanted to eat, when he lived in a world in which there were economic reasons for slavery, war and exploitation, in which man only sensed the possibilities of his new science and of its application to technique and to production—nevertheless man at the *beginning* of modern development was full of hope. Four hundred years later, when all these hopes are realizable, when man *can* produce enough for everybody, when war has become unnecessary because technical progress can give any country more wealth than can territorial conquest, when this globe is in the process of becoming as unified as a continent was four hundred years ago, at the very moment when man is on the verge of realizing his hope, he begins to lose it. It is the essential point of all the three negative utopias not only to describe the future toward which we are moving, but also to explain the historical paradox.

The three negative utopias differ from each other in detail and emphasis. Zamyatin's *We*, written in the twenties, has more features in common with *1984* than with Huxley's *Brave New World*. *We* and *1984* both depict the completely bureaucratized society, in which man is a number and loses all sense of individuality. This is brought about by a mixture of unlimited terror (in Zamyatin's book a brain operation is added eventually which changes man even physically) combined with ideological and psychological manipulation. In Huxley's work the main tool for turning man into an automaton is the application of hypnoid mass suggestion, which allows dispensing with terror. One can say that Zamyatin's and Orwell's examples resemble more the Stalinist and Nazi dictatorships, while Huxley's *Brave New World* is a picture of the development of the Western industrial world, provided it continues to follow the present trend without fundamental change.

In spite of this difference there is one basic question common to the three negative utopias. The question is a philosophical, anthropological and psychological one, and perhaps also a religious one. It is: can human nature be changed in such a way that man will forget his longing for freedom, for dignity, for integrity, for love—that is to say, can man forget that he is human? Or does human nature have a dynamism which will react to the violation of these basic human needs by attempting to change an inhuman society into a human one? It must be noted that the three authors do not take the simple position of psychological relativism which is common to so many social scientists today; they do not start out with the assumption that there is no such thing as human nature; that there is no such thing as qualities essential to man; and that man is born as nothing but a blank sheet of paper on which any given society writes its text. They do assume that man has an intense striving for love, for justice, for truth, for solidarity, and in this respect they are quite different from the relativists. In fact, they affirm the strength and intensity of these human strivings by the description of the very means they present as being necessary to destroy them. In Zamyatin's *We* a brain operation similar to lobotomy is necessary to get rid of the human demands of human nature. In Huxley's *Brave New World* artificial biological selection and drugs are necessary, and in Orwell's *1984* it is the completely unlimited use of torture and brainwashing. None of the three authors can be accused of the thought that the destruction of the humanity within man is easy. Yet all three arrive at the same conclusion: that it is possible, with means and techniques which are common knowledge today.

ORWELL COMMENTS ON WAR AND NUCLEAR ARMS

In spite of many similarities to Zamyatin's book, Orwell's *1984* makes its own original contribution to the question, How can human nature be changed? I want to speak now about some of the more specifically "Orwellian" concepts.

The contribution of Orwell which is most immediately relevant . . . is the connection he makes between the dictatorial society of *1984* and atomic war. Atomic wars had first appeared as early as the forties; a large-scale atomic war broke out about ten years later, and some hundreds of bombs were dropped on industrial centers in European Russia, Western Europe, and North America. After this war, the governments of all countries became convinced that the continuation of the war would mean the end of organized society, and hence of their own power. For these reasons no more bombs were dropped, and the three existing big power blocs "merely continued to produce atomic bombs and stored them up against the decisive opportunity which they all believe will come sooner or later." It remains the aim of the ruling party to discover how "to kill several hundred million people in a few seconds without giving warning beforehand." Orwell wrote *1984* before the discovery of thermonuclear weapons, and it is only a historical footnote to say that in the fifties the very aim which was just mentioned had already been reached. The atomic bomb which was dropped on the Japanese cities seems small and ineffective when compared with the mass slaughter which can be achieved by thermonuclear weapons with the capacity to wipe out 90 per cent or 100 per cent of a country's population within minutes.

The importance of Orwell's concept of war lies in a number of very keen observations.

First of all, he shows the economic significance of continuous arms production, without which the economic system cannot function. Furthermore, he gives an impressive picture of how a society must develop which is constantly preparing for war, constantly afraid of being attacked, and preparing to find the means of complete annihilation of its opponents. Orwell's picture is so pertinent because it offers a telling argument against the popular idea that we can save freedom and democracy by continuing the arms race and finding a "stable" deterrent. This soothing picture ignores the fact that with increasing technical "progress" . . . the whole society will be forced to live underground, but that the destructive strength of thermonuclear bombs will always remain greater than the depth of the caves, that the military will become dominant (in fact, if not in law), that fright and hatred of a possible aggressor will destroy the basic attitudes of a democratic, humanistic society. In other words, the continued arms race, even if it would not lead to the outbreak of a thermonuclear war, would lead to the destruction of any of those qualities of our society which can be called "democratic," "free," or "in the American tradition." Orwell demonstrates the illusion of the assumption that democracy can continue to exist in a world preparing for nuclear war, and he does so imaginatively and brilliantly.

DOUBLETHINK AND THE NATURE OF TRUTH

Another important aspect is Orwell's description of the nature of truth, which on the surface is a picture of Stalin's treatment of truth, especially in the thirties. But anyone who sees in Orwell's description only another denunciation of Stalinism is missing an essential element of Orwell's analysis. He is actually talking about a development which is taking place in the Western industrial countries also. . . . The basic question which Orwell raises is whether there is any such thing as "truth." "Reality," so the ruling party holds, "is not external. Reality exists in the human mind and nowhere else . . . whatever the Party holds to be truth *is* truth." If this is so, then by controlling men's minds the Party controls truth. In a dramatic conversation between the protagonist of the Party and the beaten rebel, a conversation which is a worthy analogy to Dostoyevsky's conversation between the Inquisitor and Jesus, the basic principles of the Party are explained. In contrast to the Inquisitor, however, the leaders of the Party do not even pretend that their system is intended to make man happier, because men, being frail and cowardly creatures, want to escape freedom and are unable to face the truth. The leaders are aware of the fact that they themselves have only one aim, and that is power. To them "power is not a means; it is an end. And power means the capacity to inflict unlimited pain and suffering to another human being." Power, then, for them creates reality, it creates truth. The position which Orwell attributes here to the power elite can be said to be an extreme form of philosophical idealism, but it is more to the point to recognize that the concept of truth and reality which exists in *1984* is an extreme form of pragmatism in which truth becomes subordinated to the Party. An American writer, Alan Harrington, who in *Life in the Crystal Palace* gives a subtle and penetrating picture of life in a big American corporation, has coined an excellent expression for the contemporary concept of truth: "mobile truth." If I work for a big corporation which claims that its product is better than that of all competitors, the question whether this claim is justified or not in terms of ascertainable reality becomes irrelevant. What matters is that as long as I serve this particular corporation, this claim becomes "my" truth, and I decline to examine whether it is an objectively valid truth. In fact, if I change my job and move over to the corporation which was until now "my" competitor, I shall accept the new truth, that its product is the best, and subjectively speaking, this new truth will be as true as the old one. It is one of the most characteristic and destructive developments of our own society that man, becoming more and more of an instrument, transforms reality more and more into something relative to his own interests and functions. Truth is proven by the consensus of millions; to the slogan "how can millions be wrong" is added "and how can a minority of one be right." Orwell shows quite clearly that in a system in which the concept of truth as an objective judgment concerning reality is abolished, anyone who is a minority of one must be convinced that he is insane.

In describing the kind of thinking which is dominant in *1984,* Orwell has coined a word which has already become part of the modern vocabulary: "doublethink." "Doublethink means the power of holding two contradictory beliefs in one's mind simultaneously, and accepting both of them. . . . This process has to be conscious, or it would not be carried out with sufficient precision. But it also has to be unconscious, or it would bring with it a feeling of falsity and hence of guilt." . . .

Another important point in Orwell's discussion is closely related to "doublethink," namely that in a successful manipulation of the mind the person is no longer saying the opposite of what he thinks, but he thinks the opposite of what is true. Thus, for instance, if he has surrendered his independence and his integrity completely, if he experiences himself as a thing which belongs either to the state, the party or the corporation, then two plus two are five, or "Slavery is Freedom," and he feels free because there is no longer any awareness of the discrepancy between truth and falsehood. Specifically this applies to ideologies. Just as the Inquisitors who tortured their prisoners believed that they acted in the name of Christian love, the Party "rejects and vilifies every principle for which the socialist movement originally stood, and it chooses to do this in the name of socialism." Its content is reversed into its opposite, and yet people believe that the ideology means what it says. In this respect Orwell quite obviously refers to the falsification of socialism by Russian communism, but it must be added that the West is also guilty of a similar falsification. We present our society as being one of free initiative, individualism and idealism, when in reality these are mostly words. We are a centralized managerial industrial society, of an essentially bureaucratic nature, and motivated by a materialism which is only slightly mitigated by truly spiritual or religious concerns. Related to this is another example of "doublethink," namely that few writers, discussing atomic strategy, stumble over the fact that killing, from a Christian standpoint, is as evil or more evil than being killed. The reader will find many other features of our present Western society in Orwell's description in *1984*, provided he can overcome enough of his own "doublethink."

ORWELL'S DARK VISION

Certainly Orwell's picture is exceedingly depressing, especially if one recognizes that as Orwell himself points out, it is not only a picture of an enemy but of the whole human race at the end of the twentieth century. One can react to this picture in two ways: either by becoming more hopeless and resigned, or by feeling there is still time, and by responding with greater clarity and greater courage. All three negative utopias make it appear that it is possible to dehumanize man completely, and yet for life to go on. One might doubt the correctness of this assumption, and think that while it might be possible to destroy the human core of man, one would also in doing this destroy the future of mankind. Such men would be so truly inhuman and lacking in vitality that they would destroy each other, or die out of sheer boredom and anxiety. If the world of *1984* is going to be the dominant form of life on this globe, it will mean a world of madmen, and hence not a viable world (Orwell indicates this very subtly by pointing to the mad gleam in the Party leader's eyes). I am sure that neither Orwell nor Huxley or Zamyatin wanted to insist that this world of insanity is bound to come. On the contrary, it was quite obviously their intention to sound a warning by showing where we are headed for unless we succeed in a renaissance of the spirit of humanism and dignity which is at the very roots of Occidental culture. Orwell, as well as the two other authors, is simply implying that the new form of managerial industrialism, in which man builds machines which act like men and develops men who act like machines, is conducive to an era of dehumanization and complete alienation, in which men are transformed into things and become appendices to the process of production and consumption. All three authors imply that this danger exists not only in communism of the Russian or Chinese versions, but that it is a danger inherent in the modern mode of production and organization, and relatively independent of the various ideologies. Orwell, like the authors of the other negative utopias, is not a prophet of disaster. He wants to warn and to awaken us. He still hopes—but in contrast to the writers of the utopias in the earlier phases of Western society, his hope is a desperate one. The hope can be realized only by recognizing, so *1984* teaches us, the danger with which all men are confronted today, the danger of a society of automatons who will have lost every trace of individuality, of love, of critical thought, and yet who will not be aware of it because of "doublethink." Books like Orwell's are powerful warnings, and it would be most unfortunate if the reader smugly interpreted *1984* as another description of Stalinist barbarism, and if he does not see that it means us, too.

The Paradoxes
of Time Travel

Paul A. Carter

Paul A. Carter, who has taught as professor of history at the University of Arizona, discusses the time machine as a science fiction device through which writers explore traditional philosophical issues of the individual's relationship to destiny. He credits H. G. Wells with introducing the mechanism into the genre. Carter explains that time travel stories often oppose free will with determinism, and many characters struggle against their own destiny. Time travel raises unresolved and entertaining paradoxes in its attempt to determine the mutability of the future, or the past.

It was not until 1895, with the appearance of *The Time Machine*, by H. G. Wells, that the idea [of time travel] really caught fire.

This was Wells's first book (other than a hack biology textbook written simply to put bread on the table), and it brought the young, struggling writer his first real fame. It was a book for its times; what, it asked, would become of the stagnant, class-divided society of late Victorian England if allowed to evolve along existing lines into the indefinite future? But the story far transcended its topicality. *The Time Machine*, like Mary Shelley's *Frankenstein*, is one of the great parables of Western industrial man. Those who have seen only George Pal's film version, with its made-in-Hollywood happy ending, have entirely missed what Wells was driving at in this poem of cosmic doom. It is the final emphatic denial of Darwinian evolutionary optimism; its real hero is not so much the Time Traveller as the Second Law of Thermodynamics. It is also a formal rebuttal to the Christian epic, as the world ends not with choirs of angels and a new

Excerpted from *The Creation of Tomorrow: Fifty Years of Magazine Science Fiction*, by Paul A. Carter (New York: Columbia University Press, 1977). Copyright © 1977 by Paul A. Carter. Reprinted by permission of the publisher via the Copyright Clearance Center.

Jerusalem descending but with scuttling crabs on a tideless beach and the quiet falling of the snow.

WELLS'S INFLUENCE

Since *The Time Machine* there have been hundreds, perhaps thousands, of stories written on its central theme. A writer for the science fiction pulps could confidently assume his readers' familiarity with Wells's classic; not only with its specific time-traveling gadget, which was imitated many times over, but—more important—with its mood and point of view. Wells's *fin-de-siècle* pessimism surely influenced John Campbell's "Twilight," for example. It also touched Howard Phillips Lovecraft, who seized upon the radical shock of mental displacement that travel to far-off time might entail; a terror at least as keen as the kind evoked by the yawning graveyards, sag-roofed farmhouses, and musty genealogy, which were that writer's usual stock in trade. In his "Commonplace Book" of notes for stories to be written, Lovecraft jotted down one truly hair-raising idea: "In an ancient buried city a man finds a mouldering prehistoric document *in English in his own handwriting.*" That sentence grew into one of Lovecraft's longest and most effective tales, "The Shadow Out of Time," published in *Astounding Stories* (17, June 1936).

If the event in that story really happened, says its narrator, "then man must be prepared to accept notice of the cosmos, and of his own place in the seething vortex of time, whose merest mention is paralyzing." Wrenched back into time by an ancient prehuman civilization that practices time travel as a novel method for doing scholarly research, Lovecraft's hero finds himself among other, similarly kidnapped time travelers from all eons, past and future. . . .

"To Lovecraft," anthologist Donald Wollheim perceptively wrote (in *The Portable Novels of Science*, 1945), "the millions of years gone by and the millions of years to come are sources of dread, because of his knowledge of the cold cruelty of nature." Mingled with the dread, however, is that other powerful impulse so often expressed in science fiction: the Faustian urge to know all. As Lovecraft's character converses with all these highly knowledgeable people and Things, his sense of estrangement and horror mutates insensibly into fascination.

THE INDIVIDUAL STRUGGLE AGAINST DESTINY

"Shocking secrets and dizzying marvels" were a common-place in the science fiction of the mid-1930s, when Love-craft's exercise in cosmic terror appeared in *Astounding*. But the focus of science fiction by that time was changing. The question "What's it like out there?" was being rephrased as "What difference does it make to me here?" Ralph Milne Farley, in "The Time-Wise Guy" (*Amazing Stories:* 14, May 1940), sent a time traveler 200 million years into the future, to a landscape straight out of Wells: "The time-machine stood on a rocky spit of land, jutting out into a listless sea. . . . A hollow soundlessness hung over the world. . . . Dark, indistinct clouds gathered, ruddy on one side like the smoke of a train when the fireman opens the door to shovel in coal." But the traveler, a callow Joe College type named George Worthey, couldn't care less. Lacking even a tourist's curiosity, he does not wish so much as "to set foot on this barren land of things to be."

The time machine's inventor, Professor Tyrrell—"Old Tillie" to his students—has warned George not to return from the future at the exact moment when he left. But our hero had had plans for the evening of his departure day, plans interrupted by his impromptu journey to the end of time. If he obeys the professor's warning, George is going to miss out on a fraternity dance! Therefore, disregarding "Old Tillie's" advice, he returns to the present at the very second of his departure.

At that point the story breaks off. What happened next? The editors of *Amazing Stories* offered readers a cash prize for the best answer. So conventional had time travel become in science fiction that several contestants came up with the same conclusion as the author's own: George, coming back to the laboratory at the instant he left it, finds himself once again going *forward* in time. He is caught in an eternally re-curring loop, and he will travel to and from that rocky spit of land at the end of time, forever and ever, world without end. The cosmic vision of *The Time Machine* has become comic anticlimax; the universe after all has outsmarted the wise guy. In pulp stories like this one, the vast historical and as-tronomical panorama of Wells and Lovecraft has receded into the wings. Time travel has become localized as an indi-vidual struggle against destiny.

CHEATING FATE

"If it were possible to discover the hour of death, could that death be deliberately circumvented?" Two short stories asking that ultimate question appeared in the pulps in the late summer of 1939, "Life-Line" by Robert A. Heinlein (*Astounding:* 23, August), and "The Fate Changer," by Richard O. Lewis, which carried the story blurb just quoted (*Amazing Stories:* 13, September). Of this pair, Heinlein's is the better known; it was his first published story, and its tone of quiet rationality sharply contrasted with the furnace-draft pulp style generally prevailing in 1939. Socially aware as in all his early work, Heinlein assumed that an invention which could accurately predict an individual's lifespan would be opposed (logically enough) by the insurance companies, which would have a vested interest in their customers' not learning that kind of intimate specific information. The profit motive figures in Lewis's tale also, but it is embodied in a much more crass form.

"The Fate Changer" begins: "Samuel J. Curbul, broker, let the smoke from his expensive cigar roll upward from his thick lips to drift lazily about his heavy features and to veil his close-set, piggish eyes." Samuel J. Curbul, broker, was of a type not at all unusual in magazine science fiction in that post-Crash, anti-business era. Walter Hirsch, in an essay called "The Image of the Scientist in Science-Fiction" (*American Journal of Sociology:* 63, March 1958) based on random sampling of the science fiction pulps published between 1926 and 1950, found that capitalists by and large figured in the stories as disreputable characters: "Scientists comprised the major category of both heroes and villains, but businessmen were, proportionately, more villainous than scientists." But the scientist in "The Fate Changer," given the allegorically apt name of Factsworth, appears neither as hero nor as villain, but as victim. A fast-talking operator named Jamison, armed with a power of attorney, has mortgaged Factsworth's laboratory to buy worthless stocks from broker Curbul. Pressed for margin when the securities collapse, the speculator finds no sympathy in the dealer: "I can't foretell the future of stocks," Curbul curtly informs him. Desperate for cash, Jamison reveals the secret that Factsworth knows how to foretell the future. The broker pays him off, goes to see the scientist, and asks Factsworth what he, Curbul, will be doing for the rest of the present week.

"Knowing your world line will in no way aid you as a businessman," Factsworth warns him, "for you cannot step aside from it or change it in any possible way."

Samuel J. Curbul's answer is in the best tradition of free American enterprise: "I'll take my own chances on changing my world-line. I have a strong will." . . .

We have seen here a fresh variation on one of the most compelling myths of Western man, the myth of the Bad Bargain: Faust sells his soul to the devil in exchange for various good things of this world, but the devil cheats. In this case, Faust cheated himself. From either a Marxist or a Calvinist point of view it is a fitting destiny. Jonathan Edwards himself might have relished such a retribution, in which a man's damnation is totally predestined and yet at the same time morally appropriate. Of course, a typical American executive's hypertension might have done Curbul in anyway. The story ends: "The awful pounding ceased abruptly. The newspaper slipped to the floor from nerveless fingers."

If space-time *is* a continuum, then we have no real control over our future, for what will be is all of one piece with what was. "Choice," explains Norman Spinrad in "Weed of Time" (*Vertex:* 1, August 1973), "is an illusion caused by the fact that future time-loci are hidden from those who advance sequentially along the time-stream one moment after another in blissful ignorance." The age-old philosophical question of determinism versus free will is thus resolved emphatically in favor of determinism. Nor does physical travel in time, as distinguished from mere scanning and prediction, necessarily mean escape from this predetermined fate. Traveling back and forth along the time-dimension, in "The Time Cheaters" by Eando Binder (*Thrilling Wonder Stories:* 15, March 1940), the time travelers learn that the impact of their visits has already been allowed for. If they try to change the course of events, for example by stopping the time machine in a different year from the one the records indicate, they will only confirm destiny's decree; the time machine's calibration will have been just sufficiently inaccurate that, willy-nilly, they will land in the correct year anyway. At the end of this story by Binder, the hero accepts the situation philosophically: "Time," he admitted, "is immutable."

In the course of their journey, Binder's time travelers from the year 1940 have learned of the collapse of Japan's occupation of China in 1942 and of a stalemate along the

Maginot and Siegfried lines in 1944, followed, on May 16, 1945, by the ultimate in escalation: an invasion from Mars. War shadowed many of the time-travel stories published in the early 1940s, as it touched so much other science fiction. "Forever Is Not So Long," by F. Anton Reeds, for example (*Astounding:* 29, May 1942), begins at a summer garden party in England in 1931, when "the lights of Europe still burned." Young couples are dancing, while along the sidelines sit the gray-tinged members of England's "lost generation," spiritual casualties of a previous war. While the party goes on, the hero leaves his fiancée for a brief visit to her father's laboratory a short distance away. There he becomes the subject of the first experiment in time.

Going forward ten years, to 1941, he finds that the manor house behind which he had lately danced has been bombed to rubble. Captured by a Home Guardsman as an intruder, he is told: "You look remarkably like a chap I soldiered with in Flanders. Died the last night of Dunkirk . . . a brilliant fellow. Scientist of promise, I believe, before the war." That soldier's widow survives, but is said to have been crippled in an air raid not long before.

Armed with this kind of knowledge, what does one do? Accept one's destiny, the author answered. The time traveler escapes from custody, goes back to 1931, returns to the dance, and tells his betrothed that from now on he will have time only for her. Quite unknowing of the future, she replies that they will be "the happiest people in the world . . . forever." The story closes on a bittersweet echo from the Jazz Age: "Two trumpets were taking a hot chorus, unmuted, their notes high and sharp and quivering. 'Forever,' he said."

FREE WILL VS. DETERMINISM

"A common opinion prevails that the juice has ages ago been pressed out of the free-will controversy, and that no new champion can do more than warm up stale arguments which every one has heard." So said William James, as he lectured the divinity students at Harvard in 1884 on "The Dilemma of Determinism," ten years before H. G. Wells wrote *The Time Machine.* "This is a radical mistake. I know of no subject less worn out, or in which inventive genius has a better chance of breaking open new ground." Purists may balk at attributing inventive genius to writers for the pulp magazines of the 1940s; however, their contribution to the free-will controversy by way of time-travel stories certainly broke open new ground.

We live in "a world in which we constantly have to make . . . judgments of regret," James argued. The dilemma is that if whatever will be will be, such judgments are irrational— yet, humanly, we cannot help making them. "Determinism, in denying that anything else can be in its stead, virtually defines the universe as a place in which what ought to be is impossible," James concluded. In an historical period more given to ethical and cultural relativism than the era of William James, the question was bound to arise: ought to be, from whose point of view? My own, or society's? The present generation's, or that of the yet unborn?

Alfred Bester, one of the brilliant cluster of science fictionists who began to write in 1939, explored these and other questions in a story that deserves to be better known, "The Push of a Finger" (*Astounding:* 29, May 1942). Its hero is no formal philosopher; he is that stock pulp adventure figure, the cynical/sentimental newspaperman. His beat is the Prog—short for Prognostication—Building, in which a bureaucratic government dedicated to Stability predicts the future by computer. "Prophecy is far from being a mystical function," Chief Stabilizer Groating explains. "It is a very logical science," just a matter of integrating enough accurate data. Its syntheses do not add up to absolute determinism, however; the Stabilizers, having read their daily printouts, may refrain from following the predicted course of action if they consider it detrimental. . . .

The only flaw in this carefully stablized utopia is that the massed computers—eight floors of them—in the Prog Building have just predicted the end of the universe. That event is yet a thousand years away, but from a Chief Stabilizer's viewpoint a thousand years (to paraphrase the Psalmist) are but as a watch in the night. Furthermore this particular downfall is man-made, and can therefore—perhaps—be man-prevented. The Prognosticator's viewing screen shows a jerry-built spaceship swarming with outlaw technicians and workmen, about to perform in secret a most illegal experiment. Their intention is to release unlimited energy for the betterment of man. What they accomplish instead is Doomsday. The star their spaceship is circling simply blots out; then the spaceship; then more stars, and more stars, and more stars. . . .

What can the Stabilizers do about it? Unfortunately, their equipment has not the power to isolate out the causal factor from the mass of raw data. Instead, at the reporter's suggestion, they work backward in time from the catastrophe three hundred years closer to their own time, to the debates that result in the outlawing of that particular kind of hazardous scientific research. Briefly, the hero glimpses a lovely young woman of that remote future; a glimpse, as it turns out, that is to seal his destiny.

The scanners now for the first time learn of a mysterious equation, $i = (b/a) \pi\, i\, e/\mu$, and of its brilliant, controversial author, a scientist named FitzJohn. More backtracking, and the monitor picks up FitzJohn himself, delivering a lecture on his "Tension Energy Dynamics Equations" to a raucous, hostile audience in a great amphitheater at the north end of Central Park (not built yet, Chief Stabilizer Groating remarks; they have plans to erect it about three decades hence). Egged on by other professors hostile to FitzJohn's theories, a host of undergraduates cavort in hilarious carnival, chanting anti-FitzJohn slogans and parodying his equations.

The story's point of view has insensibly shifted. FitzJohn in this scene is not the dangerous crackpot who must be stopped before he wrecks the universe; he is a heroic figure, who stands his ground against the mob and converts their jeers into applause. Silence ensues, and he begins his lecture as if nothing has happened. "No scientist is a lone adventurer, striking out into new fields by himself," FitzJohn modestly points out. "The way is always led by those who precede us, and we who seem to discover all, actually do no more than add our bit to an accumulated knowledge." Even the equation basic to his theory is not his own; fifty years prior to this day, some ten years before his own birth, "in Central Park, on the very site of this amphitheater, my father, suddenly struck with an idea, mentioned an equation to my mother." That equation was none other than the fatal $i = (b/a) \pi\, i\, e/\mu$—and fifty years prior to the day of FitzJohn's lecture brings the prognosticators to *this* evening, of the day the action in the story takes place!

It is winter, and they have only about two hours till dark. No time to computer-scan all the possible ancestors of FitzJohn, who in any case may have blotted out his past and changed his name. A cordon of police swarms around Central Park, to intercept any strolling couple who might unknowingly fall into the fateful conversation. Then down into the park whirrs a copter-load of newspaper reporters. One of them, a rookie just hired by her paper, is a girl . . . and she reminds the hero irresistibly of the woman he has glimpsed six hundred years into the future. In surprise, and in comic anticlimax, he exclaims, "I'll be a pie-eyed emu!"—which, suitably garbled into family folklore and inaccurately remembered by a loving son, might well become identified some day with the disastrous $i = (b/a) \pi\, i\, e/\mu$.

The circle is complete; the Prognosticators' frantic security precautions have brought on the very encounter they sought to forestall. Boy has met Girl, and the first step has been taken that will probably lead, at the next millennium's end, to the blotting out of the stars. . . .

Here is a philosophic and moral paradox that might baffle both Jonathan Edwards and William James—or Kant, whose "categorical imperative" (the doctrine that one ought always to act as if one's own conduct were to become universal law) does not even begin to fill this bill. Throughout the story there has been an implication that the persistence, courage, and imagination—however wrong-headed—of FitzJohn and his adherents have the moral edge over the paternalism, self-righteousness, and stagnation—however prudent and logical—of the Prognosticators. Ultimately, on this time-track, the existence of the whole world seems to depend on suppressing the liberty of one lone individual. From that individual's own point of view, to assert that there is human free will and that the future really can be changed is to renounce freedom of choice for oneself personally; conversely, to deny free will, and do what one must although the heavens fall, is existentially to affirm it. . . .

UNRESOLVED PARADOXES

Some writers left their paradoxes tantalizingly unresolved. There is, for example, P. Schuyler Miller's haunting tale, "As Never Was" (*Astounding:* 32, January 1944). A knife, made of a translucent blue metal unknown to this world, is found somewhere in the future by a time-traveling archeologist (appropriately, his name is Walter Toynbee). Defying all attempts at physical or chemical analysis, the artifact is housed in a glass case in a museum named after the time traveler. Centuries pass. Bombs fall. The building crumbles in ruins. Then at last comes the time traveler, to shovel away the debris and bring the knife back to his own time, where it will be studied and analyzed and housed in a glass case in a museum. . . . But where, or when, did it come from in the first place? "I wish I knew," the narrator cries; "I might find logic and purpose in the future instead of chaos."

Latent in that outcry may be existential revulsion against traveling in time at all. The narrator hints that in trying to solve the paradox of the knife, and utterly failing, the rational intellect of the civilization of his own era has begun to crack. Should a time machine ever actually be invented, people morally committed against venturing outside one's proper place in the continuum might vehemently oppose time travel, much in the spirit of the Apollo space program's detractors. "Tired men live in the past, ambitious men live in the future," says the protagonist of a 1970s story by Gordon Eklund, "The Stuff of Time" (*Fantastic:* 22, September 1973). "But who lives in the present? Perhaps healthy men live in the present; it's hard to say. But somebody must."

There remains moreover that elusive will-o'-the-wisp known as human freedom, which is not to be captured merely by spinning endlessly in dizzy circles of paradox. Heinlein's single/multiple hero in "By His Bootstraps" thinks he has solved that problem; "freedom" and "determinism" he neatly separates into "subjective" and "objective" categories. "Free will . . . could not be laughed off, because it could be directly experienced," he muses, "yet his own free will had worked to create the same scene over and over again. Apparently human will must be considered as one of the factors which make up the processes in the continuum— 'free' to the ego, mechanistic from the outside." But that really won't do; it still, basically, defines freedom as an illusion.

"By His Bootstraps" has most commonly been taken as comedy. That thrice-repeated conversation between the hero's first version who wants only to finish his thesis and get his degree, a second who tells him to enter the future, and a third who urges him not to, all climaxing in a three-cornered drunken fistfight that knocks Number One through the time gate and off on the first of his gyrating travels, still stands up after repeated readings as a wondrously comic invention. It might even work on television. But Alexei and Cory Panshin, in the important article "SF in Dimension: The Search for Renewal" (*Fantastic:* 22, July 1973), draw a far more bleak moral to this Heinlein story. "His character is caught in a maze of time in which he meets himself again and again, acting out what he has already seen himself act out, helpless to alter his behavior, vainly repeating himself, trapped in his own futility." Psychologically, the Panshins see this as a classic crisis of American middle age! Furthermore, it is the character's own fault: "his older self is responsible for setting the time trap for his younger self. He is the agent of his own futility." At one point in his odyssey he has the opportunity to break out of the cycle, but at a psychic cost he cannot bear to pay. "So he must turn from transcendence and run—and remain trapped in his own character, to run round and round and round the maze, without hope."

DIVERGING ROADS, ALTERNATE FUTURES

Two roads diverged in a yellow wood, said Robert Frost, and he took the one less traveled by. The twentieth-century scientific universe of Einstein and space-time is also the universe of Heisenberg and statistical indeterminacy. Perhaps, in the chinks and crevices of such a cosmos, there remains some room for acts of free human choice. "We assume that if we travel to futureward there is but one possible destination," a professor lectures in Murray Leinster's "Sidewise in Time," a story that pioneered the philosophic idea of alternate, ontologically real, parallel futures (*Astounding Stories:* 13, June 1934). "There is more than one future we can encounter, and with more or less absence of deliberation we choose among them. But the futures we fail to encounter, upon the roads we do not take, are just as real."

From this perspective, not only did two real roads diverge in the wood, but also there are two real Robert Frosts, each trudging thoughtfully along one of them. Leinster also assumed that the traveler could bushwhack through the forest from one road over to the other. Indeed, in "Sidewise in Time"—published at the height of *Astounding* editor Orlin Tremaine's vogue for "thought-variant" stories, in which marvel must be piled upon metaphysical marvel—entire societies migrate across the continuum into each other's territory. Rice fields, wide-hatted peasants, and Chinese junks suddenly appear along the Potomac, deriving from an alternative past in which the Orient colonized America; San

Francisco, displaced by a city from a time-track in which the Spaniards did not get there first, finds itself ruled by the Tsar of All the Russias. This plurality of continua was a stimulating idea, and it has generated an entire inventive subspecies of science fiction.

What if————? . . .

THE TIME SOLDIER

The restoration of free will to the time-travel equation makes possible more activist personal vocations than the seminar and library life of the Visiting Time Fellows (as H. P. Lovecraft might have called them) in "The Shadow Out of Time." Moments of choice in the past or present may become so important that soldiers from alternate potential futures are willing to go back to that point in time and fight each other to change the outcome—the stakes being not mere survival, but the possibility of ever *having* existed. Such is the theme of Jack Williamson's three-part serial, "The Legion of Time" (*Astounding:* 21, May, June, July 1938). Fighting men are plucked from the disasters of war— the Western Front, the naval battle of Jutland in 1916, the defense of Paris in 1940 (which, at the moment of writing, had not yet happened)—and recruited into the most foreign of all imagined legions. Traveling by time machine to the point where alternate world-lines diverge from a moment of choice, they must do battle in order that a good (democratic and Utopian) future may prevail over an evil (despotic and reactionary) one.

The wartorn 1930s and 1940s ideologically nurtured this kind of science fiction, much as they influenced the course of space opera. The hero of Williamson's epic has fought against Franco in the Spanish Civil War, and he is flying for China against the Japanese invader when he is caught up into the Legion of Time. This was to remain a popular form of science fiction adventure in a time-track that remained wartorn, and ideology continued to shape it. The revolutionary and counterrevolutionary currents of the Eisenhower-Dulles years were insensibly allegorized in this time-soldier literature. Thus there were temporal radicals, as in Fritz Leiber's "The Big Time" (*Galaxy:* 15, March, April 1958), who strove to change the past for change's own sake, because in change is creativity and life; and there were temporal conservatives, as in Poul Anderson's "Time Patrol"

(*Fantasy and Science Fiction:* 8, May 1955) and its several sequels, who struggled to preserve the known past from time-machined tampering, on the ground that it is better to endure the devil we know than fly to others we know not of.

As our society became ever more police-conscious, it nurtured stories like "Hawksbill Station," by Robert Silverberg (*Galaxy:* 25, August 1967; book version 1968), in which a despotic future government shunts its political dissidents back into a geological era before life had crawled out upon the land, where they cannot possibly affect the future course of history. There, subsisting on brachiopod stew and trilobite hash, they may argue about ideology to their hearts' content—and, in their futility, one by one go mad. Since H. G. Wells first put forth the idea, time travel had thus devolved from high adventure to penal servitude!—a most ominous comment on what was actually happening along our own timeline.

Moreover, despite their philosophic commitment to freedom of the will, in working out the ground rules by which their legionnaires of time were to operate, these writers quite often hedged back in the direction of determinism. There is a Law of Conservation of Reality, one of Fritz Leiber's timefighters explains, in a story warningly titled "Try and Change the Past" (*Astounding:* 61, March 1958). "The four-dimensional space-time universe doesn't *like* to be changed, any more than it likes to lose or gain energy or matter. . . . Change the past and you start a wave of changes moving futurewards, but it damps out mighty fast." Eventually the old pattern tends to reestablish itself. People move as crowds to change destiny, not as individuals; a vast organized array of soldiers may, crudely and brutally, change history, but a man by himself remains in the fell clutch of circumstance. "No, I wouldn't advise anyone to try to change the past, at least not his *personal* past." In contrast, Poul Anderson's Time Patrolmen *do* have the power to change their personal pasts—but they pledge themselves never to use it. "The Patrol exists to guard what is real," one of its leaders explains ("Gibraltar Falls," *Fantasy and Science Fiction:* 49, October 1975). "If ever a mortal takes himself that power, where can the changing end? . . . None less than God can be trusted with time."

Understanding the Alien

Gregory Benford

Gregory Benford is the author of such science fiction
novels as *Great Sky River, Tides of Light,* and
Timescape, which won the Nebula Award for best
novel of 1980. In this selection Benford analyzes one
of the genre's most time-honored conventions—the
alien. According to Benford the alien should be totally unfamiliar by scientific definition; it cannot be
conceived of in human terms, but many writers have
mistreated the alien by depicting it according to familiar concepts. The alien as a science fiction device
may then represent the unknown, but more often it
reflects some aspect of the human condition. This
function as an analog for humanity lends philosophical implications to the portrayal of encounters with
the extraterrestrial.

J. G. Ballard has said that one of the problems of science fiction is that it is not a literature won from experience. There
are several ways of interpreting this assertion. It is nowhere
more obviously true, though, than in the case of science fiction that depicts aliens.

I shall discuss some of the philosophical and literary
problems of treating aliens. My discussion will probably not
resemble most literary criticism because I am not a critic,
but a science fiction writer and a physicist. And I do not pretend to objectivity or even to impartiality, since I have written some fiction about this subject and am therefore already
biased. I shall attempt a brief catalog of the ways aliens have
been depicted in science fiction and then move on to the
philosophical problems that interest me. I shall necessarily
give only slight attention to many rich areas.

Excerpted from "Aliens and Knowability: A Scientist's Perspective," by Gregory Benford,
in *Bridges to Science Fiction,* edited by George E. Slusser, George R. Guffey, and Mark
Rose. Copyright © 1980 by Southern Illinois University Press. Reprinted by permission
of Southern Illinois University Press.

ANTHROPOCENTRIC ALIENS

By far the most common kind of alien in science fiction is the unexamined one—supposedly strange, but represented by only a few aspects, all of which are merely exaggerations of human traits. The simplest version of this kind of alien is the invader, often depicted as an implacable, mindless threat (as in Robert Heinlein's *Puppet Masters* and *Starship Troopers*). In making easy political analogies, the film *The Thing* is fairly typical of a vast body of science fiction: the Thing stands for the Communist menace, the wooly-minded scientists who try to make contact with it despite its obvious hostility represent the Adlai Stevensons of this world, and the United States Air Force stands for, of course, the United States Air Force. A more interesting version of the anthropomorphic alien is typified by Hal Clement's Mesklinites in *Mission of Gravity*. They have unusual bodies, determined by their bizarre planetary surroundings. This "biology as destiny" theme occurs often in science fiction, but, like the Mesklinites, the aliens of such stories commonly speak like Midwesterners of the 1950s and are otherwise templates of stock humans. In Larry Niven's *Ringworld*, variants on this kind of alien are represented by beings roughly equivalent to types of terrestrial animals. Niven's kzinti is a catlike carnivore, given to mindless rages. His puppeteers are herd animals (that is, cowards); their cities stink, like a corral. In *People of the Wind*, Poul Anderson has done this sort of thing with more subtlety, giving his bird aliens touches of real strangeness.

In my view, the trouble with most realizations of this much-sought strangeness is that its effect so soon wears off. Larry Niven and Jerry Pournelle's *Mote in God's Eye* explores aliens who are not bilaterally symmetric (an odd variant, indeed) and extracts some value from the feel of threeness versus twoness. In the end, though, these aliens seem no more difficult to understand than the Chinese. (Indeed, there is an uncomfortable resemblance in the old Space Navy method of dealing with them.) They are stopped from spreading by a technicality involving faster-than-light travel; this insures that alien values and threenesses do not flood through the sevagram.

Even as respected a work as Olaf Stapledon's *Star Maker* does not truly focus on the alienness of the many creatures that inhabit its future worlds. Stapledon gives them biological variations that ultimately have no impact whatever on the gross socioeconomic forces at work in the environment around them. There are no alternate realities here, no genuinely different ways of looking at the universe, but instead (on the planetary level, at least) a clockwork Marxism that drives them inevitably into tired confrontations of labor with capital, and so on. It is the larger vision Stapledon pursued, his account of the ultimate grinding down of the galaxies, that still moves us today. The Marxism is the most dated aspect of his work.

A related function of aliens in science fiction is that of a mirror (or foil). The sexual strangeness of the Gethenians in Ursula Le Guin's *Left Hand of Darkness,* for example, is a distancing device, a way to examine our own problems in a different light. In countless lesser works aliens are really stand-in humans of the Zenna Henderson sort: quasi-human, with emotions and motivations not much different from our own. Aliens as mirrors for our own experiences abound in science fiction. Arthur C. Clarke's "Rescue Party" has humans as its true focus, though the action centers on aliens who are only a dumber version of ourselves. The final lines of the story give us a human-chauvinist thrill, telling us more about ourselves than we nowadays wish to know.

The Galactic Empire motif, with its equations of planet=colony and aliens=Indians (of either variety), is a common, unimaginative indulgence of science fiction. There are generally no true aliens in such epics, only a retreading of our own history. This underlying structure is so common in science fiction, even now, that it is difficult to know whether we should attribute it to simple lack of imagination or to a deep, unconscious need to return repeatedly to the problem. It would be interesting to see an Asian science fiction writer tackle the same theme. The list of aliens-as-foils is large. Authors have treated women as aliens, children as aliens, and robots as alienlike. In such tales we are really saying something about ourselves, not about the universe beyond us. An especially pointed use of this device was made by Brian Aldiss in *The Dark Light Years,* in which aliens use excrement as a sacrament. This stress on the holiness of returning to the soil so that the cycle of life may go on mirrors some Eastern ideas, though its main target may be Western scatology.

I end this catalog of more conventional uses of aliens by bringing up a puzzle I think worth pondering. It has long been clear (to any biologist who has thought about the question for more than five minutes) that any alien planetary ecology will be utterly different from ours. The old cliché—open the helmet, sniff the air: "Smells good! We can breathe it"—is usually avoided these days, but more subtle technical difficulties are not. Even if, for example, we found alien plants we could stomach, anything they contained resembling sugar could easily have the wrong sense of rotation from Earthly ones and thus would be unusable as food. Proteins, trace minerals—all would almost certainly be incompatible with our organic systems. To make a planet habitable by humans, we would have to erase what is there and introduce an entirely new, man-oriented ecology. Yet, in thousands of otherwise respectable science fiction stories, this point is ignored. Why? If questioned, most science fiction authors would, I imagine, admit the point and plead the convenience of assuming otherwise. Yet this sidestepping of the problem is not simply a bit of insiders' footwork, as is, say, faster-than-light travel. When a new theoretical fillip for getting such high velocities appears, the hard–science fiction writers instantly snatch it up and ring some changes on it; I have done so myself. But we never really touch the ecology problem. Seldom do we admit in fiction that it *is* a problem. I can think of only two recent works that address the issue: Joanna Russ' *We Who Are About To. . . .* and Lloyd Biggle's *Monument.* The almost universal avoidance of this striking astronomical-biological fact must have some motivation. Is it a telltale signal of some deep fear? Does it indicate that we do not care to smudge the image of a difficult but generally sympathetic galaxy out there? I do not know. But I do think the problem is worth the attention of the critics.

UNKNOWABLE ALIENS

For me, the most interesting aspect of the alien lies, not in its use as a fresh enemy, an analog human, or a mirror for ourselves, but rather in its essential strangeness. Remarkably few science fiction works have considered the alien at this most basic level. One which does is Arthur C. Clarke's *Rendezvous with Rama.* The vast space vehicle, Rama, yields up some of its secrets, but leaves our solar system with its essential nature shrouded. We see the mechanisms, but not

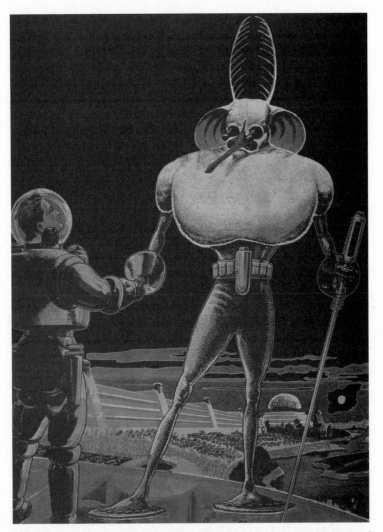

The most common interpretations of aliens contain exaggerations of human traits, as seen in the alien depicted above.

the mind behind them. Since Ringworld and Rama there has been a tendency to use giganticism as an easy signifier of alienness, as in John Varley's *Titan* trilogy, but I feel the method yields diminishing returns. Size alone is not all that significant. Let us remember that some of the most bizarre aspects of reality appear at the subatomic level.

The biggest entity of all, of course, is God. Aliens often have a strong theological role, as in the metaphors of ascension in Clarke's *Childhood's End* and *2001: A Space Odyssey.* Aliens do occasionally appear in science fiction as distant, inexplicable things, often ignored by the human characters. Making them objects of indifference does not exploit or illuminate the philosophical problems involved, though. These emerge when other beings attempt communication with them.

One of the basic devices of science fiction is the instant translator, which enables aliens to speak an Earthly language with little difficulty (in science fiction, English, often American English, at that). This device serves to speed up a story, but writers using it sidestep a knotty problem: how can beings be strange and still communicate with us easily? Some authors have been able to surmount this difficulty, but few have used the language problem itself as a major turning point. The essence of epistemology is language, for only by communicating our perceptions can we get them checked. The intuitive bedrock of perception must be given voice. Ian Watson's *Embedding* involves aliens who come to barter with us for our languages (not our sciences or arts), for languages are the keys to a deeper knowledge. By assembling all the galaxy's tongues, they believe they will transcend their species limitations and at last understand the real world. Thus the language of each species is capable of rendering a partial picture.

In another visit by aliens to the Earth (depicted in *If the Stars Are Gods* by Gordon Eklund and me), the aliens seek communion with our star, not with us. Their picture of reality involves stars as spiritual entities. The protagonist at first believes the aliens are lying, but is later drawn into their world view. He sees their vision and reaches some sort of understanding. But the paradoxes that run through the text turn about at the end, and he sees himself as trapped, by his own use of human categories, into a fundamental ignorance of the aliens. A Wittgenstein quotation, "A dog cannot be a hypocrite, but neither can he be sincere," underlines the limits of using human concepts. The emotional reaction to this view is also varied: the aliens are deliberately compared to pastel giraffes, and there are other comic touches. The layered paradoxes of the story line all suggest a possibility of "communion with the suns," but also the impossibility of knowing whether this sense, as filtered by human minds, is what the aliens mean. Reflections of this basic either-or, subject-other habitual mind-set occur throughout this work, always pointing toward an irreducible strangeness.

The most extreme view one can take is to reject the notion of any degree of possible knowledge of the alien, to declare all the aliens of science fiction inherently anthropomorphic or anthropocentric, and to state flatly that true aliens would be fundamentally unknowable. This position is perhaps best put forward in Stanislaw Lem's *Solaris*. In *New Worlds for Old* David Ketterer has explored the many images and phrases Lem uses to underline his position. The library scene adroitly satirizes science as model building, for example. In his afterword to the novel, Darko Suvin attributes Lem's renunciation of final truths to "the bitter experiences of Central European intellectuals in this century." If this were in fact the only reason to adopt such a position, *Solaris* would not be important, but of course the philosophical roots of these ideas go quite deep. . . .

My sense of *Solaris* is that it does not really talk about the physical sciences at all. There, the question of whether model building is hopelessly anthropocentric can only be settled by infinite recursion—keep trying to see whether the problem cracks, whether predictions do bear out. It is an unfortunate fact that much fiction takes the "truths" of science as absolute although they were never intended to be. Science is always provisional, yet the urge to adopt the position of *Solaris* rests, I believe, on an emotional bedrock of the sort Suvin cited, from Sartre on. I think a better understanding of *Solaris* might evolve from looking at it from the perspective of the social sciences. If in some sense the ocean were alive, then *Solaris* might, for example, be read as a reflection on the error of applying a mechanistic description to a social science, *not* to a physical one. In the social sciences, including psychology, there is a fundamental limitation: one cannot do completely reproducible experiments, even on very thin social groupings. Thus Lem's criticisms would appear to apply most directly to mechanistic social theories such as Marxism. One wonders whether the literary czars of Eastern Europe (or the Marxist critics of the West) really understand quite what Lem seems to be driving at.

BITTERSWEET IRONY

My own instincts as a theoretical physicist and a writer lie with the intuitionist school. I think that anyone who participates in science comes to realize that, by expanding our categories and using the most "universal" of descriptions (and languages—that is, mathematics), we can make of ourselves something greater. We can, in other words, ingest the alien. Yet we know from Gödel that the analytic sense of knowledge will forever escape us. It seems to me that this is fertile ground for bittersweet irony. Perhaps such philosophical pursuits can lead us finally to a deeper sense of what it does mean to be logical and fragile and human.

The Robot as Symbol

Sam Moskowitz

Sam Moskowitz (1920–1997) was a diligent and prolific scholar of science fiction, and an award was
founded in his name in 1998. In this selection he discusses the robot as a science fiction symbol. Providing a brief literary history of the "mechanical man,"
Moskowitz focuses on its development in American
science fiction. Pointing out the parallels and con-
trasts between robots and humans, Moskowitz explains that some writers imbued their robots with
feelings and intelligence, and it is through robots
that the motif of artificial intelligence was developed
in the genre. Perhaps the most significant contribution to the development of robots was made by Isaac
Asimov, whose Three Laws of Robotics not only influenced the whole genre, but also the real science
of robotics. Moskowitz suggests that the robot as a
symbol is linked to the public perception of science
fiction and the future.

It has been said, with considerable justice, that the age of robots is already here. Aircraft take off, fly, and land with no
pilots; great industrial plants, frequently many square miles
in area, function like great cities with no human workers in
sight; giant electronic computers do the work of a thousand
mathematicians in minutes and even play outstanding
games of chess against human champions. In a very real
sense, all these devices are robots, automatically doing the
work of human beings, but they are not what the man in the
street thinks of when he uses the term.

The man-like machine, preferably with two legs and two
arms, with photoelectric cells for eyes and an electronic
brain remains today and may always remain the symbol of
the robot to the general public. The public thinks of a robot
as a *mechanical man.* . . .

Excerpted from *The Coming of the Robots,* edited and with an introduction by Sam
Moskowitz (New York: Collier, 1963). Reprinted by permission of the Estate of Sam
Moskowitz.

There have been robots of one sort or another in fiction for well over 100 years, and references to mechanical men appear in records more than 2,000 years old, but the word itself, as an addition to the English language, is relatively new. It first appeared in the play *R. U. R.* by Karel Čapek, greatest of all Czechoslovakian playwrights, when that famed classic concerning the revolt of artificial men was premiered in Prague on January 26, 1921. The term was derived from the Czech word *robota,* meaning "to work."

If mechanical men are actually created in the future, their function will be to do the work formerly done by men. At first their appearance will be completely in the form of a machine, but as technology advances, a wedding of plastics and metal will result in robot devices so closely resembling humans that they will have to be marked to be distinguished.

THE LITERARY ROOTS OF THE ROBOT

The roots of man's conception of a robot go deep into literary history. It has been suggested that Publius Vergilius Maro, better known as Vergil, greatest poet of ancient Rome, constructed innumerable metal devices, including bronze archers to protect his premises. The variety of these stories linking Vergil with the building of robots is in itself a fascinating area of research.

These legends of Vergil, together with Ovid's masterful depiction of a statue come to life, are believed to have inspired the tales of the Golem, an artificial man constructed from clay by the Jews to serve them on the Sabbath and protect them from their enemies.

There are dozens of Golem legends, mostly from Eastern European sources, some of them as recent as the early nineteenth century. The most famous legends of the Golem, however, emanated from sixteenth-century Prague, where such an artificial man was said to have been the servant of the famed Rabbi Judah Loew.

The Golem is unquestionably the prototype for the monster of Mary Wollstonecraft Shelley's *Frankenstein,* a work whose importance to the literary history of the mechanical man lies in its plot innovation, the concept of an artificial man turning on his creator. *Frankenstein,* like many other early robot stories, may be considered antiscientific, insofar as it equates the advancement of knowledge with disaster.

A Hungarian nobleman, Baron Kempelen of Presburg, was inadvertently responsible for the American interest in robots. An ingenious mechanic, he devised many robots that walked, actually *talked,* and performed other mechanically mystifying operations. His most famous invention was a mechanical chess player, built out of metal to resemble a turbaned Turk, which engaged men in public contests throughout Europe. He sold this invention to a German named Johann Nepomuk Maelzel in 1769. The robot subsequently toured the United States during the early part of the nineteenth century.

Edgar Allan Poe, then editor of *The Southern Literary Messenger,* with editorial offices in Richmond, Va., performed one of the most brilliant exposés of the period after reading a report on this device. With no other evidence than published descriptions of the operation of the chess player, he proved by deductive logic that the machine was a fraud operated by a left-handed midget, concealed through the use of mirrors. His exposé, published in 1836, as well as a reference to the automatic chess player included in his short story "The Thousand-and-Second Tale of Scheherazade" (1845) influenced the entire course of literature dealing with mechanical men in the United States.

The most famous derivative of Poe's analysis of the mechanical chess player was Ambrose Bierce's classic, "Moxon's Master," the story of a chess-playing robot built by a scientist, which eventually, like Frankenstein's monster, kills its master.

Poe bears some responsibility for influencing a series of dime novels (they actually sold for five cents), beginning in 1868, dealing with steam men and steam horses invented by teen-aged geniuses and used to fight Indians and highwaymen. The most famous of these stories were the inventions of a sixteen-year-old Brooklyn boy, Luis Senarens, writing under the pen name of "Noname." His most popular character, Frank Reade, Jr., embarked on a series of adventures which Senarens began chronicling in 1879 and which he continued past the turn of the century. They are remembered nostalgically, today by thousands of boys, now grown old, because of their numerous prophecies of submarines, airplanes, spaceships, helicopters, and tanks.

The Frank Reade, Jr. robots were mindless steam and electric engines shaped like men. Most of the fictional robots that followed, however, were capable of thought, much like Ambrose Bierce's thinking machine; these were always depicted as treacherous and dangerous.

THE ROBOT IN MODERN SCIENCE FICTION

This hostile characterization continued right into the era of the science fiction magazines, the first of which, *Amazing Stories*, was launched with the dateline April 1926. Until the appearance of "The Lost Machine" by John Beynon Harris in the April 1932 issue of that magazine, authors vied with one another to contrive increasingly gruesome means by which robots could turn on mankind and assume control of the world.

Feeling, perhaps, that its readers would not immediately accept the notion of a friendly machine, Harris created an advanced *Martian* robot, who gives his first-person reaction to being stranded on the much more primitive Earth. Since the appearance of that story, Harris has become much better known under the pseudonym of John Wyndham.

Authors then began to re-examine their approach to robots. Beginning with John W. Campbell, Jr., in his short story "The Last Evolution" which appeared in *Amazing Stories* for August 1932, robots were depicted as allies of future man in his losing battle against invasion from outer space.

The theme of the robot as a menace is not likely to die out, but in the future it will be necessary to give it a special note of originality to make it palatable. Harl Vincent, writing in the June 1934, *Astounding Stories*, presented "Rex," a robot surgeon of such intelligence that he seizes control of all civilization and then tries to learn the meaning of emotions, the only area in which he was not superior to the enslaved humans.

Raymond Z. Gallun in "Derelict" (*Astounding Stories*, October 1935), taking his cue from the robot in "The Lost Machine," creates a fantastically alien automaton, whose builders have long since disappeared. In contact with a grief-stricken spaceman, the robot gradually restores the man's will to live and to face reality again. This left an opening for Robert Moore Williams to bring a race of arrogant robots back from a far star system, in the very distant future ("Robot's Return," *Astounding Science-Fiction*, August 1938) to the ruins of a dead Earth. They are sobered by the knowledge that they were created by the relatively fragile flesh-and-blood men.

ROBOTS WITH FEELINGS

Psychologically the time was now ripe to launch an assault against the reader's prejudices concerning robots. Two stories, appearing within weeks of one another, deserve the lion's share of the credit. The first was "I, Robot" (*Amazing Stories*, January 1938) by Eando Binder, which reversed the plot of *Frankenstein* and showed how the public could be made to believe that a robot, in this case Adam Link, was a threat to humanity, whereas in reality his motives were more noble than those of most men.

The second was "Helen O'Loy" by Lester Del Rey (*Astounding Science-Fiction*, December 1938) wherein robot technology has advanced to the point where robots are outwardly indistinguishable from humans. This story of a female robot, designed for housekeeping purposes, who falls in love with her owner, is one of the most tender and poignant stories in science fiction.

Reader reaction was so enthusiastic to both these stories that Eando Binder carried Adam Link through innumerable sequels and even employed him in a comic-magazine continuity. Dozens of authors immediately began to explore the potential of this science fiction plot gambit, which was to become second in popularity only to the interplanetary story.

What Binder and Del Rey had done was simple. They attributed human emotions to machines and showed the problems that result when the machines' personal feelings came in conflict with their tasks.

In "True Confession," F. Orlin Tremaine, the editor who had initially purchased and published both "Rex" and "Derelict," picked up the new formula and dramatized the credibility of a robot as a witness in a murder trial.

Clifford D. Simak, employing the plot devices in "Helen O'Loy," where the "female" robot is conditioned by soap operas and trashy novels to romantic notions, has a robot of the future who reads too many stories of science fiction in which his counterparts perform heroic deeds. He runs away from home and stows away on a spaceship making its way back to ancient, dying Earth (as in "Robots Return") in search of adventure.

ASIMOV AND THE THREE LAWS OF ROBOTICS

Of course, you can't have all those robots running helter-skelter and getting tangled up in their emotions without having some sort of check on them. The man who really brought order out of chaos was Isaac Asimov, when he propounded his Three Laws of Robotics:

1. A robot may not injure a human being, or, through inaction, allow a human being to come to harm.

2. A robot must obey the orders given it by human beings except where such orders would conflict with the First Law.

3. A robot must protect its own existence as long as such protection does not conflict with the First or Second Law.

A series of stories concerning robots, based on those laws, was written by Isaac Asimov. One of the most entertaining, "Runaround" (*Astounding Science-Fiction*, March 1942), clearly dramatizes the operation of The Three Laws of Robotics, and has the added advantage of being a robot story in an interplanetary setting.

Since Asimov postulated his robot regulations, they have either been adopted or become implicit in the robot stories of many leading science fiction writers. The careful reading of modern robot stories reveals how much they owe to these limiting factors.

The idea has not been lost on authors that, if the day arrives when robots become self-conscious personalities, it is inevitable that robot colonies, without any humans at all, may some day come into being. Such robot societies are projected in "Lost Memory," where Peter Phillips conceives a robot civilization on a world in a far galaxy, cut off so long from human contact that the robots cannot comprehend the very concept of a flesh-and-blood creature.

Of course, the humanizing of robots, while immensely popularizing that phase of science fiction, has not meant the end of good stories based on the Frankenstein-monster line. The results can often prove immensely clever, as displayed by Michael Fischer's brief but effective tale "Misfit," from *Science-Fiction Plus* for December 1953. . . .

THE ROLE OF ROBOTS

Today's robot is often one of the cast of characters, not necessarily the star of the show. The science fiction writer has a special problem which the writer of non-science fiction does not have. When the science fiction writer sits down at a type-writer he must not only write a good story, but *he must invent from start to finish the world in which the story takes place!* There is no map of the future, no book of its customs, laws, and problems.

A writer in a non-science fiction story need only say that his character stepped out of a Rolls-Royce and immediately the reader accepts the fact that the man is rich. He can also accomplish the same thing by saying: "The butler helped him to dress." But what will be the symbol of wealth of the man of the future? To give the impression of wealth, the science fiction writer must employ some other device, and what could be better than a chromium-plated robot tending to his master's every wish in response to electronic signals?

In a story of today, if a man escapes from prison, the reader expects him to be chased by bloodhounds. You can't have bloodhounds following a man who has escaped from a prison on Mars, but you can use a robot, equipped with detecting devices to track a man on that planet.

In a modern spy story, the secret agent, in order to get the information he wants, learns to talk, act, and dress like the people from whom he wants to get the information. But suppose you wanted to learn the secrets of the blue people of Venus who have six arms and four legs and breathe mustard gas instead of oxygen? A more practical means would be to build a robot that looked and acted like those Venusians.

The foregoing are just a few examples of what a very, very useful device the robot is to the science fiction writer.

As a result of using the robot so often and in so many ways, a strange thing has happened. Just as the camel reminds one immediately of Egypt, the skyscraper of New York, orange juice of Florida, and six-guns of the Old West, the robot has come to be associated with the *future*.

The writer, in effect, sets the mood and period of his story by introducing the robot, who may even lend it a note of *authenticity*. Once the robot was only the symbol of a Frankenstein monster; when the space rocket becomes commonplace, however, he may very well become the new symbol of science fiction!

CHAPTER 4

Themes of Science Fiction

Science
Fiction

Religious and Spiritual Aspects of Science Fiction

Tom Woodman

In this selection, Tom Woodman, who teaches at the University of Redding and specializes in the theme of religion in English literature, provides an overview of the treatment of religious themes in science fiction. Describing the prominence of scientism (a scientific belief system that replaces religion) in the work of many writers, Woodman examines how this perspective is contrasted with more traditional religious notions of existence. While some writers emphasize the triumph of scientism over religion, others criticize the scientific point of view from a religious, sometimes Christian, perspective. Many writers treat science and scientism as a mythology that is no more substantial than any religion, and some refuse to see religion and science as mutually exclusive categories, reconciling the two belief systems in their work. Science fiction and religion are linked by a desire to transcend the present reality. According to Woodman science fiction's greatest theme is coming to terms with the cosmos, and the genre naturally invites speculation on metaphysical and theological issues in its attempt to fathom the universe.

Samuel R. Delany has written that 'Virtually all the classics of speculative fiction are mystical' (*Extrapolation,* May 1969), and Arthur C. Clarke is reported to have called *2001* the world's first 'billion dollar religious movie'. The list of Hugo and Nebula award winners includes various novels and stories on religious themes. Anyone's list of famous

Excerpted from "Science Fiction, Religion, and Transcendence," by Tom Woodman, in *Science Fiction: A Critical Guide,* edited by Patrick Parrinder (New York: Longman, 1979). Reprinted by permission of Pearson Education Ltd.

science fiction would have to include C. S. Lewis's trilogy, Blish's *A Case of Conscience,* Miller's *A Canticle for Leibowitz* and the works of Philip K. Dick, and all of these have religion as a central theme, treat it seriously and become the vehicle for metaphysical and even theistic speculations.

If we look to the history of the genre for light on the question we see that several of its important antecedents were written by bishops or Jesuits like Godwin, Wilkins and Kircher. Later Jules Verne was to receive the papal blessing. It is true that the science fiction of the later nineteenth and early twentieth centuries often reflects the preconceptions of 'scientism' (the view that science has now explained away religion and indeed replaced it as the agent of man's salvation). The religion found in the pulp magazines is usually an exotic or barbaric magic, a caricature of pagan cults, like the gods encountered by Flash Gordon and Buck Rogers. The conscious view of religion here is that it is a base and primitive phenomenon, though an unconscious fascination with religious archetypes is also evident, as well as vague metaphysics in some stories. In the same period the epics of David Lindsay and Olaf Stapledon embody the genuine metaphysical searching that is often endemic to the genre.

ORTHODOXY AND SCIENCE

After the Second World War critiques of scientism are much more common. An intellectual resurgence of Christian orthodoxy occurred in the 1940s and early 1950s, and this is reflected in C. S. Lewis's and Walter Miller's attacks on scientism in the perspective of man as fallen. James Blish reveals a fascination with the intellectual problems of orthodoxy and science. The 1960s are the period in which the recognition that science had failed to provide values becomes widespread. The themes of science fiction begin more and more to overlap with religious aspirations rather than dismissing them. At the same time the writers of the 'New Wave' regard science itself as a mythology. Reflecting a movement in the culture at large, an undifferentiated quest for 'mystical' or spiritual experience takes the form of a new interest in non-Christian religions, as in Zelazny's *Lord of Light* (1967), and a new Californian gnosticism, the harbinger of which is Heinlein's *Stranger in a Strange Land* (1961). Philip K. Dick's work reflects the interest in the mysticism of drugs, at the same time as providing an early critique of it in

The Three Stigmata of Palmer Eldritch (1965), and his and
Vonnegut's black comedy is frequently the medium for
metaphysics. . . .

There seems no reason to doubt the legitimacy of a topic
like the future of religion, at least if it is seen as a fictional
and speculative extrapolation from history, and not as a factual prediction.

Catholicism, as a large institutional Church with a powerful cultural impact, has been the favoured religion for
such treatment, witty, irreverent or agonized. Brian Moore's
Catholics (1972) is a moving study of the tension between a
post-Vatican IV progressive papal authority and a pocket of
conservative Catholicism in Ireland. Various writers use
their understanding of the Church's historical attitude to science as a basis for predicting the suppression of scientific
activity by an all-powerful reactionary Church of the future,
as in Edgar Pangborn's *Davy* (1964). Alternatively, one may
envision an empire of the enlightened, who persecute Christians. This is the theme of an anonymous early novel, *In the
Future* (1875), and also of several modern stories of which
the best is Barry N. Malzberg's 'In the Cup', a dignified account of a future Christian martyr. Roger Ellwood's anthology *Signs and Wonders: Science Fiction Stories for the Christian Reader* (1972) puts Malzberg's story together with
another on the same theme, Eando Binder's 'All in Good
Time', in which an anti-Christian technocratic society is
converted by seeing on a time-viewer that its own future is
Christian. God has intervened through the technology by
which man attempts to control the future to show that it is in
fact in his hands. An interesting early presentation of the
twin alternatives, triumphant Church and triumphant scientism, occurs in the Catholic priest Robert Hugh Benson's
Lord of the World (1907) and *The Dawn of All* (1911). Recent
writers have been more interested in witty speculations, like
George Zebrowski's idea that the future world religion will
be a mixture of Christianity and Teilhard de Chardinism
('Heathen God', 1971). (De Chardin's *The Phenomenon of
Man* remains the most ambitious modern attempt at a synthesis of scientific and religious values, and it is not surprising that references to this famous Jesuit and evolutionist
crop up in several recent science fiction writers.) In *Deus
Irae* (1976) Philip K. Dick plays with the idea of 'teilhard de
chardin' birds that mutate forward, and envisages a post-

holocaust conflict between Christianity and a religion wor-
shipping the 'God of Wrath', the man who pressed the but-
ton. Various of these fantasies go beyond futurological extrapolation from the history of the Church as a human
phenomenon. Robert Hugh Benson's are, of course, wedded
to the idea of a divinely activated future, but several of the
others also have a genuine theological content. . . .

COMING TO TERMS WITH THE COSMOS

The ultimate theme of the genre of science fiction is man's
attempt through science to come to terms with the cosmos
he inhabits. Implications that go beyond a purely anthropological or sociological approach to religion may well develop
out of the fictional exploration of science as a human activity or as technology, the main focus of earlier writers. The
ethics of scientific activity may be examined by religious criteria or a look at the claims of scientism may involve its conflict with religion. Science fiction has always had another
aspect to its central theme as well, and from the early sixties
on writers have increasingly moved away from science as an
external activity towards considering it as a body of knowledge and a methodology. If the older prevailing mode was
humanist and ethical, the other interest is almost contemplative, emphasizing the greatness of the cosmos that man
comes to know. Writers present a fictional imitation of the
methodology of science to make quasi-cognitive assertions
about the cosmos. So they imitate the way science inevitably
overlaps to some extent with religion in making such statements. The study of the cosmos has always induced metaphysical speculations and is the source of what is traditionally called 'natural theology'. In some recent writers this
theme has taken the very different form of critical agnosti-
cism about science as a means of knowledge, so that the critique has led on to the assertion of a universe the incomprehensible richness of which transcends man's mind
altogether.

The great epic of man's scientific endeavours is simplified
into a hymn to scientism, assuming its values without analysis, in much fiction of the 1920s and 1930s. Asimov's
'Trends' (1939) is a touchstone, with its story of religious oppression trying to crush space travel until enlightenment finally triumphs. Lester del Rey's 'Evensong' (1967) is a late,
almost mythic, account of the pride and achievement of sci-

entism. By science men have become the superiors of God, whom they usurp and put in exile. The presupposition that religion is the enemy of scientific enlightenment is found in a whole set of novels involving parallel worlds like Keith Roberts's *Pavane* (1968)—where there is a papal encyclical entitled *Petroleum Veto*—or Kingsley Amis's *The Alteration* (1976). In Keith Roberts's novel it finally appears that the Church's reason for withholding science from man is paternalistic but well intentioned, but Amis's novel is a curiously dated assertion of anti-religious prejudices, including the view that science would have disproved God if the Church had not crushed it. Other writers also reflect the idea that science has explained religion away. In Heinlein's 'Universe' (1941) he provides the aetiology of a religion: the descendants of abandoned astronauts in a space-ship invent one to explain their situation. In Brian Aldiss's 'Heresies of the Huge God' (1966) mankind projects divine characteristics on to a mass of galactic debris that has fallen on to earth causing disaster. In various novels we are shown religious 'miracles' that are really powered by science, as in Fritz Leiber's *Gather Darkness* (1950), where a guild of scientists has grown afraid of the diffusion of knowledge. They establish a 'religion' that works miracles by scientific tricks. With the genuine spread of technology a golden age would have come, but the scientist-priests keep the serfs in ignorance by fostering superstition. Philip K. Dick parodies the view that science has explained away religion in *Our Friends from Frolix 8* (1970), where it is announced that God's carcase was found in space several years before the action of the book began. . . .

A more sympathetic and sophisticated method of 'explaining away' religion within a framework of scientism is the view expressed by several writers that religious phenomena are the products of para-psychology. It is announced in Frank Herbert's *The Godmakers* (1972) that the wise man prays once a week and practices 'psi' every day. The whole vast Mohammedan-style religion that dominates the same author's *Dune* (1965) has been set up by an order of clairvoyants and psychics, who sow prophecies about the coming of the messiah who is the hero of the book. In *The Godmakers* we see the process by which psychic gifts can be developed so that the protagonist becomes like a god in awareness and power. Similarly, in Clarke's *Childhood's End*

(1953) it is suggested that the traditional mystics had experienced a foretaste of 'breakthrough' into the next *gestalt* stage of human consciousness. Unfortunately, they had translated their insights into dogma. So, though this approach seems sympathetic to religion and depends on para-science (which is legitimate for a fictional genre) it does continue to carry the implication that religious phenomena are not valid in their own terms.

The same is true of the writers of the New Wave when they interpret religion rationalistically, though not unsympathetically, through a scientifically based interest in the structures of mythologies. But they see science, too, as a mythological structure of thought-patterns, which they test against more traditional mythic structures, and so the critique of scientism is a major aim. . . .

CRITIQUING SCIENCE AND SCIENTISM

The more usual perspective for the critique of a science that is trying to dislodge religion is that of Christian orthodoxy. Mary Shelley's *Frankenstein* (1818) presents the possibility that the scientist is usurping the role of God in trying to create life. This is a frequent archetype, seen, for example, in J. R. Fearn's 'Before Earth Came' (*Astounding Stories,* 1934) where a group of experimenters plan to create a new solar system. It all goes wrong, and the Chief Scientist says that the reason is that they are trying to usurp the Creator's power. Nor can fallen man create Utopias through technology, as we see in R. A. Lafferty's *Past Master* (1968), where St Thomas More is taken to a utopian planet. But the inhabitants attempt to stamp out belief in a beyond, and he has to become a martyr again. The world is condemned to repeat the pattern of trying to create new Edens and then destroying them again in *A Canticle for Leibowitz.* The most famous and popular orthodox critique of scientism is, of course, C. S. Lewis's trilogy *Out of the Silent Planet* (1938), *Perelandra* (1943) and *That Hideous Strength* (1945), and James Blish takes up Lewis's linking of scientism and the demonic when he envisages the megalopolis created by post-industrial technocratic man not as a new Eden but a new hell (*The Day after Judgement,* 1971).

Ursula Le Guin's *The Lathe of Heaven* (1971) offers a thorough-going attack on scientism from the perspective of Taoist philosophy. The universe, as she has beautifully conveyed elsewhere, is a system of dualities held in balanced harmony. Man is a part of the whole, and his fulfilment comes from the acceptance of this. Utilitarian technology, as symbolized by Dr Haber, is man's attempt to set himself above the universe and to tamper with it. Haber goes beyond utilitarianism into scientism when he boasts of a technological revolution that will transform men into gods and this world into heaven.

The Lathe of Heaven is anti-science science fiction, just as much as C. S. Lewis's, though Ursula Le Guin's other work often shows more sympathetic attitudes to science. This novel exemplifies how the critique of scientism often leads on to more general themes in the relationship between science and religion which are legitimate topics for fictional treatment within the genre. The novel deliberately sets out to associate Haber's world-view with the Judaeo-Christian tradition. So a curious situation has occurred in the fictional presentation of the relationship between the Church and science, one that reverses the preconceptions of many other writers. Despite the prejudices against science that the Church has often revealed and despite the anti-Church values of scientism, Ursula Le Guin's view is probably closer to the truth. Ernan McMullin argues in *New Blackfriars* (March 1969) that Christian revelation, which sees the universe as God's creation, and believes that God works through the historical process, is hospitable to science in a way that the Eastern religions are not. This is not to deny the special analogies between the highest levels of Eastern mysticism and modern physics that the physicist Fritjof Capra has pointed to. But the answer that *The Lathe of Heaven* gives to Haber's claim that technology will one day make a heaven of earth is to say that it is a heaven already if we could only see it. Marxism, Judaeo-Christian revelation and scientism all agree in saying that this world is not yet like heaven. Christianity agrees with Marxism, too, in seeing technology as one means that will help in the transformation. Thus, a tradition of theology, which Milton, Hartlib and Bacon were only developing, affirms, as in Hugh of St Victor, that the sciences were given by God to help man overcome the effects of the Fall, ignorance and infirmity. Historically, this is the main Christian tradition; the more negative one that sees science as Faustian self-assertion is only secondary.

RECONCILING RELIGION AND SCIENCE

Several writers do in fact treat the theme of the relationship between science and religion by presenting the Church as favourable to science, as in Philip José Farmer's parallel-world story 'Sail On, Sail On' (1952), where there is a clerical order of scientists called after 'St Roger Bacon'. The Jesuit scientist who is the hero of Blish's *A Case of Conscience* (1958) comes finally to realize that there is no ultimate conflict between his science and his religion. The same happens in a charming Ray Bradbury story of 1949 in which an elderly conservative priest comes to see that rockets are the 'Machineries of Joy' of the title, and can help man to know more of God's handiwork and so praise him better.

In some stories a religious reversal of the theme of the machine as God is used to point to what the authors see as a better version of the relationship between science and religion. In Arthur C. Clarke's 'The Nine Billion Names of God' (1953) Hindus use a computer to spell out all the possible words which could be God's name, and so bring about the end of the world. So religion uses technology for its own ends, as also in Michael Davidson's *The Karma Machine* (1975), where a computer is linked up with Eastern wisdom to produce Nirvana. The ultimate pro-religious twist to the theme is Anthony Boucher's clever 'The Quest for St Aquin' (1951), which tells of the conversion of a robot to Thomist Catholicism. The preconceptions behind Boucher's story are the Thomist ones that science deals with secondary causes which lead, when properly interpreted, to God. The end of *A Case of Conscience* is a very sophisticated presentation of the same teaching about the relationship between scientific and religious values. Blish makes use of the Thomist theology of science as the realm of secondary causes to provide a clever conclusion to the novel. At the same time as the priest exorcizes the planet he has come to see as a demonic delusion it is accidentally blown up by the scientists who wish to exploit it for armaments. So the author leaves us to make up our minds whether we want to believe supernatural or natural explanations, or whether both coexist, as in the Thomist view that God works out supernatural purposes through the natural order, which preserves its own logical autonomy.

In theological terms the most sophisticated novel on the relationship between science and religion is Walter Miller's

A Canticle for Leibowitz (1959). The book is a marvellous imaginative invention describing the time after the nuclear holocaust when a monastic order is the sole preserver of scientific knowledge. Miller creates fine comedy out of the monks' naïve reverence for pre-holocaust science and their superstitious misunderstandings of the monster 'Fallout'. But the book contains an implicit argument. It is, after all, true that it was the monks who preserved scientific wisdom in the early Middle Ages. After the nuclear disaster a movement called 'The Simplification' had blamed science, and tried to stamp it out. Miller's point is that the Church cannot set herself against any real truth, for all truth bears some relationship to the Logos. It is not science that is wrong but men's hearts. But scientism, the opposite extreme to 'The Simplification', is equally wrong. Leibowitz, the scientist-founder of the religious order, came to see that 'Great knowledge, while good, had not saved the world'. The whole book is dominated by the idea of the Fall. This is the basis of its impressive black comedy and of the genuine tragic vision which gives it, despite a rather dated view of Catholicism, a sombre power. Science has been given to help man. It is a means of overcoming the effects of the Fall. But in itself it cannot bring back the lost Eden. Science's Utopia is a blasphemous and unsatisfying parody of man's true fulfilment, which is brought about by God's grace alone, in radical disruption of this world's order. . . .

THE OTHER AND THE COSMIC VIEWPOINT

The theme of creation may also follow on from a consideration of the stars. Many writers play with the topic, from the beautiful reworking of traditional Judaeo-Christian ideas in Eric Frank Russell's 'Second Genesis' (1951) to the nihilist view of a galaxy created from the debris of the cosmos that we find in Silverberg's *The Masks of Time* (1968). Several writers explore the idea that the galaxy was created not directly by the Christian God but by a demiurge, well intentioned but weak, who makes several mistakes. George Zebrowski's 'Heathen God' (1971) makes fine use of this theme. The demiurge was loving, and has left a loving spirit among men. The ultimate God figure, the creator of all reality, recedes further and further away as the story continues, and the priest-hero realizes that the demiurge has no knowledge of such a God. All we can do is to live with the hope of perpetuating the demiurge's benevolence. The story translates Christian ideas of the Holy Spirit into its own terms. But 'Heathen God' is so complex that, despite its anthropocentric emphasis, it might also intimate the possibility at least of a benevolent creator on a vastly grander scale than the god directly responsible for this world in the story.

The interest in other planets and their possible inhabitants raises specific theological problems discussed earlier. In a much more general sense it evokes the whole mystery of man's relationship with the alien and the Other. The strangeness of bizarre forms of life in the galaxy can be an imaging of the frightening aspects of what is transcendent to the individual ego and its controls. As J. Robert King has pointed out, these aliens from other planets are often projections of father and god figures. They may also embody man's yearning to transcend his own isolations and limitations. Lord Running Clam in Dick's *Clans of the Alphane Moon* (1964) is a spore clam that sacrifices itself for the hero. There is something consoling and moving in the idea of being cared for by a creature so different from man. In Karl Barth's theology God is the wholly Other, to whom man must yet relate himself in love if he is to be made whole. Man fears Otherness at the same time as he needs it to complete himself. This theme is brilliantly explored in Dick's *The Three Stigmata of Palmer Eldritch* (1965), where the alien is a terrifying possessor who yet, because transcendent to man, is a part of God or an analogue of God. A similar speculation occurs in Lem's *Solaris.* One of the novel's central themes is man's urge to communicate with what is beyond himself, and Lem is manifestly aware of there being religious implications to this impulse.

The cosmic viewpoint that arises naturally in science fiction, the interest in ideas about the creation, and the reflections of relativity theory all evoke a special interest in the theme of time. Vonnegut's *Slaughterhouse-Five* (1969) utilizes quasi-scientific concepts to explore the difference between an earthly sense of time and an eternal perspective, as the hero is snatched out of this world to the planet Tralfamadore. The cosmic viewpoint of the inhabitants encourages quietism and determinism, which Vonnegut seems half to urge and half condemn. In *Perelandra* C. S. Lewis discussed man's deluded sense of time, which Simone Weil, like Lewis, sees as one of the primary results of the Fall. Science fiction can make us aware of this delusion by manipulating our ideas of time, by contrasting our time with a cosmic perspective, by fictionalizing versions of true science, and by using pseudo-scientific motifs like time travel. The cosmic perspective and the motif of time-travel also leads science fiction writers to the same themes as Milton's bad angels, who debated:

> Of Providence, Foreknowledge, Will and Fate,
> Fixt Fate, Free Will, Foreknowledge Absolute,
> And found no End in wandering Mazes lost.

If our time can be seen from an eternal perspective, then is there free will? Or are we involved in a predestined cosmic plot? . . .

A NATURAL CONNECTION

Metaphysics and theology have arisen naturally out of the genre's common themes, the limits and ethics of science, time, eternity, creation, and out of its radically future orientation. At the furthest limits of this development towards theology, a very specific 'theologizing' occurs; that is, the exploration of a range of speculations about the nature of God, from the mad god of Dean Koontz's *A Darkness in My Soul* (1972), through the imperfect deity of Lem's *Solaris*, and the incompetent one, powerless to bring about the end of the world in Mark Geston's *Out of the Mouth of the Dragon* (1969), to the majestic but impersonal and indifferent *Star Maker* (1937) of Olaf Stapledon. Philip K. Dick is a good example of a recent and prestigious writer who explores theistic ideas of varying degrees of bizarreness or orthodoxy such as the god whose carcase is found in space in *Our Friends from Frolix 8*, the evil god of the paranoid vision in 'Faith of Our Fathers' (1967), and the totally Augustinian theodicy that we find in *Counter-Clock World* (1967):

> *Evil is simply a lesser reality, a ring farther from Him. It's the lack of absolute reality, not the presence of an evil deity.*

Here St Thomas Aquinas, St Augustine and Erigena are quoted to back up the presentation, through fictionalized technology, of an 'after-life' experience which brings you into touch with the divine.

Various scientists and theologians have been suggesting for some time now that the views of modern science are much more compatible with religion than those of the older science. Teilhard de Chardin's is only the most ambitious attempt at a synthesis. Harold Schilling, Emeritus Professor of Physics at Pennsylvania State University, claims in *The New Consciousness in Science and Religion* that modern science acknowledges its inability to grasp in its fullness a reality that is seen as inexhaustible. Scientists now tend, in Professor Schilling's view, to see man as part of a universal creative process, not inaugurated by us and to which we must humbly submit. The word 'transcendence' is interpreted by Schilling as referring not to 'a spatial beyond but to the "infinitely more than" anything observable directly in us or the cosmos'. (This sense of science's cognitive limitations is a strong theme in *Solaris*.) The implications of various aspects of the new science for theological concepts are considerable. . . .

Transcending Our Present Reality

What finally links religious aspirations and the best science fiction is a common interest in transcending our present reality. Both have a cosmic dimension. Both have a common focus on the future of man, an interest especially built into Judaism and Christianity. Cosmic awe, the perspective that comes from contemplating the stars, makes us realize our littleness, as Troilus looks down from the eighth sphere at the end of Chaucer's poem and smiles at the triviality of our concerns. Science fiction relates us to vast cosmic forces. It is the opposite as a genre to what D. H. Lawrence once called 'wearisome sickening little personal novels'. Our earthly viewpoint is bound to be narrow and half-blind, and the epistemological sophistication of modern science confirms this: 'We see through a glass darkly', writes Philip K. Dick, quoting St Paul, and as the critic Bruce Gillespie explains, Dick's aim is not to give us an ecstatic religious vision but to show us the frailty of our reality and the intimations of another. Father Simon Tugwell says that our world and our present human status are 'provisional'. He cites St Thomas Aquinas's view that genuine religious prophecy needs imagination, a gift for seeing that things could be other than they are, a gift of seeing from God's viewpoint. We are not to be 'conformed to the present age' (Romans 12, 2). He also explains that transcendence is more a temporal than a spatial concept. In the future man will be radically different from what he is now, conformed not to the present age, but to Christ, the 'first fruits' of the new humanity:

It does not yet appear what we shall be, but we know that
when he appears we shall be like him, for we shall see him as
he is.   (1 John 3, 1–2, *Revised Standard Version*)

The genre of science fiction can help shatter the complacencies of our present views of reality, and make our imaginations enjoyably receptive to new visions of the future. Obviously the great mass of work in the genre is formulaic. Its
material is of interest to the psychologist, the sociologist and
even the theologian as a record of man's aspirations and
prejudices. It can entertain us and soothe us with pre-
dictable futures and safe horrors. But it bears the same relationship to the greatest achievements and potential of the
genre as a British country-house detective novel of the 1920s
bears to *Crime and Punishment.* The idea of transcendence
creates a common ground between aesthetic criteria for
evaluating science fiction and a degree of theological interest that goes beyond the purely diagnostic. For, in the best
science fiction with theological implications, we are startled
in some way. It may merely be that shock of newness which
is essential for the effect of a witty or even blasphemous manipulation of religious ideas. It may be the playful shock of
an intellectual puzzle in which a tired dogma is confronted
with a facet of reality that tests or breaks it. Or the aesthetic
shock may come from the comedy or the tragedy of man's
attempts to transcend himself through science and technology. Religious science fiction might condemn the attempt as
futile by the standards of a different transcendent vision altogether, or it might even celebrate it as an epic, God-given
and marvellous creative struggle, as Teilhard de Chardin
does. But the aesthetic shock to our complacencies that the
best science fiction brings is *cognitive,* a reminder of our
provisional status. We get the sense in Olaf Stapledon's *Last*
and First Men (1930) that our present humanity is only a
brief stage in the titanic mental and spiritual mutations that
man must undergo. Science fiction from a committedly religious point of view will fall into stale pieties unless it can
present old doctrines prophetically, in the challengingly cosmic and futurist dimension which is of their essence. The
best science fiction from an agnostic or atheistic point of
view has often indicated, like Stapledon's, that the inexhaustible creativity of man and the cosmos utterly transcends our present experience.

Frankenstein and the Female Voice in Science Fiction

Jane Donawerth

Instructing as a professor of English in women's studies and comparative literature at the University of Maryland in College Park, Jane Donawerth has designed courses that study the relationship of women and science fiction. She credits Mary Shelley with inventing the genre with her famous novel, *Frankenstein.* Donawerth asserts that with this novel Shelley raises complex and important issues that have had a lasting impact on the genre of science fiction, especially for the women writers who have followed Shelley's lead. In this regard, Donawerth analyzes and explains some of Shelley's prevalent concerns in *Frankenstein* such as: contending with a male-dominated science that excludes women, exploring the identity of woman as alien, and finding a voice within an overtly masculine narrative.

At the beginning of the history of science fiction stands a woman writer, Mary Shelley, but ironically one who conceived of science fiction as a male story. Her *Frankenstein* defines the genre, but male critics have taken at face value her assumption of science fiction as male, writing her own contribution out of its history. Mark Rose, for example, explains that *Frankenstein* is not really science fiction because Mary Shelley did not name it that and the genre did not yet exist (1981). And Darko Suvin dismisses *Frankenstein* as a "flawed hybrid," a portrait of failed proletariat revolution (1979). Moreover, numerous editors of science fiction histories and encyclopedias have simply left women out of their works. Nevertheless, women writers have continued,

Excerpted from *Frankenstein's Daughters,* by Jane Donawerth. Copyright © 1997 by Syracuse University Press. Reprinted by permission of Syracuse University Press.

stubbornly, to write science fiction. They have returned again and again to the complexities of the questions that Shelley raised: making a science that does not exclude women, creating an identity for woman as alien, and finding a voice in a male world.

Indeed, these three crucial problems took shape in Mary Shelley's *Frankenstein*, suggesting that they are cultural as much as literary inheritance. And just as men in the 1920s and 1930s pulps reprinted H. G. Wells, Jules Verne, and Edgar Allan Poe, modeling stories after them in order to constitute their modern genre, so women presented themselves as Frankenstein's daughters, alluding to Mary Shelley and *Frankenstein* in constituting their version of science fiction. In the 1920s and 1930s, allusions to Mary Shelley's *Franken-stein* occur in Clare Winger Harris's "The Artificial Man" (1929), Sophie Wenzel Ellis's "Creatures of the Light" (1930); Kathleen Ludwick's "Dr. Immortelle" (1930); and L. Taylor Hansen's "The City on the Cloud" (1930). Even Charlotte Perkins Gilman's *Herland* echoes *Frankenstein*, rewriting Victor's jubilation: "She alone had founded a new race!" (1979). In subsequent writers, Shelley's influence is equally important. In C. L. Moore's "No Woman Born" (1944) in *The Best of C. L. Moore*, the scientist Maltzer and the woman whom he has recreated, Deirdre, debate whether or not he is a "Frankenstein" (1975). Faced with gender restrictions, Joanna, one protagonist of Joanna Russ's *The Female Man* (1975), cries, "I am a poet! I am Shelley! I am a genius!" Phyllis Gotlieb includes a poem entitled "ms & mr frankenstein" in her collection of short stories, *Son of the Morning and Other Stories* (1983). And Joan Slonczewski's Spinel fears that he is "becoming a monster" because of Shoran breath microbes (1987). Robin Roberts further argues that Doris Lessing's *The Sirian Experiments* is a "revision of Shelley's *Frankenstein*" (1985). In an essay on writing science fiction, Cherry Wilder claims that *Franken-stein* was a turning point in two ways, "one when I realised Frankenstein was written by a woman, and another when I realised that she was nineteen years old" (1992). I suspect that the many monster stories by women, from Ellis's "The White Wizard" and Harris's "The Artificial Man," to C. L. Moore's "No Woman Born," Judith Merril's "That Only a Woman" in *Out of Bounds*, and Octavia Butler's "Bloodchild" are all to some extent reworkings of the issues of illegitimate birth and monstrosity that *Frankenstein* raises. These women's knowledge of Shelley as a predecessor quite probably enabled them to write. But they also then carried into their own works Shelley's problems with the genre. Even by the 1920s, an exclusively male science, first person male narration, and the woman as alien were established conventions in male "scientifiction." Mary Shelley's strategies for surviving the patriarchal and generic restrictions, therefore, were also helpful guides for women writers.

THE THEME OF MALE-DOMINATED SCIENCE

Let us begin with the science in *Frankenstein*. As Victor Frankenstein relates his story to Robert Walton, he gradually details a more and more disturbing picture of the male scientist. As a boy, Victor "delighted in investigating [the] causes [of things]," and early felt "the enticements of science." To him, "The world was . . . a secret" and he felt "gladness akin to rapture" through his "earnest research to learn the hidden laws of nature." His "object of pursuit" was "the inner spirit of nature" and "the physical secrets of the world." As an adult he turns to the alchemists because he thinks that he has found men who "had penetrated deeper and knew more." But he eventually learns that their knowledge is outdated. Not until college is he again stirred by enthusiasm for science: there he hears M. Waldman extoll "the modern masters" of science, who "penetrate into the recesses of nature and show how she works in her hiding-places." The "master" and the "her" are crucial: for Victor Frankenstein, the scientist is male and nature is female; science is the domination of nature. The domination is erotic: the scientist pursues nature, uncovers her and unveils her, penetrates her, and rejoices in his mastery.

As the feminist historians of science, Carolyn Merchant and Evelyn Fox Keller, have pointed out, in the words of male scientists from Bacon to DNA specialists, the history of science is the history of male study of "female" nature, and erotic and patriarchal assumptions about controlling women inform science. Nor is Victor the only male scientist in *Frankenstein* to use these metaphors. Robert Walton admires Victor Frankenstein's "penetration into the causes of things" (1985); he likewise hopes to achieve fame from science, exploring "over the untamed yet obedient element," and aiming for a "knowledge" that would give "dominion . . . over the elemental foes of our race." Exploration offers him "entice-ments" and the hope of "discovering [dis-covering?] a pas-sage near the pole" or "the secret of the magnet." Thus sci-ence is conceived of as an erotic act—Carolyn Merchant would say rape—and Victor Frankenstein's quest for life seems to typify the male scientist's activity. For Victor, sci-ence at times seems "a deformed and abortive creation"; at other times, the source of "immortality and power." By "pursu[ing] nature to her hiding-places" he "discover[s] the cause of generation and life" and experiences "the most grat-ifying consummation" of his "toils." The result, he first imag-ines, will be "[a] new species," the scientist usurping both God's and woman's powers of creation, as well as experienc-ing his own self-sufficient consummation: "No father could claim the gratitude of his child so completely as I should de-serve theirs." With great horror Victor learns instead that his illicit intercourse with nature has produced a monster, an "abortion." Thus, as Anne K. Mellor has detailed, Mary Shel-ley in *Frankenstein* "challenged any conception of science and the scientific method that rested on a gendered defini-tion of nature as female."

For Mary Shelley, then, a significant constraint in the cre-ation of her story was the exclusion of women from science in her culture, and the resulting image of a female nature as the object of male study. Indeed, Victor must leave the world of women entirely and enter the university world that ex-cludes women in order to practice his science. These as-sumptions about the nature of science determine that scien-tists must be male, and that the quest, erotic and illicit, must be profane. Elizabeth, because she is a woman, cannot be a scientist, but she can have a different, holy, relation with na-ture: "In the majestic and wondrous scenes which sur-rounded our Swiss home—the sublime shapes of the moun-tains, the changes of the seasons, tempest and calm, the silence of winter, and the life and turbulence of our Alpine Summers—she found ample scope for admiration and de-light." "With a serious and satisfied spirit," Elizabeth can achieve a union with nature because women *are* nature. Mary Shelley allows a brief glimpse of a utopian relation with nature. But she also allows the problem of science sim-ply to stand: from its illicit eroticism her story derives much of its anguish, from what Margaret Homans calls Franken-stein's "oedipal violation of Mother Nature" (1987). And from Mary Shelley, as well as from their patriarchal culture, later women writers of science fiction inherit science as a problem for women writing science fiction. Some women, like Shelley, detail the story of science as illicit intercourse. Many modern writers . . . alternatively construct a utopian science based on different metaphors, Elizabeth's metaphors—a science that places women as subjects at its center.

THE DEPICTION OF WOMAN AS ALIEN

Intimately connected with the construction of science in *Frankenstein* is the depiction of woman as alien. The women of *Frankenstein* are all marked by difference. Elizabeth— found, not created by the Frankenstein family—seems "of a distinct species, a being heaven-sent, and bearing a celestial stamp in all her features." She provides "diversity and contrast" to Victor, and is herself "saintly," "celestial," Victor seeing her function only in terms of this difference: "She was there to subdue me to a semblance of her own gentleness." After her unjust condemnation for William's murder, Justine admits, "I almost began to think that I was the monster that he said I was." Thus women in *Frankenstein,* as in much of Western literary history, are marked as either angels or monsters, both outside of normative society.

This positioning of woman as alien is most strikingly presented in *Frankenstein* in the character of Safie. Although Safie's father is "the Turk" and represents the unjust prejudice that Europeans hold toward non-Europeans, Safie herself, always called "the Arabian," functions in the novel more as a representative of gender difference than racial difference, revealing Shelley's own racial prejudice. Like Elizabeth and Agatha, Safie is "angelic," with a "complexion wondrously fair, each cheek tinged with a lovely pink." She has taken from her Christian mother not only her complexion, but also her "higher powers of intellect and an independence of spirit" unlike that of other Muslim women. But this independence marks her for Shelley as different not only from Muslim women but also from the other Christian women we see in this novel: Safie alone of the women travels and adventures, exploring foreign lands, like the men of the novel. At the center of *Frankenstein,* then, is a hinted motif receiving much elaboration in later science fiction by women: the woman as alien. In *Frankenstein,* the alienation is simply represented and not developed into story; or, rather, it is developed by similarity to another alien—the monster.

Like the monster, Safie is marked by lack of the dominant language, and it is through Felix's teaching of Safie that the monster learns the language. Indeed, it is through Felix's teaching of Safie that the monster comes to a recognition of his monstrosity—"When I looked around I saw and heard of none like me. Was I, then, a monster . . . ?"—a recognition that might equally apply to Safie. Their quests are similar: the monster "an imperfect and solitary being," a "stranger" seeking through friendship to establish "intercourse" with the cottagers; Safie, a "stranger" seeking through marriage to remain "in a country where women were allowed to take a rank in society." Thus Safie, like the monster cast out by her father-creator, freely chooses to alienate herself because of her bitter resentment. Indeed, both Safie and the monster suffer from their fathers' broken promises of intended mates. Like the monster, Safie must learn a new language, a new culture, in order to find a voice, in order to enter society. And like Safie standing, voiceless, outside European society, all the women of the novel stand outside the narration, alienated, but with their feelings displaced by Shelley onto the monster—as many recent feminist critics have shown. The monster, like the women of the novel, is willing to "be even mild and docile to my natural lord and king," if he, in return, is allowed to be king in his own home, to be given "a female who will accompany [him] in [his] exile." However, unlike the monster and like many alien women who follow in science fiction by women, Safie is not inferior to the man she seeks to reach an understanding with across cultural boundaries: she brings her own gift of cultural difference across the border, singing "to him the divine airs of her native country."

In *Frankenstein,* the problem of woman as alien is thus introduced into science fiction but displaced onto the monster and not resolved. In many later works of science fiction by women, . . . the woman as alien is returned to, explored, expanded as a symbolic category, and sometimes transformed through equality of respect for racial, gendered, and personal differences. For help in interpreting the taxonomy of alien women that later writers develop, I shall eclectically draw on feminist psychology. In any case, the woman as literally an alien, but a subject with a culture of her own, calls into question the naturalness of male superiority.

THE PROBLEM OF MALE NARRATION

If the woman remains an alien in science fiction by women, only recently in the genre does she share and then usurp the male human point of view. In the structure of male narration in *Frankenstein,* we can recognize the difficulties for a woman writer. The story is told in letters by Robert Walton to his sister. This narrator is an adventurer, wending his way further and further north towards the pole and to discoveries, further and further away from his sister-reader, Mrs. Saville ("Civil") and her "gentle and feminine fosterage." This narrator also travels further and further from the writer's own experience, the writer—Mary Wollstonecraft Shelley—lending her own initials not to the adventurer but to the supportive reader—Mrs. Margaret Walton Saville. Like Robert Walton, the second narrator, Victor Frankenstein, is male, a scientist who adventures into unknown realms not geographically but in his laboratory. Again, the spaces he inhabits, and the story he tells, are exclusively male: he must journey to the all-male university in order to make the monster. Finally, we hear in the middle of the tale from the monster, who is also male, despite his parallels to Safie. He, too, would learn patriarchy, congratulating himself on his superiority when he learns the language much faster than the woman. For Mary Shelley, male narration, of course, was a solution as well as a problem, as it has become for many later women writers of science fiction: male narration allows a woman to enact vicariously a tale of adventure, a triumph of science, in a sexist society that rarely allows the female person such freedoms.

However, for a woman writer, male narration is not only a freedom but also a constraint: where can we put a female voice when so much of the text is spoken by men? In *Frankenstein,* Shelley experiments both with male narration, and also with strategies for resisting it and subverting it. Several of these strategies become important to later women writers of science fiction. First, she interpolates a female voice: Elizabeth writes Victor two letters. As in later experiments with female voice in science fiction before 1960, Elizabeth's letters represent a misplacement in science fiction because they are bound so entirely to gender, to the middle-class domestic details of women's lives. Elizabeth could perhaps write a novel by Mrs. Gaskell, but she could not write the science fiction novel that Shelley herself writes. Second, Shelley resists male narration by providing the monster as an alien voice, an abnormal male with whom female readers can sympathize. With his insistent "Listen to my tale. . . . Listen to me, Frankenstein. . . . Listen to me," the monster interrupts and resists the tale that Frankenstein is himself telling Walton. In this subversion of male narration, the monster expresses "the barbarity of man," standing outside his gender but still retaining some of its privilege and authority.

Finally, Shelley retains the male narrator but forces him to undergo a distinctly feminine experience. Again, like many later women writers of science fiction, Shelley imposes a feminine story on a male narrator-protagonist. In *Frankenstein*, Shelley dislocates the story of illegitimacy, placing it on Victor Frankenstein. She can thus turn male narration into a conversion story; she can also explore the feminine story in terms not only of guilt but also of triumph.

The fiction of an aristocratic woman conceiving an illegitimate child was common among women writers who preceded Shelley. We may take as representative of Shelley's inheritance the story of Lady Emilia in Sarah Scott's 1762 novel, *Millenium Hall*. The Lady Emilia, in a moment of passion, conceives a child by her honorable fiancé, Lord Peyton. The next day she realizes her terrible mistake, refuses to marry him knowing that he could never respect her, bears the child secretly and gives it up in order to protect her family honor, and spends the rest of her life in penance separated from both her lover and child. After her lover's death, she reconciles with her child, revealing the truth only on her own deathbed. She is heroic because she has enacted sufficient penance, but she has, of course, also punished all those connected with her: her fiancé has been deprived of a wife and her baby of both parents, nor can her daughter marry once she learns her monstrous lineage. The story of the illegitimate mother is the story of a lifetime of anguish as a result of her secret creation.

Similarly, Victor Frankenstein, in "a moment of presumption and rash ignorance," creates the illicit monster, "the life I so thoughtlessly bestowed." Like the Lady Emilia, he immediately sees his error, deserts the monster, and spends the rest of the novel in anguished, secret penance for the "wretch whom I created." Like the Lady Emilia, Frankenstein has a "dreadful secret" that obstructs his marrying. Also like the Lady Emilia, Frankenstein avoids making himself known to his child until he dies, and so Frankenstein enacts the penitent woman on his/her deathbed. This narrative technique is, in fact, cross-dressing: the male narrator is wearing the story of the fallen woman with an illegitimate child. By displacing this feminine story onto the male narrator, Shelley enables male conversion: Victor Frankenstein eventually "felt what the duties of a creator were"—not in the form of financial responsibility like Lord Peyton, but in the form of responsibility for the "happiness" of the creature, like the Lady Emilia.

Victor's conversion comes too little and too late, but again Shelley's strategy is extended and experimented with in many later novels by women. In Marge Piercy's *Woman on the Edge of Time* (1976), for example, future science enables men and women to engender life in the laboratory, and men undergo in a utopian setting the feminine experience of nursing. In Jayge Carr's *Leviathan's Deep* (1979) and in Octavia Butler's "Bloodchild" (1984), men are raped by alien females, and in Butler's story, men undergo pregnancy, caesarean section, and all the physical and emotional dangers of unwanted childbearing. In Shelley's novel, the satisfaction of the story derives not from Frankenstein's androgyny, since he never lives up to the calling of mother, but instead, from the revenge of casting a powerful male in a woman's story, from making at least one imaginary male feel what many women had felt (including, perhaps, Mary Shelley, her mother, and her half sister—all of whom bore illegitimate children).

In creating the genre of science fiction, in fusing the romance with enlightenment rationality, Shelley created a genre that gave women writers enormous freedoms—to be adventurers and scientists, imaginatively, to be vicariously what their society denied them. But Shelley also created a genre inheriting the limitations of her patriarchal society: a society in which women were denied education and careers in science, in which women were constructed as aliens, and in which men retained the license to speak and control the stories. These, I think, are the limitations that women writers of science fiction have surmounted throughout the twentieth century in an infinite variety of ways.

Asimov and the Morality of Artificial Intelligence

Patricia S. Warrick

Patricia S. Warrick is an eminent scholar of science fiction. Contemplating the value of the genre as a means of education in the subjects of politics, anthropology, psychology, and philosophy, Warrick is particularly interested in such science fiction masters as Philip K. Dick and Isaac Asimov. In this selection Warrick examines Asimov's use of robots in his work, and especially his development of the theme of artificial intelligence. Warrick believes that Asimov, perhaps more than any other writer, has made the most significant contributions in this area, explaining that Asimov's Three Laws of Robotics formed a basis from which he continually drew for his material. She asserts that Asimov's later robot stories contemplate the ethical and philosophical implications of artificial life more than his earlier writings, a thesis which Warrick explores by comparing stories from different phases of Asimov's work.

Because the imaginative literature about computers and robots is so extensive, it is helpful to be familiar with its images, themes, and issues. For this overview there is no better source than the cybernetic fiction of Asimov. He has written thirty-five works of fiction about computers and robots, a far greater number than any other writer. The fiction extends over a long period of time: the first was published in 1940, the most recent in 1976. Asimov has been both comprehensive, thoughtful, and imaginative in creating his substantial body of fiction.

Asimov is optimistic about the relationship of man and intelligent machines. Asimov has labeled the fear of mechani-

Excerpted from *The Cybernetic Imagination in Science Fiction*, by Patricia S. Warrick. Copyright © 1980 by The Massachusetts Institute of Technology. Reprinted with permission from the MIT Press.

cal intelligence the "Frankenstein complex." He does not have this fear, nor does he approve of those who do. He believes that machines take over dehumanizing labor and thus allow humans to become more human. In his words, "the electronic computer is far superior at those mental tasks that are dull, repetitive, stultifying and degrading, leaving to human beings themselves the far greater work of creative thought in every field from art and literature to science and ethics." His optimistic attitude is notable because it is the exception to much of the SF written since World War II. . . .

In his robot stories most of the population resents robot research and resists the use of robots, so most of the development and testing goes on in outer space. In "Profession" (1957) he summarizes this phenomenon of resistance to change by creating a future world where the phenomenon has become part of the system. In this imaginary world most people have their brains wired to tapes and are programmed like machines to function in a routine, nondeviating fashion. Rare, creative individuals are set apart in a special house where they follow the creative thrust of their imagination. Asimov's view is clear: Most members of society are rigid, like machines, and resist change; the rare individual with a creative mind is the exception. The nineteenth-century Luddites, smashing weaving looms in England, were as programmed to a fixed pattern as the machines they attacked.

Asimov's cybernetic fiction can be divided into three phases. During the first, from 1940 to 1950, he wrote a dozen stories primarily about robots, with only two computer stories. Nine of these stories were collected and published as *I, Robot* in 1950. During his second period, from 1951 to 1961, he wrote another dozen or so stories and the novels *The Caves of Steel* and *The Naked Sun*. Many of the stories and the two novels were collected and published under the title *The Rest of the Robots*. In 1958 he turned from writing SF to writing about science, and not until the mid 1970s did he write more fiction about computers and robots. *The Bicentennial Man* (1976) contains a half dozen stories marking his third period and demonstrates the evolution of his ideas about the key role computers will play in man's future.

THE ASIMOVIAN VIEW AND THE SCIENTIFIC METHOD

The Asimovian view gives a kind of unity to all his fiction about computers and robots, from the first story in 1940 to the last in 1976. This view holds that man will continue to develop more sophisticated technology; he will become more skillful at solving societal and environmental problems; he will expand outward and colonize space. Many of the stories share the same characters and settings. U.S. Robots and Mechanical Men, Inc. builds the first robot in 1998 and the progress of the corporation is guided for many years by Dr. Susan Calvin, "the brilliant roboticist who had, virtually single-handedly built up the positronic robot from a massive toy to man's most delicate and versatile instrument. . . ." The most recent stories are set two hundred years later, Susan has died, and the new roboticist is Mervin Mansky.

The stories are often concerned with the same themes: the political potential of the computer, the uses of computers and robots in space exploration and development, problem solving with computers, the differences between man and machine, the evolution of artificial intelligence, the ethical use of technology. This last theme is explored through Asimov's Three Laws of Robotics, first fully stated in "Runaround," Asimov's fifth robot tale. They appear in many other stories and are crucial to three stories in *The Bicentennial Man*.

Asimov handles machine intelligence both realistically and metaphorically. In stories about computers, technology functions very much like existing technology. Large stationary machines store, process, and retrieve data; do mathematical calculations at incredible speeds; play mathematical games; make logical decisions. Asimov is knowledgeable in the concepts of computer science, and his portrayals are always intelligent and accurate. He has been wise enough to omit specific descriptions of computer technology, and consequently the material does not become dated—something that can easily happen if the writer portrays details of the technology because it is changing so rapidly in the real world. Asimov's robots are much more metaphorical than his computers. In the real world no robots comparable in form to those he pictures have been built, nor is there much possibility that they will be in the near future. Only specialized industrial robots performing limited functions are being developed. The all-purpose robots that Asimov pictures might be possible, but the specialized ones are economically more feasible. It is more meaningful to regard his robots as a metaphor for all the automated electronic technology—in a variety of forms—that will replace most of man's physical and routine mental work in the future.

Asimov rarely uses dramatic conflict to develop his plots; instead he relies almost entirely on puzzle or problem solving to create suspense and to move his plot forward. Through all his fiction runs the theme of faith in the ability of human reason to solve problems. His fiction is cerebral, grounded in sound science and logic. The action is more often mental than physical. In a typical story a problem or puzzle is defined; as much data as possible is collected and evaluated; a hypothesis is formed, providing a basis for a set of predictions about the solution to the problem; finally the predictions are tested. If they are incorrect, the process is reexamined until the difficulty is discovered. This procedure, of course, is the scientific method. The universe for Asimov is more mysterious than threatening. His use of the puzzle paradigm, rather than the conflict paradigm, seems related to his optimistic view of computer and robots. His short story "The Evitable Conflict" reflects his attitude toward conflict. The future world is one in which society has learned to avoid war. In his fiction Asimov also avoids the conflict mode. . . .

ASIMOV'S THREE LAWS OF ROBOTICS

The Three Laws of Robotics have attracted more attention than any other aspect of Asimov's cybernetic SF. In SF religious tales are rare. So are stories debating the niceties of various moral codes. SF has traditionally based itself on the natural and social sciences, which aim to be analytic not normative. Certainly no writer grounds his fiction more solidly in science than Asimov, yet he has formulated an ethical code now famous in and out of SF. . . . Even Asimov himself expresses amazement at the wide influence of those Three Laws. "It is rather odd to think that in centuries to come, I may be remembered (if I am remembered at all) only for having laid the conceptual groundwork for a science which in my own time was nonexistent." The laws are as follows:

1. A robot may not injure a human being nor, through inaction, allow a human being to come to harm.

2. A robot must obey the orders given it by human beings except where such orders would conflict with the First Law.

3. A robot must protect its own existence as long as such protection does not conflict with the First or Second Law.

The Three Laws are an important element in at least a dozen stories. Asimov explains that "there was just enough ambiguity in the Three Laws to provide the conflicts and uncertainties required for new stories, and to my great relief, it seemed always to be possible to think up a new angle out of the sixty-one words of The Three Laws." In "Robbie" (1940) the First Law apparently served no purpose other than to assure man that a robot was harmless. . . .

ASIMOV'S ROBOTS EVOLVE IN HIS LATER WORK

Asimov's imagination constantly spirals forward into new possibilities. Robbie, his first robot, was a giant toy programmed to entertain and protect a child. Later his robots labored in space. In his most recent writing robots acquire characteristics previously ascribed only to humans—characteristics like creativity and the capacity to make judgments. Finally the complexity of the robots leads Asimov in *The Bicentennial Man* to suggest that ethical considerations concerning man may need to be extended to include machine intelligence.

Several of the short stories in *The Bicentennial Man* pair with earlier fiction; comparison shows how Asimov's thinking has evolved over the last thirty-five years. "Evidence" (1946) considered whether a robot might not be as efficient a mayor as a human. In "Tercentary Incident" (1976) a robot serves as president of the United States. In both instances the general public is unaware of the substitution of machine for man but enjoys the benefits that result from more efficient government.

Another pair of stories pictures a world governance structure operated by computer. In the early story, "The Evitable Conflict," the world economy has been stabilized, underemployment and overproduction have been eliminated, and famine and war have disappeared. The recent "Life and Times of Multivac" also pictures a world system operated by computer, but the details of the process are more specific. Multivac is "a global presence knit together by wire, optical fiber, and microwave. It had a brain divided into a hundred subsidiaries but acting as one. It had its outlets everywhere and no human being . . . was far from one." Robots perform all necessary work, and mankind has an abundance of leisure time. But human nature, ever perverse, is unhappy in its peace, leisure, and economic abundance. The majority feel that their freedom has been confiscated and that they are being forced to live in slavery under the rule of Multivac. The protagonist of the story, listening to the pleas of the majority, devises and carries out a plan that irreversibly shuts down the computer system. Then he and his fellow men face one another in solemn shock at what they have done: traded peace and security for freedom.

In "The Life and Times of Multivac," as in all his other stories, Asimov has a comprehensive grasp of the issues raised by the development of artificial intelligence. Machine systems can remove the drudgery of work; they can be used in planning and decision making; they can store and process vast amounts of information, thus augmenting man's mental power. But these benefits have a cost. Man must replace his image of himself as a rugged individualist free to do as he wills with an image of himself as a systems man living in symbiosis with his machines. In *The Caves of Steel* Asimov calls this supportive relationship a C/Fe culture: carbon (C) is the basis of human life and iron (Fe) of robot life. A C/Fe culture results from a combination of the best of the two forms.

In the stories of the third period artificial intelligence has evolved substantially beyond its level in the earlier works. The goal of the computer scientists in "Feminine Intuition" (1969) is to develop a creative robot. The principle of uncertainty, explains Research Director Bogert, "is important in particles the mass of positrons." If this unpredictability of minute particles can be utilized in the robot design, it might be possible to have a creative robot. "If there's anything a human brain has that a robotic brain has never had, it's the trace of unpredictability that comes from the effects of uncertainty at the subatomic level . . . this effect has never been demonstrated experimentally within the nervous system, but without that the human brain is not superior to the robotic brain in principle." If the uncertainty effect can be introduced into the robot brain, it will share the creativity of the human brain. The research is successful, and U.S. Robots produces the first successful design of creativity in artificial intelligence.

"Stranger in Paradise" (1974) describes another aspect of the evolutionary process augmenting the capability of artificial intelligence. A robot, designed for use on Mercury, is operated via radio control by an Earth-based computer as complex as a human brain. The robot results from the collaborative research of a specialist in the human brain and a specialist in computer science. When the robot lands on Mercury, he capers in joy at reaching the paradise for which he was designed. Here is a new form of intelligence rejoicing in the environment of outer space so inimical to man's survival. Asimov suggests that the machine form may be ideal for housing intelligence as it journeys among the stars.

"That Thou Art Mindful of Him" (1974) pictures the development of the positronic brain with the capacity for judgment. Judgment is developed in the robot because it is required to cope with conflicting orders from two humans. The Second Law says he must obey—but which order? The answer is that he must obey the human most fit by mind, character, and knowledge to give that order. However, once the capacity for judgment is designed into the robots, they begin to use it in unanticipated ways. The robot George Nine decides he will "disregard shape and form in judging human beings, and . . . rise superior to the distinction between metal and flesh." He concludes, after exercising his judgment, that his fellow robots are like humans, except more fit. Therefore they ought to dominate humans. The possibility that machine intelligence may be both superior to human intelligence and likely to dominate human intelligence appears for the first time in this story. Asimov's robots have now evolved a long way from that first clumsy Robbie in 1940.

THE POWER OF "THE BICENTENNIAL MAN"

The last design for the evolution of artificial intelligence appears in "The Bicentennial Man" (1976). Here pure intelligence, irrespective of carbon or metal form, appears. This story, awarded both the Hugo and Nebula awards in 1977, is Asimov's finest fictional work. . . . Told in twenty-three episodes, it covers two hundred years in the life of the robot Andrew Martin. Asimov's approach to the puzzle of intelligence, human or machine, gives the story its power. Inverting the obvious approach—man examining artificial intelligence—he has Andrew explore the nature and implications of human intelligence. As the story opens, Andrew is an obedient household servant for the Martin family, much the role of Asimov's early Robbie. But Andrew is a mutant robot form with an unusual talent: he is creative. He produces exquisite wood carvings. Just as he has transcended the patterns of previous robots, so he aspires to transcend the limits of the role they occupied in society. He desires to be free, not a slave to man, but this seems a clear violation of the Second Law.

Andrew's struggle to evolve beyond his programmed obedience is dramatized with great economy. The Martin family represents the small group of humans who realize the potential of artificial intelligence and take actions to foster and expand it. The U.S. Robots Corporation symbolizes the economic system supported by the mass of men who wish only to exploit robot technology for profit. They feel no ethical responsibility to this emerging form of intelligence.

After a long struggle the courts declare Andrew free. Then, bit by bit over the ensuing years, Andrew moves toward fulfilling his aspiration to become like his masters. His potential, his determination, and the support of a few dedicated individuals yield slow progress. . . .

Andrew is not alone in his learning activities. The research of man into artificial intelligence and sophisticated mechanical devices continues. The science of prothestology develops rapidly and becomes increasingly skillful at replacing human parts—kidney, heart, hands—with mechanical parts. Andrew draws on this new technological expertise to have his positronic brain transplanted into an android body.

With Andrew's increasing intelligence comes increasing awareness of the price he pays for approaching humanity. Complexity yields ambiguity. The moral simplicity of his early life when he was an obedient servant is gone. To achieve what he has, he had to ask others to lie for him. He resorted to pressure and blackmail. But given his aspirations to become a man, he is willing to pay the price. Because his robot intelligence is never muddied by emotions, he can reason clearly and with utmost logic. He finally sees that he cannot be declared a man as he had hoped, despite his freedom, intelligence, and organic body, because his brain is different. The World Court has declared a criterion for determining what is human. "Human beings have an organic cellular brain and robots have a platinum-iridium positronic brain. . . ." Andrew is at an impasse. His brain is man-made;

the human brain is not. His brain is constructed; man's brain is developed.

Finally Andrew pushes the implications of this statement to its ultimate meaning. The greatest difference between robot and man is the matter of immortality. He reasons, "Who really cares what a brain looks like or is built of or how it was formed? What matters is that brain cells die; *must* die. Even if every other organ in the body is maintained or replaced, the brain cells, which cannot be replaced without changing and therefore killing the personality, must eventually die." He realizes that the price of being human is to sacrifice his immortality. In the final moving episode of the story he submits to surgery that rearranges the connection between organic nerves and positronic brain in such a way that he will slowly die. When he performs this ultimate act of sacrifice, the court at last declares him a man.

"The Bicentennial Man" is a powerful, profound story for several reasons. Foremost is what Asimov leaves unsaid. The story follows the movement of mechanical intelligence toward human intelligence and death. But Andrew's progress toward manhood and death unfolds against man's development of technology and movement toward artificial intelligence and immortality. Knowledge or information eventually dies in the organic brain, but it can survive indefinitely in a mechanical brain. Thus the inorganic form may well be the most likely form for the survival of intelligence in the universe. As machine intelligence evolves to human form, human intelligence is evolving toward machine form. A second implication of "The Bicentennial Man," again unstated, is that a line between the animate and the inanimate, the organic and the inorganic, cannot be drawn. If the fundamental materials of the universe are matter, energy, and information patterns (or intelligence), then man is not unique. He exists on a continuum with all intelligence; he is no more than the most highly evolved form on earth. This view implies that ethical behavior should extend to all systems because any organizational pattern—human or nonhuman, organic or inorganic—represents intelligence. A sacred view of the universe, the result not of religious mysticism but of pure logic, emerges from this reading of "The Bicentennial Man."

The Nature of Reality

Philip K. Dick

Philip K. Dick (1928–1982), a prolific writer, is the author of *Do Androids Dream of Electric Sheep?* (upon which the film *Blade Runner* is based), *The Man in the High Castle* (a Hugo Award winner), and *Flow My Tears, the Policeman Said* (winner of the John W. Campbell Memorial Award), as well as many other mind-bending tales. Now receiving much critical attention from scholars, he is seen as one of science fiction's greatest visionaries, and not only in an artistic sense, for Dick actually believed himself the recipient of mystic revelation. In his work he is obsessed with the themes of the nature of reality, and, by extension, what it means to be human. In this excerpt from a speech he delivered at a science fiction conference, Dick discusses his favorite themes in depth, giving some insight into philosophical concepts of the construction of reality, including the notion of a delusional, false existence. Dick relates these themes to the writing of science fiction, which he believes is one of the many mediums through which reality can be manipulated.

Science fiction writers, I am sorry to say, really do not know anything. We can't talk about science, because our knowledge of it is limited and unofficial, and usually our fiction is dreadful. A few years ago, no college or university would ever have considered inviting one of us to speak. We were mercifully confined to lurid pulp magazines, impressing no one. In those days, friends would say to me, "But are you writing anything serious?" meaning "Are you writing anything other than science fiction?" We longed to be accepted. We yearned to be noticed. Then, suddenly, the academic world noticed us, we were invited to give speeches and ap-

From "Introduction: How to Build a Universe That Doesn't Fall Apart Two Days Later," by Philip K. Dick, in *I Hope I Shall Arrive Soon*, by Philip K. Dick, edited by Mark Hurst and Paul Williams (Garden City, NY: Doubleday, 1985). Copyright © 1985 by the Estate of Philip K. Dick. Reprinted by permission of Scovil, Chichak, and Galen Literary Agency on behalf of the author's estate.

pear on panels—and immediately we made idiots of ourselves. The problem is simply this: What does a science fiction writer know about? On what topic is he an authority?

It reminds me of a headline that appeared in a California
newspaper just before I flew here. SCIENTISTS SAY THAT MICE
CANNOT BE MADE TO LOOK LIKE HUMAN BEINGS. It was a feder-
ally funded research program, I suppose. Just think: Someone in this world is an authority on the topic of whether
mice can or cannot put on two-tone shoes, derby hats, pin-
striped shirts, and Dacron pants, and pass as humans.

Well, I will tell you what interests me, what I consider important. I can't claim to be an authority on anything, but I
can honestly say that certain matters absolutely fascinate
me, and that I write about them all the time. The two basic
topics which fascinate me are "What is reality?" and "What
constitutes the authentic human being?" Over the twenty-
seven years in which I have published novels and stories I
have investigated these two interrelated topics over and over
again. I consider them important topics. What are we? What
is it which surrounds us, that we call the not-me, or the em-
pirical or phenomenal world?

In 1951, when I sold my first story, I had no idea that such
fundamental issues could be pursued in the science fiction
field. I began to pursue them unconsciously. My first story
had to do with a dog who imagined that the garbagemen
who came every Friday morning were stealing valuable food
which the family had carefully stored away in a safe metal
container. Every day, members of the family carried out paper sacks of nice ripe food, stuffed them into the metal container, shut the lid tightly—and when the container was full,
these dreadful-looking creatures came and stole everything
but the can.

Finally, in the story, the dog begins to imagine that someday the garbagemen will eat the people in the house, as well
as stealing their food. Of course, the dog is wrong about this.
We all know that garbagemen do not eat people. But the
dog's extrapolation was in a sense logical—given the facts at
his disposal. The story was about a real dog, and I used to
watch him and try to get inside his head and imagine how
he saw the world. Certainly, I decided, that dog sees the
world quite differently than I do, or *any* humans do. And
then I began to think, Maybe each human being lives in a
unique world, a private world, a world different from those

inhabited and experienced by all other humans. And that led me to wonder, If reality differs from person to person, can we speak of reality singular, or shouldn't we really be talking about plural realities? And if there are plural realities, are some more true (more real) than others? What about the world of a schizophrenic? Maybe it's as real as our world. Maybe we cannot say that we are in touch with reality and he is not, but should instead say, His reality is so different from ours that he can't explain his to us, and we can't explain ours to him. The problem, then, is that if subjective worlds are experienced too differently, there occurs a breakdown of communication . . . and *there* is the real illness.

I once wrote a story about a man who was injured and taken to a hospital. When they began surgery on him, they discovered that he was an android, not a human, but that he did not know it. They had to break the news to him. Almost at once, Mr. Garson Poole discovered that his reality consisted of punched tape passing from reel to reel in his chest. Fascinated, he began to fill in some of the punched holes and add new ones. Immediately, his world changed. A flock of ducks flew through the room when he punched one new hole in the tape. Finally he cut the tape entirely, whereupon the world disappeared. However, it also disappeared for the other characters in the story . . . which makes no sense, if you think about it. Unless the other characters were figments of his punched-tape fantasy. Which I guess is what they were.

WHAT IS REALITY?

It was always my hope, in writing novels and stories which asked the question "What is reality?", to someday get an answer. This was the hope of most of my readers, too. Years passed. I wrote over thirty novels and over a hundred stories, and still I could not figure out what was real. One day a girl college student in Canada asked me to define reality for her, for a paper she was writing for her philosophy class. She wanted a one-sentence answer. I thought about it and finally said, "Reality is that which, when you stop believing in it, doesn't go away." That's all I could come up with. That was back in 1972. Since then I haven't been able to define reality any more lucidly.

But the problem is a real one, not a mere intellectual game. Because today we live in a society in which spurious realities are manufactured by the media, by governments, by big corporations, by religious groups, political groups—and the electronic hardware exists by which to deliver these pseudo-worlds right into the heads of the reader, the viewer, the listener. Sometimes when I watch my eleven-year-old daughter watch TV, I wonder what she is being taught. The problem of miscuing; consider that. A TV program produced for adults is viewed by a small child. Half of what is said and done in the TV drama is probably misunderstood by the child. Maybe it's *all* misunderstood. And the thing is, Just how authentic is the information anyhow, even if the child correctly understood it? What is the relationship between the average TV situation comedy to reality? What about the cop shows? Cars are continually swerving out of control, crashing, and catching fire. The police are always good and they always win. Do not ignore that one point: The police always win. What a lesson that is. You should not fight authority, and even if you do, you will lose. The message here is, *Be passive.* And—cooperate. If Officer Baretta asks you for information, give it to him, *because Officer Baretta is a good man and to be trusted. He loves you, and you should love him.*

So I ask, in my writing, What is real? Because unceasingly we are bombarded with pseudo-realities manufactured by very sophisticated people using very sophisticated electronic mechanisms. I do not distrust their motives; I distrust their power. They have a lot of it. And it is an astonishing power: that of creating whole universes, universes of the mind. I ought to know. I do the same thing. It is my job to create universes, as the basis of one novel after another. And I have to build them in such a way that they do not fall apart two days later. Or at least that is what my editors hope. However, I will reveal a secret to you: I like to build universes which *do* fall apart. I like to see them come unglued, and I like to see how the characters in the novels cope with this problem. I have a secret love of chaos. There should be more of it. Do not believe—and I am dead serious when I say this—do not assume that order and stability are always good, in a society or in a universe. The old, the ossified, must always give way to new life and the birth of new things. Before the new things can be born the old must perish. This is a dangerous realization, because it tells us that we must eventually part with much of what is familiar to us. And that hurts. But that is part of the script of life. Unless we can psychologically accommodate change, we ourselves will begin to die, inwardly. What I am saying is that objects, customs, habits, and ways of life must perish so that the authentic human being can live. And it is the authentic human being who matters most, the viable, elastic organism which can bounce back, absorb, and deal with the new.

Of course, *I* would say this, because I live near Disneyland, and they are always adding new rides and destroying old ones. Disneyland is an evolving organism. For years they had the Lincoln Simulacrum and finally it began to die and they had to regretfully retire it. The simulacrum, like Lincoln himself, was only a temporary form which matter and energy take and then lose. The same is true of each of us, like it or not.

The pre-Socratic Greek philosopher Parmenides taught that the only things that are real are things which never change . . . and the pre-Socratic Greek philosopher Heraclitus taught that everything changes. If you superimpose their two views, you get this result: Nothing is real. There is a fascinating next step to this line of thinking: Parmenides could never have existed because he grew old and died and disappeared, so, according to his own philosophy, he did not exist. And Heraclitus may have been right—let's not forget that; so if Heraclitus was right, then Parmenides did exist, and therefore, according to Heraclitus' philosophy, perhaps Parmenides was right, since Parmenides fulfilled the conditions, the criteria, by which Heraclitus judged things real.

I offer this merely to show that as soon as you begin to ask what is ultimately real, you right away begin to talk nonsense. By the time of Zeno, they knew they were talking nonsense. Zeno proved that motion was impossible (actually he only imagined that he had proved this; what he lacked was what technically is called the "theory of limits"). David Hume, the greatest skeptic of them all, once remarked that after a gathering of skeptics met to proclaim the veracity of skepticism as a philosophy, all of the members of the gathering nonetheless left by the door rather than the window. I see Hume's point. It was all just talk. The solemn philosophers weren't taking what they said seriously.

FAKE REALITIES AND WORLDS OF ILLUSION

But I consider that the matter of defining what is real—that is a serious topic, even a vital topic. And in there somewhere is the other topic, the definition of the authentic human. Because the bombardment of pseudo-realities begins to produce inauthentic humans very quickly, spurious humans—as fake as the data pressing at them from all sides. My two topics are really one topic; they unite at this point. Fake realities will create fake humans. Or, fake humans will generate fake realities and then sell them to other humans, turning them, eventually, into forgeries of themselves. So we wind up with fake humans inventing fake realities and then peddling them to other fake humans. It is just a very large version of Disneyland. You can have the Pirate Ride or the Lincoln Simulacrum or Mr. Toad's Wild Ride—you can have *all* of them, but none is true.

In my writing I got so interested in fakes that I finally came up with the concept of fake fakes. For example, in Disneyland there are fake birds worked by electric motors which emit caws and shrieks as you pass by them. Suppose some night all of us sneaked into the park with real birds and substituted them for the artificial ones. Imagine the horror the Disneyland officials would feel when they discovered the cruel hoax. Real birds! And perhaps someday even real hippos and lions. Consternation. The park being cunningly transmuted from the unreal to the real, by sinister forces. For instance, suppose the Matterhorn turned into a genuine snow-covered mountain? What if the entire place, by a miracle of God's power and wisdom, was changed, in a moment, in the blink of an eye, into something incorruptible? They would have to close down.

In Plato's *Timaeus,* God does not create the universe, as does the Christian God; He simply finds it one day. It is in a state of total chaos. God sets to work to transform the chaos into order. That idea appeals to me, and I have adapted it to fit my own intellectual needs: What if our universe started out as not quite real, a sort of illusion, as the Hindu religion teaches, and God, out of love and kindness for us, is slowly transmuting it, slowly *and secretly,* into something real?

We would not be aware of this transformation, since we were not aware that our world was an illusion in the first place. This technically is a Gnostic idea. Gnosticism is a religion which embraced Jews, Christians, and pagans for several centuries. I have been accused of holding Gnostic ideas. I guess I do. At one time I would have been burned. But some of their ideas intrigue me. One time, when I was researching

Gnosticism in the *Britannica*, I came across mention of a Gnostic codex called *The Unreal God and the Aspects of His Nonexistent Universe*, an idea which reduced me to helpless laughter. What kind of person would write about something that he knows doesn't exist, and how can something that doesn't exist have aspects? But then I realized that I'd been writing about these matters for over twenty-five years. I guess there is a lot of latitude in what you can say when writing about a topic that does not exist. A friend of mine once published a book called *Snakes of Hawaii*. A number of libraries wrote him ordering copies. Well, there are no snakes in Hawaii. All the pages of his book were blank.

Is Science Fiction True?

Of course, in science fiction no pretense is made that the worlds described are real. This is why we call it fiction. The reader is warned in advance not to believe what he is about to read. Equally true, the visitors to Disneyland understand that Mr. Toad does not really exist and that the pirates are animated by motors and servo-assist mechanisms, relays and electronic circuits. So no deception is taking place.

And yet the strange thing is, in some way, some real way, much of what appears under the title "science fiction" is true. It may not be literally true, I suppose. We have not really been invaded by creatures from another star system, as depicted in *Close Encounters of the Third Kind*. The producers of that film never intended for us to believe it. Or did they?

And, more important, if they did intend to state this, is it actually true? That is the issue: not, Does the author or producer believe it, but—Is it true? Because, quite by accident, in the pursuit of a good yarn, a science fiction author or producer or scriptwriter might stumble onto the truth . . . and only later on realize it.

The Manipulation of Reality

The basic tool for the manipulation of reality is the manipulation of words. If you can control the meaning of words, you can control the people who must use the words. George Orwell made this clear in his novel *1984*. But another way to control the minds of people is to control their perceptions. If you can get them to see the world as you do, they will think as you do. Comprehension follows perception. How do you

get them to see the reality you see? After all, it is only one reality out of many. Images are a basic constituent: pictures.
This is why the power of TV to influence young minds is so
staggeringly vast. Words and pictures are synchronized. The
possibility of total control of the viewer exists, especially the
young viewer. TV viewing is a kind of sleep-learning. An
EEG of a person watching TV shows that after about half an
hour the brain decides that nothing is happening, and it goes
into a hypnoidal twilight state, emitting alpha waves. This is
because there is such little eye motion. In addition, much of
the information is graphic and therefore passes into the
right hemisphere of the brain, rather than being processed
by the left, where the conscious personality is located. Recent experiments indicate that much of what we see on the
TV screen is received on a subliminal basis. We only imagine that we consciously see what is there. The bulk of the
messages elude our attention; literally, after a few hours of
TV watching, we do not know what we have seen. Our memories are spurious, like our memories of dreams; the blank
spaces are filled in retrospectively. And falsified. We have
participated unknowingly in the creation of a spurious reality, and then we have obligingly fed it to ourselves. We have
colluded in our own doom.

And—and I say this as a professional fiction writer—the
producers, scriptwriters, and directors who create these
video/audio worlds do not know how much of their content
is true. In other words, they are victims of their own product, along with us. Speaking for myself, I do not know how
much of my writing is true, or *which* parts (if any) are true.
This is a potentially lethal situation. We have fiction mimicking truth, and truth mimicking fiction. We have a dangerous overlap, a dangerous blur. And in all probability it is not
deliberate. In fact, that is part of the problem. You cannot
legislate an author into correctly labeling his product, like a
can of pudding whose ingredients are listed on the label . . .
you cannot compel him to declare what part is true and
what isn't if he himself does not know.

It is an eerie experience to write something into a novel,
believing it is pure fiction, and to learn later on—perhaps
years later—that it is true.

CHAPTER 5

Assessing Science Fiction

Science Fiction

An Un-Credible Genre

Michel Butor

To the French novelist Michel Butor, science fiction
is a literature that explores what is possible according to the principles of science. With this specific definition in mind, Butor questions the credibility of
the genre; he criticizes the writers for what he believes is only the displacement of the mundane real
world onto alien settings and forms. Butor believes
that all too often science fiction visions of the future
are merely projections of the present. Furthermore,
he contends that the genre is weakened by the frag-
mentary visions of individual writers. As a remedy,
Butor prescribes that the genre should be ap-
proached as a collective dream; once artists are unified in a single vision, the genre will be able to rise
above its present flaws.

If the genre Science Fiction is rather difficult to define—
disputes among the experts afford superabundant proof of
that—it is, at least, one of the easiest to designate. It is
enough to say: "You know, those stories that are always
mentioning interplanetary rockets," for the least-prepared
interlocutor to understand immediately what you mean.
This does not imply that any such apparatus occurs in
every SF story; it may be replaced by other accessories
which will perform a comparable role. But it is the most
usual, the typical example, like the magic wand in fairy
tales.

Two remarks are immediately relevant:

1. There exists for the moment no interplanetary rocket.
If there ever has been one, or there is one now, the ordinary
reader knows nothing about it. A narrative in which a device
of this kind occurs is therefore a narrative of fantasy.

2. But we all believe quite firmly that such devices will
soon exist, that the question is no more than one of time—a

Excerpted from *The Crisis in the Growth of Science Fiction*, by Michel Butor, translated
by Richard Howard. Copyright © 1967 by Michel Butor. Originally published in French
in *Repertoire*. Copyright © 1960 by Les Éditions de Minuit. Reprinted with permission
from Georges Borchardt on behalf of Editions de Minuit.

few years of development. The apparatus is possible. This notion is fundamental, and requires some explanation.

It might be claimed that for the Arab storytellers, who believed in the power of magicians, flying carpets were also "possible." But for most of us, the possibility of rockets is of an altogether different order. It is guaranteed by what we might call, by and large, *modern science,* a sum of doctrines whose validity no serious Occidental dares to question.

If the author of a narrative has taken the trouble to introduce such a device, it is because he chooses to depart from reality only to a certain degree, he wants to prolong, to extend reality, but not to be separated from it. He wants to give us an impression of realism, he wants to insert the imaginary into the real, anticipating results already achieved. Such a narrative naturally situates its action in the future.

We can imagine, taking modern science in its broadest acceptation, not only other devices, but technologies of all kinds—psychological, pedagogical, social, etc. . . . This scientific guarantee may become increasingly loose, but it nonetheless constitutes the definable specificity of SF: a literature which explores the range of the possible, as science permits us to envision it.

It is, then, a fantasy framed by a realism.

The work of Jules Verne is the best example of SF to the first degree, which is justified by the results achieved and which uniquely anticipates certain applications. Wells inaugurates a SF to the second degree, much more audacious but much less convincing, which anticipates the results themselves. He lets us assume behind Cavor's machine, which will take the first men to the moon, an explanation of a scientific type, one that conforms to a *possible* science which will develop from the science of his time.

THE SPECTACLES OF SCIENCE FICTION

The SF tourist agencies offer their customers three main types of spectacles which we can group under the following rubrics: life in the future, unknown worlds, unexpected visitors.

1) Life in the Future

We start from the world as we know it, from the society which surrounds us. We introduce a certain number of changes whose consequences we attempt to foresee. By a projection into the future, we open up the complexity of the present, we develop certain still larval aspects. SF of this type is a remarkable instrument of investigation in the tradition of Swift. It readily assumes a satiric aspect. We shall find excellent examples in the works of Huxley (*Brave New World*), Orwell (*1984*), Werfel (*Star of the Unborn*), Hesse (*Magister Ludi*), Bradbury, etc.

2) Unknown Worlds

It suffices to mention the name Ray Bradbury, whose best-known work is called *The Martian Chronicles*, to see that an altogether different element occurs here, almost of necessity.

Technological progress has for its goal not only the transformation of our daily life, but also the satisfaction of our curiosity. The new instruments, the new sciences must allow us to discover domains of reality which are hidden from us today. Within the scientific representation of the world, there are enormous districts which our imagination is free to populate with strange beings and landscapes according to its whim, subject to several very broad restrictions. Here we can project our dreams.

This aspect of SF links up with a very respectable tradition. Dante, when he locates his inferno inside the globe, his purgatory at the antipodes and his paradise in the stars, is merely projecting his theology, and a good deal more, into the empty spaces which medieval cosmology reserved.

Thus Verne scrupulously inventoried the lacunae [gap] of the geography of his age and filled them with myths inscribed within the extension of the known facts, achieving a synthesis which strikes us as naive but which by its breadth and harmony outstrips anything his successors have attempted.

When an author of the eighteenth century wanted to give his story some appearance of reality, he had a ready-made site in which to locate it: the islands of the Pacific. (*Cf.* Diderot: *Supplement to Bougainville's Voyage.*) Today, when the exploration of the earth's surface is quite advanced, we prefer to locate our islands in the sky. But if we once knew nothing, of course, of the archipelagos which had not yet been discovered, we were at least quite sure that apart from certain remarkable peculiarities they could not be very different from those we knew already. We were still on the same Earth, with the same general conditions.

On the contrary, the little we know today about the islands in the sky proves to us that everything must be very different there. We know that gravity is more powerful on Venus, less powerful on Mars, than on Earth, etc. These several elements oblige the writer who respects them to make an enormous effort of imagination, force him to invent something truly new. Unfortunately, the creation of another "nature," even when based on elementary information, is a task so arduous that no author, so far, has undertaken it methodically.

In order not to acknowledge ourselves vanquished, we raise our sights: instead of describing what might happen on Mars and Venus, we leap at once to the third planet of the *Epsilon* system of the Swan, or else, since in fact there is nothing to stop us once we have started on this path, planet *n* of star *n* in galaxy *n*. At first the reader is impressed by these cascades of light years; the solar system was certainly a wretched little village, here we are launched into the universe *at large*. But he soon realizes that these ultra-remote planets resemble the earth much more than they do its neighbors. Out of the immense number of stars which populate space, it is always permissible to imagine one on which the conditions of life are very close to those we know. The authors have rediscovered the islands of the eighteenth century. They employ a vaguely scientific jargon and decorate the sky with charming fantasies; the trick is turned.

This infinite freedom is a false freedom. If we flee infinitely far into space or time, we shall find ourselves in a region where everything is possible, where the imagination will no longer even need to make an effort of coordination. The result will be an impoverished duplication of everyday reality. We are told of an enormous war between galactic civilizations, but we see at once that the league of the democratic planets strangely resembles the UN, the empire of the nebula Andromeda stands for the Soviet Union as a subscriber to *Reader's Digest* might conceive that nation, and so on. The author has merely translated into SF language a newspaper article he read the night before. Had he remained on Mars, he would have been obliged to invent something.

At its best moments, the SF that describes unknown worlds becomes an instrument of an extreme flexibility, thanks to which all kinds of political and moral fables, of fairy tales, of myths, can be transposed and adapted to modern readers. Anticipation has created a language by whose aid we can in principle examine everything.

3) Unexpected Visitors

The description of unknown worlds, in SF, necessarily becomes part of our anticipation, however rudimentary it may be; it is natural that it should affect that anticipation. It is not so much by the improvement of commercial relations that the invention of the compass transformed the Old World, but by the discovery of America. The description of unknown worlds and beings involves the description of their intervention in the future history of humanity.

We can easily imagine that the inhabitants of other planets have a civilization in advance of our own, hence that they have a realm of action superior to our own, that they are ahead of us in discovery.

All of space becomes threatening; strange beings may intervene even before we know of their existence. Most of the pre-Columbians had no expectation that a deadly invasion would come out of the East.

It is in Wells's *War of the Worlds* that we encounter this theme for the first time, and his countless imitators have not added much to it. It is a profoundly modern theme (it never occurred to anyone in the sixteenth century that Europe might be discovered in its turn) and an extremely powerful one (as several memorable radio broadcasts have demonstrated).

Thanks to this notion of intervention, SF can assimilate those aspects of the fantastic which at first seem most opposed to it: all that we might classify under the heading: "Superstitions."

In the *Divine Comedy*, Beatrice transports Dante from planet to planet; in Father Kircher's *Iter Extaticum*, an angel does the job; we are not yet in SF, which implies that the journey is made as a result of techniques developed by man. But these techniques will allow us to enter into contact with beings to whom we can attribute knowledge we do not possess, techniques we do not understand. It might, of course, occur to one of them to come to Earth, to carry off one of *us* and transport him elsewhere by means which there is no longer any need to explain. The difference between such a being and

Kircher's angel becomes infinitesimal; only the language has changed. As a matter of fact, it is necessary today, in order to gain a sufficient suspension of disbelief, that the being be described in the same way as a being that man might have discovered on another planet. Thus we could unite within SF all the narratives of phantoms and demons, all the old myths dealing with superior beings which intervene in the life of men. Certain tales by H.P. Lovecraft illustrate this possibility.

C.S. Lewis begins his curious antimodern trilogy with a novel which has all of SF's characteristics: *Out of the Silent*

AN UNFAIR JUDGMENT

In this excerpt, science fiction writer and critic James Blish responds directly to what he believes to be Michel Butor's unfounded and outrageous critique of the genre.

Michel Butor's "Science Fiction: The Crisis of its Growth" (*Partisan Review*, Fall 1967) has two serious deficiencies: it gives a completely misleading impression of the present state of the genre, and it proposes a future course for it which would destroy everyone's interest in either writing or reading it.

For some reason, most critics who undertake to discuss science fiction for a literary but non-specialised audience do so from a limited and largely antiquarian knowledge of the field, heavily weighted toward Jules Verne (d. 1905). That this is true of M. Butor may be seen in the fact that he mentions no living science-fiction author but Ray Bradbury. . . .

Clothing quite ordinary Earth settings (and, it might be added, plots) in a few futuristic trappings is a common failing of routine commercial science fiction. M. Butor stresses this point, but omits the two key words: "routine commercial." As specialists in the field are bitterly aware, no other genre in literary history has been so consistently judged by its worst examples. This observation, too, was made some years ago by [Theodore] Sturgeon, who went on to note that non-specialist critics seem to take a positive delight in pointing out that ninety per cent of all science fiction is worthless—without pausing to reflect that there is *no* field of human endeavor which is immune to exactly the same stricture.

If a field is to be considered worthy of critical examination for an audience of non-specialists, the critic owes it to that audience to weigh the field's achievements as well as its failures. If its failures are vastly more numerous, why should we

Planet. Two wicked scientists transport a young philologist to Mars by means of a spaceship furnished with every modern convenience. In the second volume, *Perelandra,* the author drops his mask: it is an angel who transports the philologist to Venus; as for the scientists, they are Satan's henchmen.

THE DOUBTFUL CREDIBILITY OF THE GENRE

We see that all kinds of merchandise can be sold under the label SF; and that all kinds of merchandise seek to be pack-

---

be surprised—or, worse, gratified? Good work in any field is always scarce; why otherwise do we prize it at all? . . .

From his gallery of dead authors M. Butor proceeds to derive a prescription of his own for science fiction: "It must become a collective work, like the science which is its indispensable basis." . . .

The prescription would freeze the very worst elements of routine commercial science fiction—its paucity of imagination and its tendency to conventionalise the future—into a set of dogmas much like thirteenth century canon law. At best it would limit the scientific or technological substrate of all science fiction to whatever some appointed tenth-rate engineer deemed "possible" at the time of writing (as all of Verne's stories were limited, though apparently M. Butor doesn't know this); no room would be left in which to extrapolate from the known to the unrealised possibilities, in the sciences alone, although science itself is today in a ferment of speculation utterly unlike the body of dogma M. Butor imagines it to be. (In fact M. Butor knows nothing about science either, as his remarks on gravity, his vagueness over what is meant by a "galaxy," and his failure to differentiate between science and technology make painfully evident.)

Secondly, such an agreed-upon or dictated city (or universe) would preclude the individual human speculation upon the future which is the life blood of the *fiction* part of science fiction. Let us not forget that it is above all else a branch of fiction that we are talking about here, not a body of myth, or an attempt at a self-fulfilling prophecy like *Das Kapital.*

James Blish, "On Science Fiction Criticism," *SF: The Other Side of Realism.* Bowling Green, OH: Bowling Green State University Popular Press, 1971.

aged under this label. Hence it seems that SF represents the normal form of mythology in our time: a form which is not only capable of revealing profoundly new themes, but capable of integrating all the themes of the old literature.

Despite several splendid successes, we cannot help thinking that SF is keeping very few of its promises.

This is because SF, by extending itself, is denaturing itself; it is gradually losing its specificity. It furnishes a very particular element of credibility; this element is increasingly weakened when it is utilized without discernment. SF is fragile, and the enormous circulation it has achieved in recent years merely renders it more so.

We have already noted that the flight to ultra-distant planets and epochs, which seems at first glance a conquest, actually masks the authors' incapacity to imagine in a coherent fashion, in conformity with the requirements of "science," the planets or the epochs which are closer at hand. Similarly the divination of a future science affords, surely, a great freedom, but we soon discover that it is above all a revenge of the authors against their incapacity to master the entire range of contemporary science.

The day is long past when an Aristotle could be the first researcher of his age in every domain, and the day when a Pico could claim to defend a thesis *De Omni Re Scibili;* but the day is almost past when a Verne could easily handle the notions implied in all the technological applications achieved in his age, and anticipate other applications while remaining perfectly clear to the high school students who formed his public.

Today the notions implied in devices as common as a radio set or an atomic bomb exceed by a good deal the average reader's level of scientific culture. He uses without understanding; he accepts without asking explanations; and the author takes advantage of this situation, which frequently causes him to multiply his blunders, for he too generally lacks a sufficient knowledge of the notions he is obliged to use or else seem backward, a grave possibility when one is claiming to reveal the mysteries of two hundred thousand years hence.

As a result SF, which should derive the greatest part of its prestige from its precision, remains vague. The story does not truly manage to *take shape.* And when the scientists themselves begin writing, they quite often prove their igno-

rance of the disciplines unfamiliar to them and their difficulty in vulgarizing their specialty.

SF is distinguished from the other genres of the fantastic
by the special kind of plausibility it introduces. This plausibility is in direct proportion to the solid scientific elements
the author introduces. If they fail, SF becomes a dead form,
a stereotype.

THE FRAGMENTED VISION OF SCIENCE FICTION

Hence we understand why few authors risk specifying the
details of their image of a transformed world. It is an under-
taking, indeed, which supposes not only a scientific culture
far above the average, but also a knowledge of present reality comparable to that supposed by a novel of the realistic
type, and finally an enormous effort of coordination. The author is generally content to evoke a future world "in general," one which might just as well be located in 1975 as in
19750, a world characterized by the widespread use of plastic substances, of television and of atomic-powered rockets.
It is within this setting that he will briefly develop what is often a highly ingenious idea. In another tale, he will use this
same background in order to develop another idea, without
taking the trouble to coordinate them. The result is an infinity of variously sketched futures, all independent of one another and generally contradictory. We shall have, in the
same way, an infinity of Venuses, each of which diminishes
the plausibility of the rest.

This dispersion has monotony as its direct consequence,
for the authors, since they renounce constructing systemati-
cally, can describe only in a rudimentary fashion and depart
only slightly from banality.

It appears that SF has begun with the cake. It had things
too much its own way: it was once enough to mention Martians to enthrall the reader. But the time has come when the
reader will notice that most of these monsters, despite their
crests, their tentacles, their scales, are much less different
from the average American than an ordinary Mexican. SF
has cut the grass under its own feet, has spoiled thousands
of ideas. The doors have been thrown open to start on a great
quest, and we discover we are still walking round and round
the house. If the authors scamp their texts, it is because they
realize that an effort to improve them would lead to an impasse.

The SF narratives derive their power from a great collective dream we are having, but for the moment they are incapable of giving it a unified form. It is a mythology in tatters, impotent, unable to orient our action in any precise way.

SCIENCE FICTION IS A COLLECTIVE DREAM

But the last word has not been said, and it is certainly possible that SF will surmount this crisis in its growth.

It has the power to solicit our belief in an entirely new way, and it is capable of affording, in its description of the possible, a marvelous precision. But to realize its full power, it must undergo a revolution, it must succeed in unifying itself. It must become a collective work, like the science which is its indispensable basis.

We all dream of clean, well-lighted cities, so that when an author situates a narrative in such a place, he is certain of striking a sympathetic note. But we find ourselves, in the present state of SF, facing an enormous choice of barely sketched future cities among which the imagination hesitates, unsatisfied.

Everyone knows Heraclitus' famous fragment: "Those who are awakened are in the same world, but those who sleep are each in a separate world." Our dreamers' worlds are simultaneously without communication and very much like one another. The classical mythologies united the common elements of these dreams into unique and public myths.

Now let us imagine that a certain number of authors, instead of describing at random and quite rapidly certain more or less interchangeable cities, were to take as the setting of their stories a single city, named and situated with some precision in space and in future time; that each author were to take into account the descriptions given by the others in order to introduce his own new ideas. This city would become a common possession to the same degree as an ancient city that has vanished; gradually, all readers would give its name to the city of their dreams and would model that city in its image.

SF, if it could limit and unify itself, would be capable of acquiring over the individual imagination a constraining power comparable to that of any classical mythology. Soon *all* authors would be obliged to take this predicted city into account, readers would organize their actions in relation to its imminent existence, ultimately they would find themselves obliged to build it. Then SF would be veracious, to the very degree that it realized itself.

It is easy to see what a prodigious instrument of liberation or oppression it could become.

Good and Bad Mythmaking

Ursula K. Le Guin

One of science fiction's most important writers, Ursula K. Le Guin is the Hugo and Nebula award-
winning author of many classics, including *The Left
Hand of Darkness, The Dispossessed,* and *The Lathe
of Heaven;* she has also received awards for her fantasy fiction. Among her many accomplishments Le
Guin is noted for her significant contributions in the
field of feminism, and she has devoted much time to
the study of women and science fiction. In this essay,
however, Le Guin contemplates science fiction's relationship to mythology. Criticizing the literary theft
of mythic material in some substandard work, she
appreciates the careful artistic use of living mythologies and collective archetypes by the great science
fiction writers, asserting that they produce true modern mythology. By releasing archetypes from individual minds into the world, science fiction acts as a
bridge between the unconscious and the conscious
realms.

"Science fiction is the mythology of the modern world." It's
a good slogan, and a useful one when you're faced with
people ignorant and contemptuous of science fiction, for it
makes them stop and think. But like all slogans it's a half-
truth, and when used carelessly, as a whole truth, can cause
all kinds of confusion.

Where care must be taken is with that complex word
"mythology." What is a myth?

What Is a Myth?

"Myth is an attempt to explain, in rational terms, facts not yet
rationally understood." That is the definition provided by

Excerpted from, "Myth and Archetype in Science Fiction," by Ursula K. Le Guin, in *The
Language of Night* (New York: HarperCollins, 1989). This article first appeared in
Parabola magazine (1976). Copyright © 1976 by Ursula K. Le Guin. Reprinted with
permission from the author and the author's agents, the Virginia Kidd Agency, Inc.

the reductive, scientistic mentality of the first half of the twentieth century and still accepted by many. According to this definition, the god Apollo "is merely" an inadequate effort made by primitive minds to explain and systematize the nature and behavior of the Sun. As soon as the Sun is rationally understood to be a ball of fire much larger than the Earth, and its behavior has been described by a system of scientific laws, the old mythological pseudoexplanation is left empty. The fiery horses and the golden chariot vanish, the god is dethroned, and his exploits remain only a pretty tale for children. According to this view, the advance of science is a progressive draining dry of the content of mythology. And, in so far as the content of myth is rational and the function of myth is explanatory, this definition is suitable. However, the rational and explanatory is only one function of the myth. Myth is an expression of one of the several ways the human being, body/psyche, perceives, understands and relates to the world. Like science, it is a product of a basic human mode of apprehension. To pretend that it can be replaced by abstract or quantitative cognition is to assert that the human being is, potentially or ideally, a creature of pure reason, a disembodied Mind. It might, indeed, be nice if we were all little bubbles of pure reason floating on the stream of time; but we aren't. We are rational beings, but we are also sensual, emotional, appetitive, ethical beings, driven by needs and reaching out for satisfactions which the intellect alone cannot provide. Where these other modes of being and doing are inadequate, the intellect should prevail. Where the intellect fails, and must always fail, unless we become disembodied bubbles, then one of the other modes must take over. The myth, mythological insight, is one of these. Supremely effective in its area of function, it needs no replacement. Only the schizoid arrogance of modern scientism pretends that it ought to be replaced, and that pretension is pretty easily deflated. For example, does our scientific understanding of the nature and behavior of the Sun explain (let alone explain away) Apollo's remarkable sex life, or his role as the god of music and of the divine harmony? No, it has nothing whatever to do with all that; it has nothing to do with sex, or music, or harmony, or divinity; nor *as science*, did it ever pretend to—only scientism made the claim. Apollo is not the Sun, and never was. The Sun, in fact, "is merely" one of the names of Apollo.

Reductionism cuts both ways, after all.

So long, then, as we don't claim either that the science in science fiction replaces the "old, false" mythologies, or that the fiction in science fiction is a mere attempt to explain what science hasn't yet got around to explaining, we can use the slogan. Science fiction is the mythology of the modern world—or one of its mythologies—even though it is a highly intellectual form of art, and mythology is a nonintellectual mode of apprehension. For science fiction does use the mythmaking faculty to apprehend the world we live in, a world profoundly shaped and changed by science and technology, and its originality is that it uses the mythmaking faculty on new material.

LITERARY THEFT OF MYTHIC MATERIAL

But there's another catch to look out for. The presence of mythic material in a story does not mean that the mythmaking faculty is being used.

Here is a science fiction story: its plot is modeled directly upon that of an ancient myth, or there are characters in it modeled upon certain gods or heroes of legend. Is it, therefore, a myth? Not necessarily; in fact, probably not. No mythmaking is involved: just theft.

Theft is an integral function of a healthy literature. It's much easier to steal a good plot from some old book than to invent one. Anyhow, after you've sweated to invent an original plot, it very often turns out to be a perfect parallel to one of the old stories (more on this curious fact later). And since there are beautiful and powerful stories all through world legendry, and since stories need retelling from generation to generation, why not steal them? I'm certainly not the one to condemn the practice; parts of my first novel were lifted wholesale from the Norse mythos (Brisingamen, Freya's necklace, and episodes in the life of Odin). My version isn't a patch on the original, of course, but I think I did the gods of Asgard no harm, and they did my book some good. This sort of pilfering goes on all the time, and produces many pleasant works of art, though it does not lead to any truly new creations or cognitions.

There is a more self-conscious form of thievery which is both more destructive and more self-destructive. In many college English courses the words "myth" and "symbol" are given a tremendous charge of significance. You just ain't no

good unless you can see a symbol hiding, like a scared gerbil, under every page. And in many creative writing courses
the little beasts multiply, the place swarms with them. What
does this Mean? What does that Symbolize? What is the Underlying Mythos? Kids come lurching out of such courses
with a brain full of gerbils. And they sit down and write a lot
of empty pomposity, under the impression that that's how
Melville did it.

Even when they begin to realize that art is not something
produced for critics, but for other human beings, some of
them retain the overintellectualizing bent. They still do not
realize that a symbol is not a sign of something known, but
an indicator of something not known and not expressible
otherwise than symbolically. They mistake symbol (living
meaning) for allegory (dead equivalence). So they use
mythology in an arrogant fashion, rationalizing it, conde-
scending to it. They take plots and characters from it, not in
the healthily furtive fashion of the literary sneakthief, but in
a posturing, showy way. Such use of myth does real disser-
vice to the original, by trivializing it, and no good at all to the
story. The shallowness of its origin is often betrayed either
by an elaborate vocabulary and ostentatiously cryptic style,
or by a kind of jocose, chatty discomfort in the tone. Watch
me up here on Olympus, you peasants, being fresh with
Aphrodite. Look at me juggling symbols, folks! We sophisti-
cates, we know how to handle these old archetypes.

But Zeus always gets 'em. ZAP!

LIVING MYTHOLOGIES

So far I have been talking as if all mythologies the writer
might use were dead—that is, not believed in with some degree of emotion, other than aesthetic appreciation, by the
writer and his community. Of course, this is far from being
the case. It's easy to get fresh with Aphrodite. Who believes
in some old Greek goddess, anyhow? But there are living
mythologies, after all. Consider the Virgin Mary; or the State.

For an example of the use in science fiction of a living religious mythos one may turn to the work of Cordwainer
Smith, whose Christian beliefs are evident, I think, all
through his work, in such motifs as the savior, the martyr,
rebirth, the "underpeople." Whether or not one is a Christian, one may admire wholeheartedly the strength and passion given the works by the author's living belief. In general,

however, I think the critics' search for Christian themes in science fiction is sterile and misleading. For the majority of science fiction writers, the themes of Christianity are dead signs, not living symbols, and those who use them do so all too often in order to get an easy emotional charge without working for it. They take a free ride on the crucifix, just as many now cash in cynically on the current occultist fad. The difference between this sort of thing and the genuine, naïve mysticism of an Arthur Clarke, struggling to express his own, living symbol of rebirth, is all the difference in the world.

COLLECTIVE SUBMYTHS

Beyond and beneath the great living mythologies of religion and power there is another region into which science fiction enters. I would call it the area of Submyth: by which I mean those images, figures and motifs which have no religious resonance and no intellectual or aesthetic value, but which are vigorously alive and powerful, so that they cannot be dismissed as mere stereotypes. They are shared by all of us; they are genuinely collective. Superman is a submyth. His father was Nietzsche and his mother was a funnybook, and he is alive and well in the mind of every ten-year-old—and millions of others. Other science-fictional submyths are the blond heroes of sword and sorcery, with their unusual weapons; insane or self-deifying computers; mad scientists; benevolent dictators; detectives who find out who done it; capitalists who buy and sell galaxies; brave starship captains and/or troopers; evil aliens; good aliens; and every pointy-breasted brainless young woman who was ever rescued from monsters, lectured to, patronized or, in recent years, raped, by one of the aforementioned heroes.

It hurts to call these creatures mythological. It is a noble word, and they are so grotty. But they are alive, in books, magazines, pictures, movies, advertising, and our own minds. Their roots are the roots of myth, are in our unconscious—that vast dim region of the psyche and perhaps beyond the psyche, which Jung called "collective" because it is similar in all of us, just as our bodies are basically similar. The vigor comes from there, and so they cannot be dismissed as unimportant. Not when they can help motivate a world movement such as fascism!—But neither can they furnish materials useful to art. They have no element of the true myth except its emotive, irrational "thereness." Writers who deliberately submit to them have forfeited the right to call their work science fiction; they're just popcultists cashing in.

TRUE MYTHS AS A CONNECTING BRIDGE

True myth may serve for thousands of years as an inexhaustible source of intellectual speculation, religious joy, ethical inquiry and artistic renewal. The real mystery is not destroyed by reason. The fake one is. You look at it and it vanishes. You look at the Blond Hero—really look—and he turns into a gerbil. But you look at Apollo, and he looks back at you.

The poet Rilke looked at a statue of Apollo about fifty years ago, and Apollo spoke to him. "You must change your life," he said.

When the genuine myth rises into consciousness, that is always its message. You must change your life.

The way of art, after all, is neither to cut adrift from the emotions, the senses, the body, etc., and sail off into the void of pure meaning, nor to blind the mind's eye and wallow in irrational, amoral meaninglessness—but to keep open the tenuous, difficult, essential connections between the two extremes. To connect. To connect the idea with value, sensation with intuition, cortex with cerebellum.

The true myth is precisely one of these connections.

Like all artists, we science fiction writers are trying to make and use such a connection or bridge between the conscious and the unconscious—so that our readers can make the journey too. If the only tool we use is the intellect, we will produce only lifeless copies or parodies of the archetypes that live in our own deeper mind and in the great works of art and mythology. If we abandon intellect, we're likely to submerge our own personality and talent in a stew of mindless submyths, themselves coarse, feeble parodies of their archetypal origins. The only way to the truly collective, to the image that is alive and meaningful in all of us, seems to be through the truly personal. Not the impersonality of pure reason; not the impersonality of "the masses," but the irreducibly personal—the self. To reach the others, artists go into the self. Using reason, they deliberately enter the irrational. The farther they go into the self, the closer they come to the other.

If this seems a paradox it is only because our culture overvalues abstraction and extroversion. Pain, for instance, can work the same way. Nothing is more personal, more un-shareable, than pain; the worst thing about suffering is that you suffer alone. Yet those who have not suffered, or will not admit that they suffer, are those who are cut off in cold iso-lation from their fellow men. Pain, the loneliest experience, gives rise to sympathy, to love: the bridge between self and other, the means of communion. So with art. The artist who goes inward most deeply—and it is a painful journey—is the artist who touches us most closely, speaks to us most clearly.

Of all the great psychologists, Jung best explains this process, by stressing the existence, not of an isolated "id," but a "collective unconscious." He reminds us that the re-gion of the mind/body that lies beyond the narrow, brightly lit domain of consciousness is very much the same in all of us. This does not imply a devaluing of consciousness or of reason. The achievement of individual consciousness, which Jung calls "differentiation," is to him a great achieve-ment, civilization's highest achievement, the hope of our fu-ture. But the tree grows only from deep roots.

So it would seem that true myth arises only in the process of connecting the conscious and the unconscious realms. I won't find a living archetype in my bookcase or my televi-sion set. I will find it only in myself: in that core of individ-uality lying in the heart of the common darkness. Only the individual can get up and go to the window, and draw back the curtains, and look out into the dark.

Sometimes it takes considerable courage to do that. When you open curtains you don't know what may be out there in the night. Maybe starlight; maybe dragons; maybe the secret police. Maybe the grace of God; maybe the horror of death. They're all there. For all of us.

ARCHETYPES RELEASED INTO CONSCIOUSNESS

Writers who draw not upon the words and thoughts of oth-ers but upon their own thoughts and their own deep being will inevitably hit upon common material. The more origi-nal the work, the more imperiously *recognizable* it will be. "Yes, of course!" say I, the reader recognizing myself, my dreams, my nightmares. The characters, figures, images, motifs, plots, events of the story may be obvious parallels, even seemingly reproductions, of the material of myth and legend. There will be—openly in fantasy, covertly in natu-

ralism—dragons, heroes, quests, objects of power, voyages
at night and under sea, and so forth. In narrative, as in paint-
ing, certain familiar patterns will become visible.

This again is no paradox, if Jung is right, and we all have
the same kind of dragons in our psyche, just as we all have
the same kind of heart and lungs in our body. It does imply
that nobody can invent an archetype by taking thought, any
more than we can invent a new organ in our body. But this
is no loss; rather a gain. It means that we can communicate,
that alienation isn't the final human condition, since there is
a vast common ground on which we can meet, not only rationally, but aesthetically, intuitively, emotionally.

A dragon, not a dragon cleverly copied or mass-produced,
but a creature of evil who crawls up, threatening and inexplicable, out of the artist's own unconscious, is alive: terribly
alive. It frightens little children, and the artist, and the rest of
us. It frightens us because it is part of us, and the artist forces
us to admit it. We have met the enemy, as Pogo remarked,
and he is us.

"What do you mean? There aren't any dragons in my living room, dragons are extinct, dragons aren't real . . ."

"Look out of the window . . . Look into the mirror . . ."

The artist who works from the center of being will find
archetypal images and release them into consciousness. The
first science fiction writer to do so was Mary Shelley. She let
Frankenstein's monster loose. Nobody has been able to shut
him out again, either. There he is, sitting in the corner of our
lovely modern glass and plastic living room, right on the
tubular steel contour chair, big as life and twice as ugly.
Edgar Rice Burroughs did it, though with infinitely less
power and originality—Tarzan is a true myth-figure, though
not a particularly relevant one to modern ethical/emotional
dilemmas, as Frankenstein's monster is. Capek did it, largely
by *naming* something (a very important aspect of archetyp-
izing): "Robots," he called them. They have walked among
us ever since. Tolkien did it; he found a ring, a ring which
we keep trying to lose. . . .

SCIENCE FICTION IS MODERN MYTHOLOGY

Scholars can have great fun, and can strengthen the effect of
such figures, by showing their relationship to other mani-
festations of the archetype in myth, legend, dogma and art.
These linkages can be highly illuminating. Frankenstein's

monster is related to the Golem; to Jesus; to Prometheus. Tarzan is a direct descendant of the Wolfchild/Noble Savage on one side, and every child's fantasy of the Orphan-of-High-Estate on the other. The robot may be seen as the modern ego's fear of the body, after the crippling division of "mind" and "body," "ghost" and "machine," enforced by post-Renaissance mechanistic thought. In "The Time Machine" there is one of the great visions of the End, an archetype of eschatology comparable to any religious vision of the day of judgment. In "Nightfall" there is the fundamental opposition of dark and light, playing on the fear of darkness that we share with our cousins the great apes. Through Philip K. Dick's work one can follow an exploration of the ancient themes of identity and alienation, and the sense of the fragmentation of the ego. In Stanislaw Lem's works there seems to be a similarly complex and subtle exploration of the archetypal Other, the alien.

Such myths, symbols, images do not disappear under the scrutiny of the intellect, nor does an ethical, or aesthetic, or even religious examination of them make them shrink and vanish. On the contrary: the more you look, the more there they are. And the more you think, the more they mean.

On this level, science fiction deserves the title of a modern mythology.

Most science fiction doesn't, of course, and never will. There are never very many artists around. No doubt we'll continue most of the time to get rewarmed leftovers from Babylon and Northrop Frye served up by earnest snobs, and hordes of brawny Gerbilmen ground out by hacks. But there will be mythmakers, too. Even now—who knows?—the next Mary Shelley may be lying quietly in her tower-top room, just waiting for a thunderstorm.

Chronology

1818

Mary Wollstonecraft Shelley first publishes *Frankenstein: or, The Modern Prometheus.*

1826

Mary Shelley, *The Last Man.*

1835–1849

Prolific genre fiction by Edgar Allan Poe, including a number of science fiction tales, such as "The Narrative of Arthur Gordon Pym of Nantucket," "Mesmeric Revelation," and "A Tale of Ragged Mountains."

1864

Jules Verne, *Journey to the Center of the Earth.*

1870

Verne, *Twenty Thousand Leagues Under the Sea.*

1872

Samuel Butler, *Erewhon.*

1886

Robert Louis Stevenson, *The Strange Case of Dr. Jekyll and Mr. Hyde.*

1888

Edward Bellamy, *Looking Backward.*

1895

H.G. Wells, *The Time Machine.*

1896

Wells, *The Island of Doctor Moreau.*

1897

Wells, *The Invisible Man, The War of the Worlds* (serialized).

1907

Jack London, *The Iron Heel*.

1912

Edgar Rice Burroughs serializes his first story, "Under the Moons of Mars," in the pulp magazine *All-Story*.

1914–1918

World War I realizes the nightmares of the nineteenth-century future war tales.

1917

Burroughs publishes his earlier serial as the novel *A Princess of Mars*; sequels follow.

1921

Czech playwright Karel Căpek introduces robots into science fiction (and science) with his play *R.U.R.*

1926

Hugo Gernsback founds *Amazing Stories*, the first pulp title specializing in all–science fiction content; the film *Metropolis* (director Fritz Lang).

1929

Gernsback loses control of *Amazing*, launches *Science Wonder Stories*.

1930

Olaf Stapledon, *Last and First Men: A Story of the Near and Far Future*.

1932

Aldous Huxley, *Brave New World*.

1934

Jack Williamson, *The Legion of Space* (serialized in *Astounding*).

1936

The first World Science Fiction Convention is held in Philadelphia.

1937

Sf writer John W. Campbell Jr. becomes editor of *Astounding Science Fiction;* Stapledon, *Star Maker*.

1938

C.S. Lewis begins his allegorical sf trilogy with *Out of the Silent Planet;* Williamson, *The Legion of Time* (serialized in *Astounding*).

1939

Campbell edits a second magazine, *Unknown;* early stories by Isaac Asimov, Robert A. Heinlein, Theodore Sturgeon, and A.E. van Vogt appear in *Astounding* and competing magazines; the golden age of science fiction begins approximately at this time and continues roughly to 1960.

1940

Williamson, *Darker than You Think* (serialized in *Unknown*).

1941

Asimov and Campbell devise the Three Laws of Robotics; Asimov begins his robot stories; the United States officially enters World War II.

1942

Asimov serializes the first stories of his Foundation cycle.

1943

Lewis, *Perelandra.*

1944

Astounding is investigated by military intelligence after Campbell publishes Cleve Cartmill's "Deadline," which predicts the development of the atomic bomb.

1945

The United States uses the atomic bomb on Japan; Lewis, *That Hideous Strength.*

1948

Williamson, *The Humanoids* (serialized in *Astounding*).

1949

George Orwell, *1984;* the *Magazine of Fantasy and Science Fiction* is launched, editor Anthony Boucher.

1950

Fritz Leiber, *Gather, Darkness!;* Asimov, *I, Robot;* Heinlein, *The Man Who Sold the Moon; Galaxy* magazine is launched, editor Horace L. Gold.

1951

Ray Bradbury, *The Martian Chronicles, The Illustrated Man;* Arthur C. Clarke, *Prelude to Space, The Sands of Mars;* John Wyndham, *The Day of the Triffids;* Asimov, *Foundation.*

1952

Kurt Vonnegut Jr., *Player Piano; Beyond Human Ken* (anthology), editor Judith Merril; Asimov, *Foundation and Empire.*

1953

The Hugo Awards are initiated to honor the previous year's best sf as voted on by fans; Alfred Bester's *The Demolished Man* wins the first Hugo for best novel; Frederik Pohl and C.M. Kornbluth, *The Space Merchants;* Asimov, *Second Foundation;* Bradbury, *Fahrenheit 451;* Clarke, *Childhood's End;* Sturgeon, *More than Human.*

1954

Poul Anderson, *Brain Wave;* Hal Clement, *Mission of Gravity;* William Golding, *Lord of the Flies;* Asimov, *The Caves of Steel.*

1955

Leigh Brackett, *The Long Tomorrow;* Philip K. Dick, *The Solar Lottery;* Clarke, *Earthlight.*

1956

Lester del Rey, *Nerves;* Richard Matheson, *The Man Who Shrank;* Bester, *Tiger! Tiger!*

1957

Fred Hoyle, *The Black Cloud;* C.L. Moore, *Doomsday Morning;* Asimov, *The Naked Sun;* van Vogt, *The Mind Cage.*

1958

Brian W. Aldiss, *Non-Stop;* James Blish, *A Case of Conscience.*

1959

Gordon Dickson, *Dorsai!;* Robert Sheckley, *Immortality, Inc.;* Heinlein, *Starship Troopers;* Pohl and Kornbluth, *Wolfbane;* Vonnegut, *The Sirens of Titan.*

1960

Campbell changes *Astounding* to *Analog;* Walter M. Miller Jr., *A Canticle for Leibowitz;* Harry Harrison, *Deathworld;* Philip Jose Farmer, *Strange Relations;* Kingsley Amis, *New*

Maps of Hell (sf criticism); Aldiss, *Galaxies Like Grains of Sand.*

1961

Stanislaw Lem, *Solaris;* Harrison, *The Stainless Steel Rat;* Heinlein, *Stranger in a Strange Land.*

1962

J.G. Ballard, *The Drowned World;* Anthony Burgess, *A Clockwork Orange;* Dick, *The Man in the High Castle.*

1963

Clifford D. Simak, *Here Gather the Stars;* Vonnegut, *Cat's Cradle.*

1964

Michael Moorcock becomes editor of the British magazine *New Worlds* and initiates the New Wave; Ballard, *The Burning World;* Blish, *The Issue at Hand* (influential sf criticism written under the pseudonym William Atheling Jr.); Dick, *The Three Stigmata of Palmer Eldritch;* Leiber, *The Wanderer.*

1965

Sf writer, critic, and editor Damon Knight founds the Science Fiction Writers of America, serving as its first president and initiating the prestigious Nebula Awards; Frank Herbert's *Dune* wins the first Nebula for best novel; John Brunner, *The Squares of the City;* William Burroughs, *The Nova Express.*

1966

Samuel R. Delany, *Babel-17;* Daniel Keyes, *Flowers for Algernon;* Ursula K. Le Guin, *Planet of Exile, Rocannon's World;* Michael Moorcock, "Behold the Man"; Roger Zelazny, *This Immortal;* Ballard, *The Crystal World;* Heinlein, *The Moon Is a Harsh Mistress.*

1967

The *Dangerous Visions* anthology, edited by Harlan Ellison, is the definitive statement of the American New Wave; Anna Kavan, *Ice;* Robert Silverberg, *Thorns;* Delany, *The Einstein Intersection;* Zelazny, *Lord of Light.*

1968

Norman Spinrad's novel *Bug Jack Barron* is serialized in *New Worlds,* stirring controversy; Thomas M. Disch, *Camp Concentration;* Joanna Russ, *Picnic on Paradise;* James Tiptree Jr. (Alice Sheldon) makes first appearance in *Analog;*

Brunner, *Stand on Zanzibar;* Dick, *Do Androids Dream of Electric Sheep?* (later adapted as the film *Blade Runner*); Silverberg, *The Masks of Time;* the film *2001: A Space Odyssey* (director Stanley Kubrick, Arthur C. Clarke coauthors).

1969

The Apollo moon landing realizes the dreams of decades of sf; Harlan Ellison, "A Boy and His Dog"; Dick, *Ubik;* Herbert, *Dune Messiah;* Le Guin, *The Left Hand of Darkness;* Silverberg, *To Live Again, Up the Line;* Vonnegut, *Slaughterhouse-Five.*

1970

Larry Niven, *Ringworld;* Anderson, *Tau Zero;* Ballard, *The Atrocity Exhibition;* Russ, *And Chaos Died;* Silverberg, *Downward to the Earth, Tower of Glass.*

1971

Campbell dies; Kate Wilhelm, *Margaret and I;* Blish, *And All the Stars a Stage;* Farmer, *To Your Scattered Bodies Go;* Le Guin, *The Lathe of Heaven;* Silverberg, *The World Inside, A Time of Changes.*

1972

Ben Bova becomes editor of *Analog;* Norman Spinrad, *The Iron Dream;* Asimov, *The Gods Themselves, The Early Asimov;* Ellison (editor), *Again Dangerous Visions;* Harrison, *Tunnel Through the Deeps;* Silverberg, *Dying Inside, The Book of Skulls.*

1973

Thomas Pynchon, *Gravity's Rainbow;* Aldiss, *Frankenstein Unbound, Billion Year Spree* (sf criticism); Clarke, *Rendezvous with Rama;* Tiptree, "Love Is the Plan, the Plan Is Death."

1974

Dick, *Flow My Tears, the Policeman Said;* Le Guin, *The Dispossessed;* Silverberg, *Born with the Dead.*

1975

Michael Bishop, *A Funeral for the Eyes of Fire;* Ian Watson, *The Embedding;* Brunner, *The Shockwave Rider;* Clarke, *Imperial Earth;* Delany, *Dhalgren;* Ellison, *Deathbird Stories;* Niven, *Inferno;* Russ, *The Female Man.*

1976

Kingsley Amis, *The Alteration;* Octavia Butler, *Patternmaster;* C.J. Cherryh, *Brothers of Earth;* Herbert, *Children of*

Dune; Wilhelm, *The Clewiston Test, Where Late the Sweet Birds Sang.*

1977

Gregory Benford, *In the Ocean of Night;* George R.R. Martin, *Dying of the Light;* Bruce Sterling, *Involution Ocean;* Dick, *A Scanner Darkly;* Dickson, *Timestorm;* Pohl, *Gateway;* the film *Star Wars* (director George Lucas) announces the end of the New Wave.

1978

Anderson, *The Avatar;* Sheckley, *Crompton Divided;* Tiptree, *Up the Walls of the World.*

1979

Bishop, *Transfigurations;* Butler, *Kindred;* Disch, *On Wings of Song;* Darko Suvin, *Metamorphoses of Science Fiction* (sf criticism).

1980

David Brin, *Sundiver;* Gene Wolfe, *The Shadow of the Torturer;* Benford, *Timescape;* Butler, *Wild Seed;* Sterling, *The Artificial Kid.*

1981

Cherryh, *Downbelow Station;* Dick, *Valis, The Divine Invasion;* Wolfe, *The Claw of the Conciliator.*

1982

Bishop, *No Enemy but Time.*

1983

Tim Powers, *The Anubis Gates;* Asimov, *Foundation's Edge;* Brin, *Startide Rising.*

1984

William Gibson's *Neuromancer* establishes the cyberpunk subgenre; Kim Stanley Robinson, *The Wild Shore;* Butler, *Clay's Ark.*

1985

Margaret Atwood, *The Handmaid's Tale;* Greg Bear, *Blood Music, Eon;* Orson Scott Card, *Ender's Game;* Brin, *The Uplift War; The Postman;* Robinson, *The Memory of Whiteness;* Sterling, *Schismatrix.*

1986

Mirrorshades, edited by Bruce Sterling, is the definitive cyberpunk anthology; Asimov, *Foundation and Earth;* Brin and Benford, *Heart of the Comet;* Card, *Speaker for the Dead;* Gibson, *Count Zero.*

1987

Butler, *Dawn.*

1988

Butler, *Adulthood Rites;* Gibson, *Mona Lisa Overdrive.*

1989

Butler, *Imago.*

1990

Dan Simmons, *The Fall of Hyperion;* Asimov and Silverberg, *Nightfall;* Bear, *Queen of Angels;* Brin, *Earth*; Clarke and Benford, *Beyond the Fall of Night;* Robinson, *Pacific Edge.*

1991

Gibson and Sterling, *The Difference Engine.*

1992

Harry Turtledove, *The Guns of the South.*

1993

Vernor Vinge, *A Fire upon the Deep;* Connie Willis, *The Doomsday Book;* Brin, *Glory Season;* Butler, *Parable of the Sower.*

1994

Bear, *Moving Mars, Legacy;* Benford, *Sailing Bright Eternity;* Robinson, *Green Mars.*

1995

Neal Stephenson, *The Diamond Age;* Bishop, *Brittle Innings;* Brin, *Brightness Reef;* Turtledove, *Worldwar: Tilting the Balance.*

1996

Jack Vance, *Night Lamp;* Brin, *Infinity's Shore;* Robinson, *Blue Mars;* Willis, *Bellwether;* Wolfe, *Exodus from the Long Sun.*

1997

Joe Haldeman, *Forever Peace;* Walter John Williams, *City on Fire;* Miller and Terry Bisson, *St. Leibowitz and the Wild Horse Woman;* Bear, */Slant;* Robinson, *Antarctica.*

1998

Bishop, *Time Pieces;* Butler, *Parable of the Talents;* Card, *Future on Ice.*

1999

Benford, *Deep Time;* Card, *Enchantment;* Vinge, *A Deepness in the Sky.*

FOR FURTHER RESEARCH

SCIENCE FICTION HISTORY AND CRITICISM

Brian W. Aldiss with David Wingrove, *Trillion Year Spree: The History of Science Fiction.* New York: Atheneum, 1986.

Kingsley Amis, *New Maps of Hell: A Survey of Science Fiction.* New York: Harcourt, Brace, 1960.

William Atheling Jr. (James Blish), *The Issue at Hand.* Chicago: Advent, 1964.

———, *More Issues at Hand.* Chicago: Advent, 1970.

Reginald Bretnor, ed., *Science Fiction: Today and Tomorrow.* Baltimore: Penguin, 1974.

Thomas D. Clareson, ed., *Extrapolation: A Journal of Science Fiction.* Wooster, OH: The College of Wooster and the Collier Printing Company, since 1959.

———, *SF: The Other Side of Realism.* Bowling Green, OH: Bowling Green University Popular Press, 1971.

———, *Voices for the Future: Essays on Major Science Fiction Writers.* Vol. 1. Bowling Green, OH: Bowling Green University Popular Press, 1976.

I.F. Clarke, *The Tale of the Future: From the Beginning to the Present Time.* London: Library Association, 1972.

L. Sprague de Camp and Catherine Crook de Camp, *Science Fiction Handbook: Revised.* Philadelphia: Owlslick Press, 1975.

Damon Knight, *In Search of Wonder.* Chicago: Advent, 1967.

Willis E. McNelly, ed., *Science Fiction: The Academic Awakening. The CEA Critic.* Vol. XXXVII, No. 1. Shreveport, LA: The College English Association, November 1974.

Sam Moskowitz, *Strange Horizons: The Spectrum of Science Fiction.* New York: Charles Scribner's Sons, 1976.

R.D. Mullen and Darko Suvin, eds., *Science Fiction Studies.* Terre Haute: Indiana State University Press, since 1974.

Robert Reilly, ed., *The Transcendent Adventure: Studies of Religion in Science Fiction/Fantasy.* Westport, CT: Greenwood, 1985.

Mark Rose, ed., *Science Fiction: A Collection of Critical Essays.* Englewood Cliffs, NJ: Prentice-Hall, 1976.

Robert Scholes and Eric S. Rabkin, *Science Fiction: History, Science, Vision.* New York: Oxford University Press, 1977.

Darko Suvin, *Metamorphoses of Science Fiction.* New Haven, CT: Yale University Press, 1979.

Donald A. Wollheim, *The Universe Makers: Science Fiction Today.* New York: Harper & Row, 1971.

NOTABLE SCIENCE FICTION ANTHOLOGIES

Harlan Ellison, ed., *Dangerous Visions.* New York: Berkley, 1967.

Harvey A. Katz et al, eds., *Introductory Psychology Through Science Fiction.* Chicago: Rand McNally College Publishing, 1977.

Carol Mason et al, eds., *Anthropology Through Science Fiction.* New York: St. Martin's, 1974.

Robert Silverberg, ed., *Science Fiction Hall of Fame.* Vol. 1, *The Greatest Science Fiction Stories of All Time.* Garden City, NY: Doubleday, 1970.

Bruce Sterling, ed., *Mirrorshades: The Cyberpunk Anthology.* New York: Ace, 1986.

ABOUT INDIVIDUAL SCIENCE FICTION WRITERS

Dani Cavallaro, *Cyberpunk and Cyberculture: Science Fiction and the Work of William Gibson.* New Brunswick, NJ: Athlone, 2000.

Elizabeth Cummins, *Understanding Ursula K. Le Guin.* Columbia: University of South Carolina Press, 1990.

Colin Greenland, *The Entropy Exhibition: Michael Moorcock and the British 'New Wave' in Science Fiction.* London: Routledge & Kegan Paul, 1983.

Mark R. Hillegas, *The Future as Nightmare: H.G. Wells and the Anti-Utopians.* New York: Oxford University Press, 1967.

Andrew Martin, *The Mask of the Prophet: The Extraordinary Fiction of Jules Verne.* New York: Oxford University Press, 1990.

Alexei Panshin, *Heinlein in Dimension, a Critical Analysis.* Chicago: Advent, 1968.

Robin Anne Reid, *Arthur C. Clarke: A Critical Companion.* Westport, CT: Greenwood, 1997.

William F. Toupence, *Isaac Asimov.* Boston: Twayne, 1991.

———, *Ray Bradbury and the Poetics of Reverie: Fantasy, Science Fiction, and the Reader.* Ann Arbor, MI: UMI Research Press, 1984.

Samuel J. Umland, ed., *Philip K. Dick: Contemporary Critical Interpretations.* Westport, CT: Greenwood, 1995.

Patricia S. Warrick, *Mind in Motion: The Fiction of Philip K. Dick.* Carbondale: Southern Illinois University Press, 1987.

INDEX